A SELECTIVE GUIDE

WESTERN fLY-FISHING vacations

NANCI & KIRK REYNOLDS

Chronicle Books • San Francisco

We dedicate this book to our daughter
Annelise. May she grow up with
a sense of wonder and awe
for the grandeur of nature.

Library of Congress Cataloging in
Publication Data

Reynolds, Nanci.
    Western fly-fishing vacations: a selective guide /
Nanci and Kirk Reynolds.
        p. cm.
    Includes index.
    ISBN 0-87701-425-6
    1. Fly fishing—West (U.S.) 2. Vacations—West
(U.S.) 3. Dude ranches—West (U.S.)
I. Reynolds, Kirk. II. Title.
SH464.W4R49   1988   88-6603
799.1′1′0978—dc19   CIP

Photography: Nanci Reynolds
Editing: Deborah Stone
Book design: Fearn Cutler
Cover design: Julie Noyes
Front cover photograph:
Copyright ©1987 by Tom Montgomery
Back cover photograph: Nanci Reynolds
Maps: Fearn Cutler

Distributed in Canada by Raincoast
Books, 112 East Third Avenue,
Vancouver, B.C. V5T 1C8

10 9 8 7 6 5 4 3 2 1

Chronicle Books
San Francisco, California

TABLE OF CONTENTS

IDAHO

MONTANA

OREGON

WASHINGTON

WYOMING

INTRODUCTION

Western Fly-fishing Vacations began to germinate on a snowy winter evening in 1983. We were sitting in front of the fire musing, as people often do, about what we'd do with our lives, given our "druthers." We both love the outdoors, fly fishing, fine cooking, and getting to know all sorts of people. Putting these disparate considerations together, we came up with the dream of someday owning or operating a fly-fishing guest lodge. We decided to do a little research and, as they say, one thing led to another—namely, this book.

It took two summers, 35,000 dusty miles, and 163 on-site interviews to complete the basic research. Along the way, we probably saw more gorgeous country than a person has a right to see in a lifetime. Spectacular sunrises and sunsets, free-flowing rivers, crystalline streams and lakes, wildflower-covered alpine meadows, and dramatic thunderstorms are but a few of the memories we will carry with us forever. A large part of our memories, however, centers around the genuine hospitality and western tradition that remains the true heritage of these lodges and guest ranches.

Yet, none of this answers the question, "Why write a book about fishing lodges and guest ranches?" The first reason is easy to express. We are among an estimated 50 million Americans who like to fish. Fishing and, increasingly, fly fishing, are America's favorite pastime. The second reason is a little more personal. We want to dispel the misconception, held by many, that a western fishing vacation necessitates the exclusion of loved ones who don't like to fish. Fully 75 percent of the lodges and ranches included in this guide are family-oriented operations; that they also offer excellent access to terrific fishing is of secondary importance.

Lodges have been assigned one of three rate categories: inexpensive ($50/day and under), moderate (between $50/day and $120/day), and expensive ($120/day and over). These are general guidelines only; readers should carefully examine the specific charges of the lodges they are considering when they make reservations. An inexpensive lodge that charges by the hour for horse rentals and guided fishing trips may turn out to be more expensive when all the extra charges have been added to the tab than an expensive lodge whose price includes everything. All lodges gladly provide brochures with current rate sheets.

We hope you find this guide useful when planning future vacations. A trip to one of these locations in the summer is sure to foster memories best cherished in front of a warm fire on a cold winter's night.

Good luck and tight lines.

ACKNOWLEDGMENTS

We wish to extend our heartfelt thanks to Betty Sechser, without whose help and encouragement this book might never have gone to press.

We are grateful to the many spokesmen and women of each lodge, guest ranch, and outfitters who took time out of their already busy schedules to answer our letters and phone calls and show us around their facility. Without their enthusiastic cooperation, this project would have been impossible.

Our thanks also go out to guides Mike Craig, Vern Bressler, Jack Dennis, Jr., Dave Hall, Rick Piscitello, and Neal Cantwell for imparting an intimate respect and love for the rivers they know so very well.

A special thanks to Loren and Sally Irving for kindly reviewing our first chapter and giving us valuable feedback.

And finally, we send our love to our families and friends, whose continual interest and support buoyed us up whenever we lost sight of the light at the end of the tunnel. Thanks.

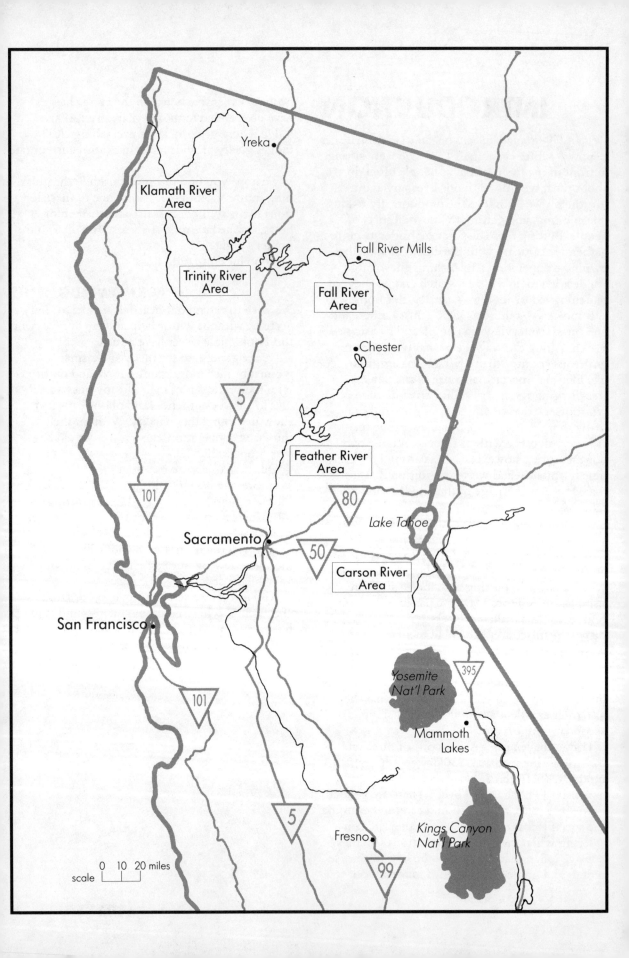

CALIFORNIA

SOUTH LAKE TAHOE

SORENSON'S RESORT

Hope Valley, CA 96120. Phone: (916) 694-2203. Contact: John and Patty Brissenden. Total capacity: 40–80. Open year round. Peak season: July 1–October 15. Reserve 2–10 weeks in advance. Two cabins reserved for guests with pets. No smoking.

Accommodations: Housekeeping cabins with kitchenettes and wood-burning stoves sleep up to 4; 2 group cabins sleep 6–8. Conference space available.

Meals: Cafe offers continental breakfast daily, a la carte lunch menu, and gourmet country-fare dinners. Wine and beer served in cafe. Restaurants also located in South Lake Tahoe.

Rates: Moderate; special rates for stays of 4 or more days. Package rates for Historic Emigrant Trail Walking Tour, river rafting on East Fork of Carson River, and day rafting trips. Cash or check only.

How to Get There: Located 15 miles south of Lake Tahoe at junction of highways 88 and 89. Airline and bus service to South Lake Tahoe and Reno, NV, daily. Small airstrip located between Woodford, CA, and Markleville, CA. Rental car recommended for local travel.

In the Hope Valley of Alpine County, a little niche of pioneer Americana just south of Lake Tahoe, lies one of the oldest resorts in the Sierra Nevadas. Sorenson's, "your all-season resort in the Sierra Nevada," is ideal for adults and sports enthusiasts who want to enjoy spending a few quiet days out of mainstream California.

Homesteaded in 1893, Sorenson's was originally a base camp for Basque sheepherders in the Hope Valley. It was established around 1900 as a fishing, hunting, and family vacation camp with canvas tents set up to accommodate guests. Today, the resort sits on 164 private acres. Rustic cabins have sleeping lofts and wood-burning stoves. Norway House, used for small conferences, was brought over piece by piece in 1971 and stands complete with sod roof and beautifully carved exterior. Furnishings have gradually been updated since the Brissendens bought the lodge. Charming country decor features patterned curtains and colorful quilts. This attention to detail has brought recognition to the resort in publications such as *Bed and Breakfast Inns of California*, *Small Hotels of California*, and the outdoor section of the San Francisco *Examiner*.

Things to Do

Sorenson's offers package deals that include a combination of lodging and Sierra country adventure. The Historical Emigrant Trail Walking Tour covers parts of the Mormon-Emigrant Trail and the early Pony Express Route once used over Kit Carson Pass. Special-interest hikes to identify alpine flora and fauna are also arranged through Sorenson's in spring, summer, and fall.

A river rafting package that includes a soak in natural hot springs at the end of an exhilarating day on the East Fork of the Carson River goes through old West's badlands country.

Easy, scenic day drives include a tour through the Amador Wine Country and a trip to Lake Tahoe. Nearly a dozen wineries are located along

Highway 49, which meanders through the Amador Wine Country. Because the Amador Valley does not receive the tourist pressure that the Napa Valley does, visitors can enjoy the wineries with far fewer crowds to contend with. The Lake Tahoe loop, via Highway 89, winds around one of the most beautiful alpine lakes found anywhere. A day on and around the lake is a must for water sports, golf, sightseeing, and, of course, gambling in world-famous casinos. Horses are also available at the south end of the lake at Camp Richardson.

Other local attractions include Elton Rodman's Roaring Camp Mining Co., which offers a tour through an old-time forty-niner gold camp on the Mokelumne River and Indian Grinding Rocks State Historic Park, which has the largest known Indian grinding rock on exhibit in California. Grover Hot Springs State Park, located just down the road from Sorenson's, features soothing soaks in a spa setting.

Hikers will enjoy trekking on the Pacific Crest Trail through the Eldorado National Forest and Mokelumne Wilderness. For longer back-country hikes and pack trips, Mama's Llamas in El Dorado provides clients with pack animals, naturalist guides, and three gourmet meals a day.

Hope Valley and South Lake Tahoe have one of the busiest calenders of summer events. Write the Amador/Alpine Chamber of Commerce or South Lake Tahoe's Chamber of Commerce for a complete listing of dates and events. The Brissendens will also help guests select the more noteworthy events when reservations are confirmed.

Fishing

Some of the best fishing on the West Fork of the Carson River is located right off the road next to the resort. The West Fork is a small, meandering stream through Woodfords Canyon abounding with rainbows, native browns, and brooks. Three-pound browns aren't an everyday occurrence, but they happen often enough. A few cutthroats, some as long as twenty-five inches, also make their way into the West Fork from Heenan Lake. This fork of the Carson is a fairly good fly-fishing stream. A lightweight rod coupled with long, light leaders works well on short casts. Mosquitos, royal coachmen, gray hackle patterns, and adams (#14–16) are recommended. Caddis

activity is sparse, but when there is a hatch, the fish quickly become selective so it's a good idea to have some elk hair caddis (#14–16) along.

The East Fork of the Carson River is a twenty-minute drive from Sorenson's. Raft fishing for cutthroats is the preferred method early in the season, with bank fishing for an abundance of browns later on.

A wide selection of walk-in stream fishing is reached within thirty minutes to three hours hiking time from Sorenson's. Pleasant Valley Creek, primarily a late June through early fall fishery, is an easily waded trophy brown and rainbow trout stream restricted to fly fishing with single point barbless hooks only. A three-fish limit is placed on the average catch of sixteen inches. Mayflies are the primary food resource here with standard attractor patterns such as adams, royal wulffs, humpies, and hair-winged variants working well. Productive nymph patterns include muskrats and hare's ear nymphs.

Slinkard Valley Creek, an early summer fishery, is a small spring-fed creek with brook trout up to sixteen inches and some cutthroats. Fly fishing is excellent here but is recommended for anglers in good physical condition as it is a long hike in. Poison Creek is a six-mile trek on foot or horseback and is a great eastern brook trout stream. Both of these fisheries are prime examples of wilderness brook trout streams at their peak: remote, picturesque, and loaded with hungry fish. Mickey finns, woolly worms, black flying ants, and mosquito patterns (#8–16) are sure to provoke action for anglers willing to take the time to visit these two small creeks. Small fisheries are delicate and these are no exception; barbless hooks and a catch-and-release policy are encouraged to preserve them for future generations.

There are also plenty of lakes to fish nearby. Upper and Lower Blue lakes are small and fun to float tube for rainbows and cutthroats. Tamarack Lake yields native rainbows and brooks and Upper and Lower Sunset lakes produce rainbows. Fourteen-inch to sixteen-inch brook trout have been taken from Red and Caples lakes, which are good spring and fall fisheries. Caples Lake is also famous for its mackinaws (weighing up to nineteen pounds), fall browns, and winter ice fishing. Heenan Lake is catch-and-release, artificial flies and lures only, with streamers

working very effectively on its population of large cutthroats.

Throughout the year, Sorenson's offers on-site classes in rod building and fly tying conducted by local artisan Judy Warren. Ms. Warren is an avid fly-fishing enthusiast who knows the high Sierras of Alpine County well.

Sorenson's sells licenses and a limited amount of angling supplies. Fishing supplies are available nearby in Woodford Station; Monty Wolfe's Sporting Good Store in Markleville and the Outdoorsman in South Lake Tahoe carry the widest selection of gear and tackle. The Reno Fly Shop is another good source for flies, equipment, and up-to-the-minute fishing information.

NORTHEASTERN CALIFORNIA

RICK'S LODGE

Glenburn Star Route, Fall River Mills, CA 96028. Phone: April–November (916) 336-5300; November–April (916) 336-6618. Contact: Rick and Linda Piscitello, owners. Total capacity: 24. Open April 1–November 15. Peak season: July 20–September 10. Reserve 1 month in advance in peak season; 1 week other times. Two-day minimum stay. No pets.

Accommodations: Thirteen nonhousekeeping motel units sleep 1–2 people; units equipped with fly-tying bench. Maid service; laundry facility.

Meals: A la carte from main lodge dining room; open to public. River lunches prepared at extra charge. Full service bar.

Rates: Moderate; rates include lodging only. Twenty-five percent discount in off season. Packages include Fly Fishing School, Fall River Fly Shop Guides, and 7-Day Fishing Expedition. Boat rentals extra. Nonguests with boats pay daily rod fee. Cash, check, MasterCard, VISA, travelers check.

How to Get There: Located 80 miles south of Redding on good paved roads. Take I-5 north to Route 299, east to Fall River Mills. Rick's will provide exact directions when reservations are confirmed. Airlines and buses service Redding and Reno, NV. Free pick-up from Fall River Mills airport for guests arriving in private planes. Rental car recommended for local travel.

Located in the northeastern corner of California, Rick's Lodge sits on the bank of the Fall River in a large valley framed by Mount Shasta to the northeast. While the landscape is reminiscent of the high plains of central Montana, the spectacular backdrop of the northern Sierra Nevadas provides the mountain vistas every angler looks for.

Rick's Lodge was originally a private getaway place for friends and family of the late California senator Metzger. His widow ran it as a bar for lumbermen before Rick took it over fifteen years ago. Since then, Rick has rebuilt the main lodge, bar, dining room, and cabins only yards away from the marshy banks of the river. Rick's Lodge is one of the few catch–and–release fly-fishing lodges still open to the public and is an ideal destination resort for serious anglers.

Nonhousekeeping motel units are modern, wood-paneled rooms, each with a fly-tying bench equipped for two people.

Things to Do

There are numerous short drives to local points of natural and historical interest within an easy day's ride from the lodge. A scenic drive through Lassen Volcanic National Park is worth a day on the road. The alpine terrain is covered with wildflowers in summer, and park service exhibits are both entertaining and informative. Indian and pioneer artifacts on display in nearby Fort Crook are also engaging. Recreationists can enjoy a variety of water sports on nearby Lake Shasta and golfing at the Fall River Country Club.

Fishing

Fall River, a spring-fed tributary of the Pit River, is an extremely productive stream averaging three thousand fish per mile. It offers prime fishing for native trout, mostly rainbows running to six pounds and larger with an average size of fifteen to eighteen inches from April through October. Some large browns are taken in April, but the best time of year for them is in October and

November. There are few small fish.

The river is typical of a spring creek. It is slow moving and gin clear and supports an abundance of natural vegetation that provides an incredibly food-rich habitat for trout and aquatic insects alike. This overabundance of natural trout fodder creates a challenging situation for fly fishers. Rick estimates that, on the average, it takes four to five hours to hook one or two "good fish" (eighteen to twenty-two inches). This is finesse fishing at its best. Even when the lodge is booked to capacity, "guests can be on the river all day and not see two other boats," Rick claims. Knowledgeable guides, limited fishing pressure, and a copious trout population are right out the front door.

Fishing is from small boats outfitted with an electric motor on six to seven miles of private access water on the upper Fall River. Wading is prohibited because of the water's depth and the marshy and reedy banks that make wade fishing from shore extremely difficult. Since strong legs and good wading technique are unnecessary here, Rick's is a great spot for older anglers.

Three additional blue-ribbon trout streams within an hour from Rick's Lodge include the well-known Pit River, Hat Creek, and the McCloud River. All are wadeable wild trout streams with excellent hatch activity all season long.

Three-day fly-fishing schools are held at Rick's by Fall River guide Bob Quigley. "The schools are designed to be both a learning *and* fishing experience," he says. Dry fly-fishing clinics emphasize on-stream instruction covering slack line, dead drift, proper striking techniques, and basic fly selection. Nymph fishing clinics cover wet-tip mending tactics, proper fly selection/relationship to motion, and analysis of spring creek flow and currents for presentation.

A fly shop on the premises offers a complete line of angling gear and tackle for fly fishers. Flies tied to match the local hatches are a specialty. Licenses can be purchased at the Dana store one mile west. Four full-time guides see that guests are outfitted properly with a 3-5 weight rod, 16-foot to 20-foot leader and 6-8X tippet. A strict

policy of catch-and-release on a single barbless hook is enforced on all private waters.

Fishing season opens for streams in late April with excellent streamer fishing for rainbow and brown trout. Sculpin, leech, matuka patterns, and small trout imitations work best. Golden stone (#10), drake, and pale morning dun hatches begin the dry fly activity. May represents the peak of green drake (#12), salmon fly (#4), and pale morning dun (#16–18) hatches with excellent dry fly and nymph fishing after the hatch. Caddis, cranefly nymphs (#8), and mayfly nymphs (#10–18) are also productive. Evening caddis hatches become very heavy. June is the peak of dries and nymphs, with large hexagenia (#6–8) and yellow stones working best. The hex hatch continues into July along with pale morning dun and heavy green caddis (#14–18) activity which continues through August. September repeats the July hatches with large orange caddis becoming effective as well. Pale morning duns, green drakes, and orange caddis (#8) produce into November, when dry and streamer fishing is hot for browns.

NORTHERN SIERRAS

Feather River Area Fisheries

Located in the picturesque portion of north-eastern California where the Sierra Nevadas meet the Cascades, the Feather River area includes the communities of Chester, Greenville, Portola, and Quincy. This part of northern California lies approximately a hundred miles north of Lake Tahoe. Peaks rise up to ten thousand feet and tower over the many river canyons below. Once famous for its mining and timber industries, this area is quickly gaining a reputation as one of the best outdoor recreation spots in California.

Middle Fork Drainage

The Feather River area is a fly fisher's dream. An angler could stay here two weeks and never fish the same fishery twice. There are over one hundred lakes and a thousand miles of streams to fish within 1.5 million acres of watershed and timberland in this scenic area of northern California.

The Middle Fork, one of six rivers originally protected under the Wild and Scenic Rivers Act of 1968, and the North Fork of the Feather River, together with their feeder streams, are the principal river fisheries. Altogether nearly 108 miles in length, the Middle Fork begins in the Sierra Valley near Beckwourth and flows gently westward until it plunges down the Sierra's west slope into Lake Oroville. Because this fork of the Feather is so rugged and tough to access, it is considered to be one of the better trout rivers in California. The opportunity to catch large fish exists for anglers in good physical condition. The river is well known for stocked and native rainbow, brown, and brooks averaging eleven to fourteen inches with some anglers claiming they've caught browns and rainbows as "long as your arm."

North Fork Drainage

The scenic North Fork of the Feather River is also known for quality dry and wet fly fishing for rainbow and brown trout. The Hamilton Branch, whose headwaters are near Lake Almanor, is a canyon river with excellent fly fishing for browns and rainbows. General fishing season on the Feather River opens Memorial Day weekend, almost one month later than other California fisheries, in order to protect spring-spawning rainbows. Early on in the season, the flooded meadows at the mouth of the Feather River are popular for fly fishing and are easily handled with hip boots or waders. The summer-run german browns begin their sprawning journey from Lake Almanor into surrounding streams in mid-July, continuing through August. A big fall run in October receives relatively little pressure because the local sportsmen turn their attention to hunting season.

The North Fork of the Yuba River, with some spectacular rainbow fishing, is an hour's drive south of the Feather River heartland. Though the fish are not huge (ten to fourteen inches average), there are some excellent caddis hatches in July and August, best imitated with the old standby, an elk hair caddis (#14).

Lake Fishing

Lake fishing is very productive, popular, and easily reached in the Feather River area. Antelope Lake yields rainbows, browns, catfish, and smallmouth bass. Buck's Lake is good for kokanee salmon, rainbows, and browns. Davis Lake produces rainbows, browns, and mackinaws, and browns and rainbow trout are taken from Gold Lake. Below Plumas Eureka State Park, more than thirty natural lakes along the Gold Lake Loop are within hiking distance of each other. PG&E powerhouses form a series of lakes, including Lake Almanor and Butt Valley Reservoir, that interconnect with one another, producing some rather interesting ecological situations that foster the growth of trophy-size trout.

The major draw for lake fishing is Lake Almanor, with its abundant yield of kokanee, rainbow and brown trout, smallmouth bass, and catfish. Bass are taken from shore all summer long whereas salmon and trout are fished in deeper water. Eagle Lake has produced some prize rainbows; however, Butt Valley Reservoir is regarded as *the* spot for trophy rainbows. The reservoir holds California's record for the largest inland water rainbow, taken in 1984, which weighed eighteen pounds, six ounces. In 1985, nearly forty fish in the twelve- to fourteen-pound class were brought in from the power-house end of Butt Valley Reservoir.

The recommended fly-fishing gear for upper lakes is a 7½-foot to 8-foot, 5-7 weight rod with a floating line, long leaders (12–20 foot), and lightweight tippets. Heavier rods (6–8 weight) with shorter leaders (9 foot) and three- to four-pound tippets work well on all major rivers of the region. When fishing Butt Valley Reservoir, heavy gear and terminal tackle are musts.

Abundant mayflies in both the adult and nymph stages provide a large portion of the food source for rainbows, browns, and brookies. Hatch activity varies tremendously with the weather and changes in water flow so it's a good idea to check with one of the local fly shops to see what's working. Bill Kiene's Fly Shop in Sacramento and the Fly Shop in Redding are both reputable outfitters and carry a wide selection of gear and tackle. Bob's Bait 'n Bull in Chester also has an assortment of flies and is helpful in identifying spots where the fishing's hot.

Feather River Area Attractions

Visitors touring the Lakes Basin area, Lake Tahoe, and Reno will enjoy watching the hang-gliders hovering and soaring around nearby Mount Hough. Hikers and backpackers can trek along miles of the Pacific Crest Trail, which winds around Buck's Lake and through the Caribou Wilderness Area and Plumas State Park. Recreationists will find Antelope, Bucks, Davis, Frenchmen, and Little Grass Valley lakes popular spots for a variety of water sports including boating, fishing, waterskiing, and windsurfing. Golfers have seven nine- and eighteen-hole courses in the area to choose from.

History buffs will enjoy the Heritage Walk through Quincy or a visit to the thirty-seven-acre Railroad Museum in Portola. There's also a local museum in Taylorsville and one in Johnsville, the later of which is a restored stamp mill with a unique collection of mining equipment and relics on display.

Summertime events include a Shakespeare Festival, the Old Time Fiddlers Contest, Gold Digger Days, the Plumas County Fair, and numerous rock and gem shows, music performances, and square dances.

DRAKESBAD GUEST RANCH

June 16–September 16: Drakesbad Guest Ranch, Chester, CA 96020. Phone: (916) 529-1512. September 30–June 15: California Guest Services, 2150 North Main Street #7, Red Bluff, CA 96080. Phone: (916) 529-1512. John and Pam Koeberer, concessionaires. Total capacity: 50–60. Open mid-June to end of September. Peak season: July and August. Reserve 1 year in advance; cancellations may be available. No pets.

Accommodations: Rustic 1-bedroom cabins sleep 2–3, share bathhouse; guest lodge and bungalows offer AAA-rated bedrooms with private bath. Larger units reserved for parties of 4 or more, depending on need. Daily housekeeping services; laundry facilities.

Meals: Three family-style meals on American Plan; buffet-style or trail lunch; full-course dinners. Menus change weekly according to what's fresh. Beer and wine; all other alcohol is BYOB.

Rates: Moderate; daily rates; 10 percent discount for 7 or more days. Children charged half if sharing adult accommodations; under 2, free. Saddle horses extra. Cash, check, MasterCard, or VISA.

How to Get There: Highway 89 north and south to Chester; Highways 36 and 44 east and west. Ranch can only be reached by 17-mile dirt road winding north out of Chester. Airlines service Redding and Chico, CA, and Reno, NV. Free pick-up from Chester airport for guests arriving in private planes. Guests arriving by train to Redding must arrange own travel. Rental car recommended for local travel.

First founded by E. R. Drake in the 1860s, Drakesbad Guest Ranch passed into the Sifford family in 1900. They named the ranch for the warm-water baths and pool filled by natural hot springs on the property and operated it as a guest ranch for over fifty years. It continues to run as a guest ranch under the direction of the National Park Concessions and is located within Lassen Volcanic National Park.

Rustic lodgings are modestly furnished; most rely on kerosene lamps for lighting as there is no electricity. The main lodge houses the dining room and a spacious western-style lounge; a library is in the North East Annex.

Things to Do

Guests are in charge of their time at informal Drakesbad. A swimming pool fed from hot springs and a bathhouse are set in a grassy meadow below the cabins. Horseback riding is an enjoyable way to see the surrounding country. Scheduled rides last several hours and cover many Lassen Volcanic National Park sites.

Lassen, full of volcanic and geothermal sites, surrounds the ranch. Hiking trails climb to the summits of Lassen Peak, Cinder Cone, Prospect Peak, and Mount Harkness. Boiling Springs Lake, Devil's Kitchen, Drake Lake, Lake Almanor, Brokeoff Mountain, Kings Creek Falls, and Manzanita Lake are easily accessible by car and short hikes. National park maps indicate where smaller volcanoes and lava flows, fumaroles, hot springs, mud volcanoes, boiling lakes, and mud pots are located. Subway Cave, a lava tube that winds its way through a lava flow less than two thousand years old, is only a short drive away. The scenic Pacific Crest Trail also traverses the park north to south.

Fishing

Warner Creek, with a predominate population of native german browns, flows through Drakesbad and is rated as good fly-fishing water by locals. Six miles downstream from the ranch, the creek joins with the North Fork of the Feather River, which then descends through a four- to five-mile stretch of canyon, the Feather River Gorge. There is no road access to this challenging stretch of rough whitewater. However, it is worth the hike as it has yielded native browns and rainbows weighing up to eight pounds, with three- and four-pounders not uncommon.

Willow Creek, running out of Willow Lake, is another fun-to-fish stream within easy reach from Drakesbad. For a stream of its small size, averaging four to fifteen feet in width, it has produced some surprisingly large browns weighing up to four pounds.

Drakesbad will arrange special horseback rides and pack trips for anglers interested in fishing in Lassen Volcanic National Park. The park's eastern sector is strung with a number of alpine lakes extending from Butte Lake near the eastern base of Prospect Peak in the north to Juniper Lake at the northern base of Mount Harkness in the south. These lakes are home to rainbow, brook, and brown trout. The closest lake to the ranch, Dream Lake, offers good fishing for brooks and is only a ten-minute hike from the lodge. Typical brookie patterns such as mickey finns, woolly worms, and black-nosed daces (#6–8) work well. Anglers should come well equipped as the ranch does not sell licenses or tackle. See Feather River Area Fisheries for more fishing information.

GREENHORN CREEK GUEST RANCH

Spring Garden P.O. Box 11, Quincy, CA 95971-7010. Phone: (916) 283-0930. Murray Howard, owner. Total capacity: 80. Open March–November. Peak season: June–August. Reserve in advance. No pets.

Accommodations: Modern duplex and fourplex cabins with private baths and front-porch swings. Daily maid service; laundry facility.

Meals: Three hearty meals daily on American Plan; lunches available on the trail; full dinners include weekly barbecue, campfire marshmallow roast. Chef will prepare fresh-caught trout to preference. Ribs are ranch specialty.

Rates: Moderate; weekly rates include lodging, meals, horseback riding, riding lessons, and all ranch activities; daily rates also available. Add 25 percent for single occupancy; super-saver, referral, senior citizen, and repeat discounts. Special group rates. Check, MasterCard, or VISA.

How to Get There: Located south of Quincy off highways 89 and 70. Free pick-up from Quincy for guests arriving in private planes or by bus; commercial airlines serving Reno provide transportation to the ranch.

Greenhorn Creek Guest Ranch, touted as the "Shangri-La of the Feather River Country," is an 840-acre dude ranch surrounded on three sides by a million acres of Plumas National Forest. Lush flowered meadows interlaced by miles of cool streams encompass the ranch, creating an atmosphere of serenity and seclusion. Estray Creek, flowing through the ponderosas nearby, lulls the senses. Greenhorn Creek is just the place for those who want to acquire good horsemanship skills while enjoying good food and relaxation. Cabins with knotty pine walls and comfortable furnishings exude a feeling of warmth.

Things to Do

From beginning to end, Greenhorn's weekly schedule is filled with activities; there's also plenty of time out for relaxation. Two- to five-year-olds have their own program supervised by a trustworthy female wrangler.

Horseback riding is the main emphasis; daily morning and afternoon rides for beginners and experienced riders alike take guests across flowered meadows and into forests of giant firs, pines, cedars, and quaking aspens. Free riding lessons are available to those who want to brush up on their skills. Hikers and anglers will also appreciate the beauty of the surrounding Plumas National Forest, laced with miles of trails alive with deer, raccoons, and birds.

Swimming in a large heated pool or in a swimmin' hole in Greenhorn Creek are activities for guests to enjoy when taking a break from the saddle. Meanwhile, young fly fishers can practice their angling techniques on the ranch's stocked pond before venturing out on their own. Additional activities include volleyball, Ping-Pong, horse-shoes, badminton, softball, frog races, and rope-spinning contests. After dinner, most guests participate in singalongs, square dancing, card playing, and amateur nights held in the dance hall.

Fishing

A well-known veteran fly fisherman visits Greenhorn quite regularly to conduct fly-casting exhibitions and to give a few pointers on technique and fly selection. His favorite patterns include the bucktailed royal coachman and yellow palmer. Licenses, equipment, and tackle are avail-

able in Quincy at the Quincy Sports Center or the Sportsmen's Den. Independent guides can also be arranged through local sports shops or through the ranch. Refer to the fishing information in the Feather River Area Fisheries section, paying particular attention to the Middle Fork of the Feather River.

LAYMAN RESORT

P.O. Box 8, Blairsden, CA 96103. Phone: (916) 836-2356. Contact: Steve and June Waasdorp, owners/managers. Total capacity: 45–55. Open April–October. Peak season: mid-June–mid-September. Book 3 months in advance.

Accommodations: One- and 2-bedroom cabins with kitchenette and private bath sleep 2–5; larger units with kitchenette, private bath, and screened-in porch sleep 8–12. All units heated with propane or wood-burning stoves. Clean linens supplied weekly; laundry facility in nearby towns.

Meals: N/A. Groceries available in town.

Rates: Inexpensive; weekly and daily rates include lodging only. Prices vary according to the number of people in party. Discount for senior citizens. Cash or check only.

How to Get There: Located 4 miles west of Blairsden on Highway 89-70. Commercial airlines service airport in Reno, NV; airstrip for small planes in Quincy and Beckwourth. Rental car recommended for local travel. Layman will pick up guests at intersection of highways 89 and 70 with advance notice.

Located just off highways 70 and 89 on the banks of the Middle Fork of the Feather River, the Layman is one of the few remaining old resorts developed during the advent of the railroad in the vicinity. It is ideal for families and fishermen who desire comfortable low-cost housekeeping accommodations on their holiday in Feather River country. The weathered exteriors of Layman Resort's rustic housekeeping cabins, built circa 1920 to 1930, lend a historic patina to the dated resort.

Things to Do

The cabins share a common area with a barbecue and campfire pit, horseshoe pit, and shuffleboard court. A deep-pit barbecue can be used to roast an entire pig on special occasions. Close by, the Layman has easy access to a private bathing beach on the Middle Fork of the Feather River. The resort also has a small office that sells a very limited supply of tackle, cards, and postage stamps.

Guests will most likely want to explore the numerous fishing and hiking opportunities found nearby. Steve and June Waasdorp, owners of Layman Resort, know the area well and will help make arrangements with just about any sort of guide or recreational service visitors are interested in. Tennis, golf, and horseback riding can be arranged in nearby Graeagle and Blairsden.

Fishing

Refer to Feather River Area Fisheries section.

NORTHERN CALIFORNIA

JH GUEST RANCH

8525 Homestead Land, Etna, CA 96027. Phone (916) 467-3468. Contact: Gene and Joy Johnston, owners. Total capacity: 60–75; 90 with conference facilities. Open: June–mid-September. Peak season: July–August. Last week in June and last 2 weeks in July for families only; childcare provided. Reserve 3 months in advance; groups 1 year in advance. No pets.

Accommodations: Five deluxe cabins equipped with kitchen, bath, and wood-burning stoves; 10 motel-type cabins sleep 1–6, no kitchen facilities; some cabins have porches. Dormitory reserved for groups and retreats sleeps 20–30; shower, bathroom, and dressing room. Maid service; laundry facility.

Meals: Three family-style meals served in dining room or on patio. Snack bar stays open between meals. Beer, wine, and liquor are BYOB.

Rates: Inexpensive; daily rates include lodging, meals, and ranch activities in motel-type cabins. Meals are a la carte for housekeeping cabins. Special rates for children; children under 2, free. Special conference rates. Horseback riding extra. Package rates for high country lake fishing, photographic excursions, whitewater raft trips. Cash or check only.

How to Get There: Six-hour drive from San Francisco, CA, or 2½-hour drive from Medford, OR. From San Francisco, take I-5 to Yreka; Highway 3 through Fort Jones and Etna; turn-off to ranch is 4 miles south of Etna. From Medford, take I-5 south to Yreka, CA and follow directions above. Nearest airport and bus depot are in Yreka; free pick-up from ranch. Free pick-up from Scott Valley Airport in Fort Jones for those with private planes.

The JH Guest Ranch, a year-round resort on 275 acres of meadows, forested hills, and meandering streams, offers relaxation in an atmosphere of warm Christian hospitality. While June through September are reserved for family vacations, the ranch is used the remainder of the year as a religious retreat and center for educational and business seminars. Located in the heart of northern California's Marble Mountains, JH enjoys access to two spectacular primitive areas within the Klamath National Forest: the Marble Mountain Wilderness and Salmon–Trinity Alps Primitive Area.

Lodging

Cabins and motel-type cabins have knotty pine paneling and wood-burning stoves; covered back porches on some provide a quiet place to recline under a tree-filled sky near rushing Payne's Creek. A dormitory reserved for groups and retreats of twenty to thirty people has two sides, each complete with separate shower, bathroom and dressing facilities, sleeping lofts with skylights and full balcony decking, and high-beamed ceilings. The main lodge houses a log-sided living room with a huge stone fireplace and library.

Things to Do

Activities at JH Guest Ranch are structured very informally. A shooting range, tennis courts, and solar-heated swimming pool are available to guests; guests are welcome to join impromptu games of volleyball, shuffleboard, Ping-Pong, and horseshoes. Daily activities for children include hayrides, lawn games, pond fishing, and minihikes to waterfalls close by. A special petting zoo down by the barn allows children to get to know and learn how to take care of tame farm animals.

Customized four-wheel drive excursions and horseback rides into the wilderness can be arranged for an extra charge. The ranch staff will also make arrangements with local guides for guests interested in pack trips into more remote areas of the Marble Mountain Wilderness. Organized raft trips on the Klamath River or innertubing on the Scott River also cost extra but are well worth the exhilarating experience.

Evening festivities include outside barbecues, games in the meadow, rodeos, and mock shootouts; on Fridays the lighted tennis courts are used for square dancing. An old barn has also been converted into a social center for live entertainment.

Scenic day trips include the seventy-five-mile Salmon River Loop crossing Etna Summit into the heart of the historical Northern Mines region. It eventually circles back through the once bustling prospecting and mill towns of Salmon, Cecilville, and Callahan. Along the way, visitors have ample opportunities to pan for gold, explore hydraulic mines of the last century, and get a glimpse of rural ranch life that hasn't changed much in the last fifty years. A drive through the Trinity Alps to Lake Trinity for a day of waterski-

ing is another fun adventure the whole family will enjoy. Golfers have easy access to the Lake Shastine Golf Resort in the nearby town of Weed.

Other interesting side trips include a visit to the Siskiyou County Museum in Yreka, the nationally acclaimed Shakespeare Festival in Ashland, Oregon, and the restored Victorian town of Jacksonville, Oregon. Summertime festivities climax with Yreka's Siskiyou Golden Fair in mid-August.

Fishing

The principal local fishery, the Klamath River, supports probably the longest season for steelhead in the Klamath Knot, a diversified geographic region encompassing several river drainages in northern California and southern Oregon. Steelhead in the Klamath River average five to seven pounds. These chrome-colored sea-run rainbows are vigorous fighters and offer a real challenge even for more experienced anglers.

In fall and winter, two other local fisheries, the Scott and Salmon rivers, also offer good fishing for steelhead and salmon.

The Klamath is a deep, fast-moving river that demands respect. Anglers new to the area are well advised to enlist the services of a professional guide for the first day or two. Kutzkey's Lodge, outside of Hornbrook, is a reputable steelhead outfitter; several guides who operate out of Fomes Bar can be contacted through sporting goods stores in Yreka, Etna, or Fort Jones. Heavier gear—a 7–9 weight rod with either a sink-tip line or a shooting head and reels with plenty of backing—is recommended for steelhead fishing as long casts are often required.

Trout fishing for rainbows averaging eight to twelve inches in the Klamath reaches its peak during late summer and early fall. Lighter gear such as a 6–7 weight rod with a floating line and 7–9 foot leaders are quite adequate for catching these smaller rainbows. Darker fly patterns (#8–12) such as black gnats, flying black ants, and mosquitos are dependable. On the Scott and Salmon rivers, mosquitos, buzz hackle, and other gray patterns (#10–12) are productive. Smaller white patterns such as the white miller (#10–12) work especially well on the Salmon.

Surfaced roads provide access to the Carter Meadows–Cecilville areas, Salmon River, Trinity Lakes, Klamath River, and the lower Scott River. The Scott River is closed to salmon fishing during spawning season, September through October. It is open for steelhead and salmon fishing from November 1 to March 1.

The Marble Mountain Wilderness and Salmon–Trinity Alps Primitive Area contain nearly two hundred lakes, most of which are limited to trail access. Many of these lakes, usually ice-free by mid-June, are stocked regularly with fingerling rainbow and brook trout and graylings. Kangaroo Lake and Lily Pad Pond east of Callahan offer good trout fishing and are an easy day's trip from the ranch. A popular outing JH guests look forward to is a four-wheel drive to Paynes Lake for feisty rainbow, brook, and brown trout. As is the case with all high-mountain lakes, both the weather and the fishing can be unpredictable so anglers should try not to have unreasonable expectations. A couple of productive high-lake fly patterns (#12–16) to pack include flying black ants, black gnats, mosquito imitations, adams, and streamers (#6–10). Eastern brooks, rainbows, and german browns are found in lower lakes that feed over five hundred miles of tributary streams. These streams also act as spawning beds for steelhead and salmon.

Fishing licenses, gear, and a limited selection of tackle can be purchased in the True Value Hardware Store in Etna and in Fort Jones. Don's Sporting Goods and Ken's Sporting Goods in Yreka also carry a good selection of fishing supplies.

NORTHERN CALIFORNIA

COFFEE CREEK GUEST RANCH

P.O. Star Route 2, Box 4940, Trinity Center, CA 96091. Phone: (916) 266-3343. Contact: Mark and Ruth Hartman, managing owners. Total capacity: 45. Open late April to end of October. Peak season: mid-June–Labor Day. Several adult-only weeks during season; please inquire. Reserve 1 year in advance. Small pets allowed.

Accommodations: Six 2-bedroom cabins; 8 1-bedroom cabins; all with private bath, outdoor decks, and wood-burning stoves. Two larger cabins with extra bath and stone fireplace. Maid service; laundry facility.

Meals: Three family-style meals daily on American Plan; lunch buffet or sack lunches, special dinners include barbecue, steak fry, and Thanksgiving dinner. Beer and wine served; all other alcohol is BYOB.

Rates: Inexpensive; weekly rates include lodging, meals, ranch activities, use of ranch facilities, babysitting, and cribs. Children under 2, free. Discounts on off-season rates. Extra charges: horseback riding and round-trip pick-up services from Redding airport. Cash, check, travelers check, American Express, or Discovery Card.

How to Get There: Six-hour drive north of San Francisco, 2-hour drive from Redding, CA. From Redding, take Highway 299 past Whiskeytown Lake to Highway 3; north on Highway 3 just past Trinity Center to Coffee Creek Road; ranch is 7 miles up Coffee Creek Road. Free pick-up from Trinity Center airport for guests arriving in private planes. Commercial airlines service Redding; rental car recommended for local travel.

Coffee Creek Guest Ranch is located on the edge of the rugged Salmon–Trinity Alps Wilderness of the Trinity National Forest in northwestern California. Compared with other summer mountain playgrounds in the state, the Trinity Alps area receives relatively little tourist pressure; backcountry hikers encounter very few, if any, other travelers during a day's trek.

Originally a boardinghouse for miners in the early 1900s, Coffee Creek Guest Ranch today is a 127-acre family resort. The way the Hartmans, ranch owners and hosts, see it, "People come up from the city tired of the battles. When they get here they can just be themselves." A high rate of return clientele attests to a job well done. Additionally, Coffee Creek's children's program lends a special appeal to families with youngsters.

Wood-paneled cabins are tucked into a densely forested hillside above the main lodge. A spacious lodge houses the main dining room, gift shop, and video game room. Located nearby is a recreation room equipped with a pool table.

Things to Do

Coffee Creek's casual ambience frees guests to come and go as they please. On-ranch activities include swimming in a heated pool, hayrides, shuffleboard, badminton, volleyball, horseshoes, and Ping-Pong. An archery range equipped with bows and arrows and a rifle range and trap range are located on the property. Ammunition and clay pigeons are sold in Coffee Creek's gift shop. A special Kiddie Korral, for youngsters two to nine years old is in session Sunday through Thursday. Supervised activities include pony rides, archery, fishing, gold panning, and nature walks. Canoes are kept on a stocked pond for their use.

Many anglers and hikers use the ranch as a base camp from which to branch out into the surrounding wilderness areas. For an extra charge, Coffee Creek's Trinity Trail Rides will arrange overnights and extended stays in the Trinity Alps Wilderness or put together short breakfast and picnic rides for guests who are interested.

Local attractions include Trinity Lake, the Lewiston Fish Hatchery (the world's most automated salmon and steelhead hatchery), the J. J. Jackson Memorial Museum in Weaverville, and the Joss State House Historical Monument. Tours of working sawmills and abandoned ore mines can easily be included in a day's agenda. Family members will also enjoy a drive to Burnt Ranch Falls in the Trinity River Gorge or to Deerlick Springs, which is believed to have curative powers.

Special summertime events include the local July Fourth Celebration, Big Foot Days, and the Trinity County Fair in August. Community theater productions presented by the Trinity Players are also scheduled throughout the summer season.

Fishing

Guests have exclusive use of a half-mile stretch of Coffee Creek that runs through ranch property. The first seven miles of the creek flowing out of Trinity Lake are closed to angling, which gives ranch guests a fresh chance at catching eager native rainbows between fifteen to twenty-two inches and fall-spawning kokanee. Above the ranch, Coffee Creek runs through private property until a ten-mile stretch of public-access fishing opens up below the trout farm. Higher up, the north and east forks of Coffee Creek yield small rainbows and brooks.

The Trinity River, located five miles from Coffee Creek, was once acclaimed as one of California's premier native steelhead and salmon streams. However, two dams built twenty-some years ago upriver from the town of Lewiston have effectively destroyed the river's anadromous rainbow population. Today, the Trinity is primarily a wild brown trout stream with fish, in rare instances, running up to twenty-three inches and

six pounds. The bulk of the browns, however, remain in the ten- to twelve-inch class. Stocked and native rainbows also inhabit the river. Special regulations intended to remove the carnivorous browns in order to promote the survival of small salmon and steelhead have been somewhat successful. In the fall of 1985, the Lewiston hatchery recorded record runs of king salmon. Light cahills (#18) and large grayish-brown stoneflies (#8–12) work effectively early in the season. Later on, rubberleg nymph patterns (#6–8) such as bitch creeks, yuk bugs, and girdle bugs become productive. A section of the river from below the Lewiston Dam to the old bridge is opened to fly angling only from the end of May to mid-September.

Secondary fisheries yielding small- and largemouth bass, rainbows, german browns, and ten- to twelve-inch kokanee include Swift Creek, Stuart's Fork, and Trinity Lake.

Guided trips into the Trinity Alps Wilderness put fly fishers within easy reach of at least twenty-five lakes stocked by the Fish and Game Department. High lakes harbor rainbows averaging twelve to eighteen inches and brooks in the ten- to twelve-inch class. Browns up to two pounds are also recorded infrequently. Mark claims that fly fishing in the lakes "is spectacular!" and will follow up his statement with suggestions for specific lakes. Standard patterns (#12–16) such as adams, royal wulffs, flying ants, and mosquito imitations work well when fish are surface feeding. Woolly worms, woolly buggers, and bright streamers work best when fish are deep during the hot days.

Coffee Creek's Trading Post sells a limited supply of tackle. Licenses and a wider variety of angling supplies can be purchased at the Wyntoon Resort and Store in Trinity Center, the Fly Shop in Redding, and Brady's Sporting Goods in Weaverville.

MAMMOTH LAKES

ARCULARIUS RANCH

Route 1, Box 230, Mammoth Lakes, CA 93546. Summer phone: (619) 648-7807. Winter phone: (805) 238-3830. Contact: John Arcularius, owner; phone: (619) 872-1716. Total capacity: 45. Open end of April to end of October. Reserve in advance; reservation for following year accepted at opening of each fishing season. Pets allowed on a leash.

Accommodations: Eleven 2-, 3-, and 4-bedroom cottages sleep 6–8 people; private bath with showers and kitchens. Some have screened-in porches for extra sleeping room. Three 2-room apartments with private bath and kitchenettes. One 6-bedroom cabin with two baths and kitchen available to groups staying 1 week or longer.

Meals: N/A; freezers available for guests to store fish.

Rates: Inexpensive; daily rates; discounts for stays of 7 or more days. Children 5 and under, free; 6 and over, ½ daily rate. Additional charge for pets. Cash or check only.

How to Get There: Located 180 miles south of Reno, NV, and 50 miles north of Bishop, CA. Take U.S. 395 7½ miles north of Highway 203 intersection; ranch is 3½ miles east on Owens River Road. Free pick-up from Mammoth Lakes airport for guests arriving in private planes or by bus. Rental car recommended for those flying into Bishop.

This 1,080-acre ranch has belonged to the Arcularius family since 1919, when it was purchased as pastureland for sheep and cattle. Fishing privileges back then cost a dollar a day. There were no guest facilities until 1927, when seven cabins were built. John Arcularius has been in control of the ranch since 1976 and since that time has developed the catch-and-release fly-fishing resort as well as launched an extensive program of stream management. Modernizing the accommodations has also been included in the latest development of the ranch.

Cottages are simply but comfortably furnished. The ranch headquarters building is located a short distance upstream from the lodgings. A comfortable living room for guests, with a fireplace, pool table, television, and video unit for viewing a growing collection of cassettes on fly-fishing techniques has an adjoining country store with one of the area's largest selections of wet and dry flies and stocks a few grocery items, as well as beer and wine.

Things to Do

The most obvious and world-renowned attraction in the Mammoth Lakes region is Yosemite National Park. The scenic Tioga Pass Road connects the park with Highway 395 where it passes through Mono Lake. Visitors travel along this route through Tuolumne Meadows, a valley cradled between rock pinnacles dotted with climbers enrolled in one of the mountaineering schools sponsored by the park and independent agencies. Motorists can tour the many well-marked sites of Yosemite by themselves or join one of the tours offered by the park service. Devils Postpile National Monument and Bodie State Historical Park are two other parks within easy driving distance. A gondola ride up Mammoth Mountain provides a breathtaking panorama of the Sierras. Other day trips include a drive to Topaz or Crowley lakes where a variety of water sports are offered— waterskiing, sailboarding, boating, and fishing—

or an outing to Bridgeport to tour the Mono County Museum.

Numerous outfitters service pack trips and horseback rides into remote high-country regions for the adventuresome. Many packers tailor their trips specifically to anglers.

For a listing of concerts and stage shows scheduled throughout the summer, write c/o Festival Stage. The Mammoth Lakes Resort Association has information on festivals, fairs, athletic and motor competitions, western days celebrations, and sports tournaments.

Fishing

The area surrounding the resort town of Mammoth Lakes contains some of the most rugged and spectacular terrain in California and has long enjoyed a reputation for having some of the best fly-fishing waters in the state. From the east slope of the Sierra Nevada range flow such legendary streams as the Owens and Walker rivers and a tiny tributary of the Owens, Hot Creek. Literally hundreds of high alpine lakes, many of which are accessible by car, are within an easy day's outing from Mammoth Lakes and the larger town of Bishop to the south. In spite of fishing pressure that gets extremely intense at times, these lakes continue to produce good quantities of large fish. Additional high-lake fishing opportunities are reached by contracting the services of local outfitters who pack into the John Muir and Minaret Wilderness areas, Yosemite National Park, Pioneer and Convict lake basins, McGee and Baldwin canyons, and Majestic Fish Creek.

The upper Owens River is a twisting, meandering stream reached by a short walk or drive

from the cabins. Approximately five miles of private stream are reserved for guests only. The trout habitat in this section of the river has been greatly enhanced by the present owner's program of stream management. Gravel has been hauled in to shore up eroding banks of oxbow turns, and boulders have been placed in dead water spots to provide holding pockets and riffle water.

The season starts with native rainbows spawning around May and winds up in late September and October with the brown spawning run. October is considered an especially hot month for large browns. In order to provide the Owens River with abundant trout populations in the future, anglers are asked to abide by ranch rules which impose a two-fish limit, eighteen inches and over, with the use of pinched down or barbless hooks. Dry and wet fly imitations are the only tackle allowed.

Productive dry flies (#14–16) include adams, elk hair caddis, and light cahills. A good selection of wet fly patterns (#6–8) include hornbergs, marabou muddlers, woolly buggers, and various rubberleg patterns. May- and stonefly nymph patterns (#12–16) are productive just prior to and during the natural hatches coming off the river. Patterns (#12–16) such as the amber hare's ear nymph, zug bug, pheasant tail nymph, and golden stonefly nymph occasionally take some good-sized fish.

Fly fishers should come equipped with rods and reels; licenses and tackle can be purchased at one of a number of sporting goods stores in Mammoth Lakes or in Bishop. Arcularius' country store stocks tippets, leaders, terminal tackle, and a large selection of dry and wet flies. It also has an impressive display of preserved local flies and nymphs as examples for anglers who prefer to tie their own flies.

HOT CREEK RANCH

Summer: Route 1, Box 206, Mammoth Lakes, CA 93546. Phone: (619) 935-4214. Contact: Mr. and Mrs. John Eggleston, managers. Total capacity: 36. Open April 27–October 31. Peak season: mid-May–end of July. Most guests are repeat customers who book a year in advance. Pets allowed.

Accommodations: One-bedroom housekeeping units sleep 2–4; with living room and fully equipped kitchenette. Linens furnished.

Meals: N/A

Rates: Inexpensive; weekly and daily rates; weekend rates with 3-day minimum stay. Cash or check only.

How to Get There: Located across the road from Mammoth Lakes airport, just off Highway 395 between June Lake and the town of Bishop. Guests arriving in Mammoth Lakes met free of charge. Rental car recommended for those arriving in Bishop.

Hot Creek was homesteaded in the early 1900s as a 720-acre sheep and cattle ranch. In the 1940s, William Lawrence began operating it as a fishing lodge by adding on a few shacks. Today, those shacks have been replaced by nine modern wood-sided structures that resemble small tract homes rather than cabins. Each has a carport and enclosed front porch overlooking a lawn that fronts Hot Creek.

Fishing

Hot Creek is a tributary of the Owens, but while the Owens has a migratory population of brown and rainbow trout, Hot Creek's trout population is in a uniquely locked-in situation. Fish are prevented from migrating upstream from the lakes because of a series of hot springs directly below the ranch. This condition creates an abundance of vegetation and aquatic insect life and keeps the water ice-free year round. Consequently, average-size rainbows and browns (twelve to fifteen inches) in the creek are larger than fish found in streams with more limited growing seasons.

The average width of this section of Hot Creek varies from fifteen to thirty feet. It is a slow-moving stream through sagebrush meadows with virtually no obstacles to hinder casting. Since fish have a long time to look at food floating by on the surface, they tend to be very selective. Correct fly presentation is critical. Guests must abide by a strictly enforced policy of catch-and-release, dry fly fishing with single barbless hooks. Streamer and nymph fishing are prohibited. All fishing is done from the bank (wading is not permitted) with recommended gear being a 7- to 9-foot, 3–4 weight rod.

Numerous small may- and caddisfly hatches occur throughout summer and early fall. Productive patterns (#18) include the gray sedge (caddis imitation), pale morning dun, adams, and quill gordon. Also see fishing section for Arcularius Ranch for further information.

A fly shop on the premises carries a complete selection of tackle suitable for Hot Creek, including specially designed dry flies. The ranch does not sell licenses; they can be purchased along with any additional equipment in sporting goods stores in Mammoth Lakes or Bishop.

CENTRAL SIERRA NEVADAS

MUIR TRAIL RANCH

June–October: P.O. Box 176, Lakeshore, CA 93634; no phone. October–mid-June: P.O. Box 269, Ahwahnee, CA 93601. Phone: (209) 966-3195. Contact: Adeline Smith, owner. Total capacity: 25. Open June 15–October 15. Peak season: July and August. Reserve 1 year in advance.

Accommodations: Seven tent cabins, simply furnished; 8 log cabins with private commodes and sinks. No linens or bedding. Hydro-generator supplies camp with electricity.

Meals: Three family-style meals daily on American Plan; trail lunches available. All alcohol is BYOB.

Rates: Moderate; weekly rates. Discount for children under 12. One-week minimum stay. Cash or check only.

How to Get There: Located 90 miles northeast of Fresno, CA, on Highway 168. Drive is about 4 hours; last 10 miles is very slow going. Fresno is nearest terminal for airline and bus services. No pick-up; rental cars must be left at Florence Lake boat dock.

Nestled among peaks rising over twelve thousand feet, Muir Trail Ranch is located in the remote high Sierra wilderness midway along the John Muir Trail. The two-hundred-acre ranch is completely surrounded by the Sierra National Forest, three miles to the north of the boundary of Kings Canyon National Park. The South Fork of the San Joaquin River, one of the few unspoiled high-mountain rivers left in California, runs through the ranch—the only privately owned outpost on the Muir Trail between the Devils Postpile National Monument and Mount Whitney.

An experience visitors are not likely to forget, the trip to the ranch leaves civilization far behind. After traveling along a winding one-lane road, travelers arrive at Florence Lake—a pristine, emerald gem of an alpine lake. From there, it's a twenty-minute shuttle across the lake to the edge of the wilderness, where wranglers with saddle and pack horses await to portage guests the rest of the way. High Sierra vistas along the five-mile stretch of Muir Trail to the ranch are resplendent with air so clean it almost hurts to breathe. Muir Trail Ranch is the ideal destination for adventurous families and couples who enjoy the physical out-of-doors and basic creature comforts.

Cabins are made up of a canvas roof tied onto a wooden platform and situated along the bank of the South Fork of the San Joaquin. Simply furnished with double and single beds and wooden shelves to store gear on, they share outdoor campfire pits and centrally located plumbed facilities. The ranch has an intimate log dining lodge and a common room in the main lodge comfortably furnished for reading and socializing. Nearby, two spring-fed soaking pools perched above a wide meadow are enclosed by simple log siding. Open frame windows and ceilings allow guests to soak away their cares in 108-degree water while enjoying a view of the surrounding mountains by day and a breathtaking view of the star-filled sky by night.

Things to Do

Guests are in charge of their own daily agendas at Muir Trail. A roster is posted each evening for guests to sign up for riding lessons and guided horseback rides. Wranglers know where the prime fishing spots are located for anglers interested in alpine lake and stream fishing away from the ranch. Many guests simply accompany the wranglers to enjoy the magnificent and rugged scenery of the high Sierra while picnicking and photographing along the way. Hikers and backpackers also use the numerous riding trails branching out from the ranch into the surrounding John Muir Wilderness. Evolution Valley, Mount Goddard, and Mount Humphrey are all within Muir Trail's pack vicinity.

After several days of strenuous activity, visitors may want to just settle back with a book from the ranch's well-stocked library or head up to a swimming lake partially warmed by hot springs.

Fishing

The main angling attraction at Muir Trail is a stretch of the South Fork of the San Joaquin River that runs through one mile of ranch land and is reserved exclusively for guests. Although heavy damming and irrigation have destroyed fishing on the lower reaches of the main San Joaquin River, the upper mountain tributaries and forks remain productive fisheries, with large populations of browns and rainbows up to fifteen to sixteen inches. The best fly fishing starts after the spring runoff, around July Fourth, and continues through September.

The South Fork is primarily a mayfly river with some caddis hatches occuring from midsummer on. In this swift river with an abundance of riffle water, standard attractor patterns (#14–18) such as elk hair caddis, royal wulffs, adams, and humpies work well. Grasshopper and ant patterns produce a lot of action during August. A good selection of wet flies (#12–14) to include are hare's ear and pheasant tail nymphs and zug bugs. During autumn, large browns up to 18 inches will strike hard at olive matukas and woolly buggers (#6–8).

Before the South Fork clears, anglers stick to fishing in nearly a dozen high-country lakes and smaller tributary streams found within a five-mile radius of the ranch. Golden trout found in nearby Sally Keyes Lake are descendants of fingerlings planted by Adeline's husband's grandfather, who served as Fresno County's first head of the Fish and Game Department. These beautiful fish tend to be a little smaller, six to thirteen inches, but the way they rise to a dry fly is heartstopping! Brooks and a few eight- to fourteen-inch browns are found downstream in numerous beaver ponds. Productive lake patterns include flying black ants, black gnats and mosquitos (#12–16), and black woolly worms (#6–10).

Hip waders with stream cleats and a 8- to 8½-foot, 6-weight rod will suffice for both river and lake fishing. The ranch strongly encourages catch-and-release fly fishing and has published a booklet to aid novices developing their angling techniques. A few of the wranglers are also old hands at teaching the basics of tying on a fly, casting, and catch-and-release tactics.

A selection of locally tied flies is available at the ranch. Licenses and equipment can be purchased at Herb Bauer's Sporting Goods in Fresno or at the Red Barn Hardware Store in Shaver Lake on the way up to Florence Lake.

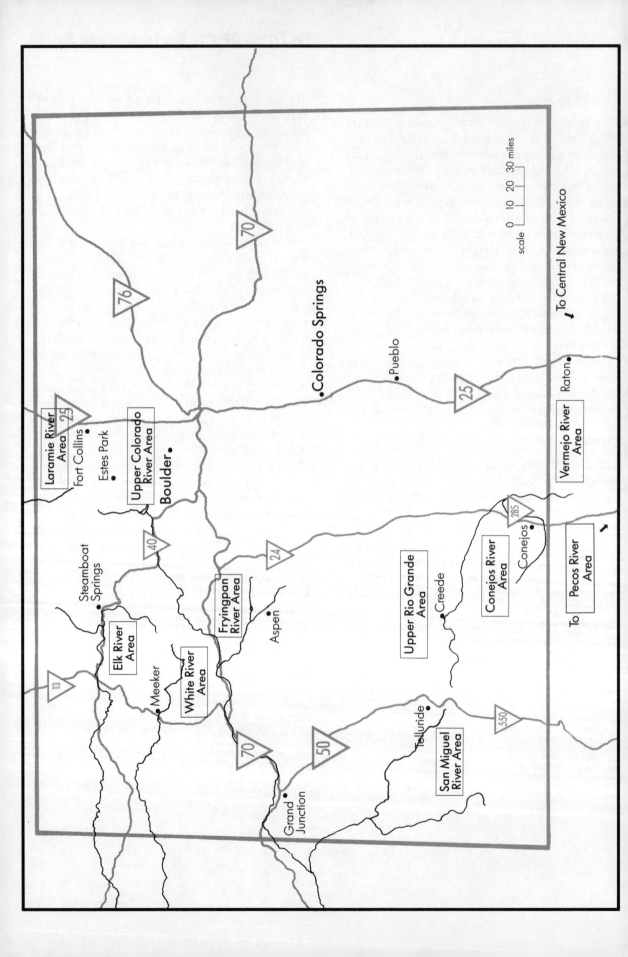

COLORADO
&
NORTHERN NEW MEXICO

SAN JUAN MOUNTAINS

Conejos River Area Fisheries

The San Juan Mountains form a part of the Rocky Mountain chain, which creates the great Continental Divide in northern New Mexico and southern Colorado. In spite of their relative lack of notoriety, the San Juans have long been a favorite spot for vacationers and fishermen who want to sample the scenic wonders of the Rockies without having to put up with the tourist pressure of more highly developed areas of central Colorado.

The San Juan Mountains possess some of the most productive fisheries found in either Colorado or New Mexico. Principal river systems include the Conejos and Los Pinos, along with their major tributaries and feeder streams — many of which are quite difficult to fish but nonetheless rewarding for the patient angler. Dozens of high-mountain lakes and reservoirs also offer spectacular fishing for large trout.

Conejos River Drainage

The Conejos River begins about thirty miles southwest of Del Norte, Colorado, near the town of Platoro. Headwaters flow south through the San Juan Wilderness, then east through the Conejos River Valley to Antonito. From there, the river flows north until finally joining the Rio Grande. Prime fishing is found on the stretch west of Antonito, which has more than sixty miles of almost unrestricted access. Parts of this beautiful mountain stream have been designated wild trout waters and are protected by special regulations. The Conejos averages fifty feet in width and, for the most part, is wadeable except during spring runoff. Riffle and pocket water provide abundant cover for small browns predominating in the upper half and for larger browns and rainbows up to twenty inches in the lower half.

The main Conejos has good fishing from Memorial Day through mid-October, with the best fishing for browns occurring between the first of September and mid-October. Midge, mayfly, and caddis hatches occur all summer long, and flies such as the adams, blue dun, and humpy (#10–14) will consistently take fish. The house and lot (#10–14) — basically a hair-winged variant — is another dry fly favorite on local waters, as well as on fisheries throughout southern Colorado. Standard nymphs such as the gold-ribbed hare's ear and muskrat (#12–16) work when fish aren't interested in dry flies.

Lake and South Forks Drainages

The Lake Fork branch of the Conejos enters the main river below the town of Platoro and has several sections of water where special restrictions are enforced to protect its population of Rio Grande cutthroat. The Conejos's South Fork enters the main river twenty miles downstream from the Lake Fork branch. It has good fishing for smaller rainbows, brookies, and cutthroats up to twelve and thirteen inches. No Name Lake, an alpine lake in the upper reaches of the South Fork, produces cutthroats from fifteen inches to five pounds plus. Elk Creek, another major tributary of the Conejos River, offers fine meadow fishing for browns and brookies. Anglers who are willing to hike a few extra miles will find their success on Elk Creek in direct proportion to the distance they put between the end of the road and where they cast a fly.

Los Pinos River Drainage

The Los Pinos River flows down out of the San Juan Mountains joining the Conejos above Antonito. Its scenic course is visible as it follows along the Cumbres and Toltec Railroad through rough high-desert terrain. The Los Pinos intersects the New Mexico state line in several spots and anglers should have both Colorado and New Mexico state fishing license. Fishing licenses for both states can be purchased in Chama, New Mexico, or Antonito, Colorado.

The upper section of the Los Pinos is easily reached by car at the top of the Cumbres Pass separating New Mexico and Colorado. The relative ease of access to this section causes it to suffer moderate fishing pressure, primarily on weekends. Native brookies and browns up to thirteen inches willingly take the same flies that produce on the Conejos. A few miles farther downstream, the river enters a box canyon section. It is in this rugged and hard-to-reach section of the river that the best fishing is encountered. Fish average ten to fourteen inches and larger fish up to twenty inches are not uncommon. Due to the lack of pressure, fish are not nearly as selective and the opportunity to hook thirty to fifty fish per day is there for the angler who has legs to match his or her desire.

Conejos River Area Attractions

One of the more intriguing features of this area is that, regardless of how remote it feels, it is still within easy commuting distance to out-of-the-way artistic and cultural communities that have sprung up all over the American Southwest. The galleries of Santa Fe and the picturesque town of Taos with its unique blend of Indian culture and slick commercialism are but a few short hours away.

Other nearby relics of the past include the Cumbres and Toltec Scenic Railroad and the Christ of the Desert Monastery. The Cumbres and Toltec Scenic Railroad travels daily between Chama, New Mexico, and Antonito, Colorado.

This sixty-four-mile trip over the crest of the San Juans travels along one of the last remaining stretches of narrow gauge lines that once crisscrossed this region. The scenery is spectacular; this is a must for a family outing. Avoid wearing white clothes as the locomotive is coal-powered, and a bath at the end of the day is necessary to remove the soot! Protective head covering is a good idea, too. Christ of the Desert Monastery, near Abiquiu, New Mexico, is an authentic Benedictine monastery that is home to a small community of monks who still adhere to the fourteenth century rule of St. Benedict. The monks work at weaving, pottery, and other crafts to support the monastery. Write ahead to make reservations and plan to spend the day as the drive is long and dusty.

Other local attractions worth a visit are Fort Garland and Pike's Stockade (remnants of western cavalry days), Jack Dempsey's Birthplace and Museum in Manassa, and the oldest church in Colorado, Our Lady of Guadalupe Church, near Antonito. The Alamosa National Wildlife Refuge and Monte Vista National Wildlife Refuge offer opportunities for viewing a variety of bird life. The Rio Grande Arts Center in Alamosa offers programs in visual arts, crafts, film, theater, dance, music, humanities, and education. The San Luis Museum Cultural and Commercial Center in the town of San Luis off Highway 159, with educational exhibits depicting the history and peoples of the Southwest and San Luis Valley, is also worth a visit.

LOBO LODGE

Box 565, Chama, NM 87520. Phone: (505) 756-2150. Contact: Dick and Vimmie Ray, managers. Total capacity: 20. Open late June–mid-September. Peak season: July and August. Reserve 4 months in advance. No pets.

Accommodations: Five housekeeping cabins sleep up to 6; bedding and linen provided.

Meals: Meals prepared only for guided pack trips; inexpensive restaurants in Chama.

Rates: Inexpensive; daily rates on per-person basis. Reduced rates for children under 12. Special packages for trail rides (3-person minimum) and pack trips. Spot drops and moving camps available. Cash, check, or travelers checks.

How to Get There: Located on Highway 17 north of Chamas, NM. Closest airport for commercial and private air travel in Alamosa, CO. Car rentals available at airports in Alamosa and Durango, CO, and in Albuquerque, NM.

Lobo Lodge, located high on an alpine slope in the San Juan Mountains of northern New Mexico, has access to over 10,000 acres of private land through which the Chama River flows, along with countless small feeder streams interspersed with alpine lakes. The simplicity of the accommodations and the ruggedness of the surrounding terrain are such that this lodge appeals mostly to fishermen looking for an inexpensive place to hang their hats while wetting their lines in a variety of private and scenic fisheries nearby.

Accommodations at Lobo Lodge consist of five log cabins that while not lavish are modern and fully equipped for housekeeping. A one-story ranch house serves as the gathering place for guests to swap fishing stories and compare notes at the end of the day.

Things to Do

Most Lobo Lodge guests come primarily to fish and pack into the back country. Those staying in cabin facilities are left entirely to themselves, although lodge managers Dick and Vimmie Ray are knowledgeable about what the area has to offer and very helpful to newcomers. Visitors should consider enlisting the services of Dick or one of his wranglers, who conduct horseback rides through aspen, spruce, and fir-covered ridges where enormous populations of wild game—elk, deer, bear, and an occasional mountain lion—abound. Scenery this vast may be tough to put on film but take a camera along anyway.

Fishing

The Chama River, with primary access from Lobo Lodge range land, starts high in the Colorado San Juans and flows south into New Mexico through the town of Chama. The canyon below the lodge up to the first bridge offers approximately two miles of good fly-fishing-only water with special creel restrictions. The river varies from five to twenty feet in width; riffles and undercut banks harbor native browns, cutthroats, and a few stocked rainbows. Fish average ten to twelve inches with good fishermen hooking larger fish, especially in the fall during brown trout spawning season. Two small feeder creeks, Wolf Creek and the East Fork of Wolf Creek,

provide excellent fishing for small brookies and cutthroat. Rio grande kings and royal wulffs (#10–14) will consistently hook fish in this drainage, as will flies that work on the Conejos River.

Most of the best fishing in this area is reached by horseback; folks at Lobo Lodge will gladly provide for your pack-trip needs.

HAMILTON'S RAINBOW TROUT LODGES

Antonito, CO 81120. Phone: (303) 376-5659. Contact: the Hamilton Family, owners/managers. Total capacity: 65–80. Open June 1–Labor Day. Peak season: July and August. Reserve 1 year in advance. No pets.

Accommodations: Two-bedroom pine-paneled cabins with two baths and porch; some with fireplace. One cabin sleeps up to 8. Maid service; laundry facility.

Meals: Three family-style meals daily; sack lunch available; special weekly meals include barbecue, breakfast horseback ride. Snack bar open during day.

Rates: Moderate; daily rates; 15 percent discount in off season. Rates include lodging, meals, horseback riding, ranch activities, use of ranch facilities. Extra charges: all-day horseback ride, overnight pack trip, Taos and Santa Fe day trips (3-person minimum), and round-trip airport pick-up from Alamosa. Cash or check only.

How to Get There: Located 23 miles west of Antonito, CO up the Conejos River Canyon off Highway 17. Commercial airline service Alamosa airport; guests will be picked up by prior arrangement. Alamosa airport also services private airplanes. Ranch vehicles available for fishing local waters.

Originally conceived as a private fishing club, this 750-acre ranch has been in the Hamilton family since the Depression. An immense log lodge surrounded by rustic and modern cabins commands a majestic view overlooking the western end of the Conejos River Valley through which flow nearly five miles of fly-fishing-only water on the upper Conejos River. This stretch is reserved exclusively for guests. The lodge's proximity to many fisheries in the Conejos Valley combined with its old western–style flair makes this a vacation retreat that both anglers and their families will enjoy.

Pine-paneled cabins are located slightly uphill from the main lodge and dining room. Built for members of the original club, each cabin has been renovated with modern baths, electricity, and front porches perfect for an afternoon siesta. Cabins are named after charter members who customarily used them and, even today, there are families who stay in the same cabin their grandparents did fifty years ago. Rainbow's main lodge is claimed to be one of the largest log cabin buildings still standing in the United States today.

Things to Do

Hamilton's holds the camaraderie between staff and guests in high regard. The ranch crew arrange special activities and trips on request and entertain guests every Friday night with a festive amateur theater.

Daily activities include horseback rides, tennis, volleyball, Ping-Pong or shuffleboard, and swimming in a heated pool. The lodge also offers supervised programs for children and teenagers daily; guided sight-seeing tours to Taos and Santa Fe and wildflower walks are other amusements available. Babysitting is provided by the staff on a voluntary basis.

Besides the staff's weekly amateur hour, evening entertainment includes family movies and lectures and nature films narrated by local game wardens and forest rangers. Some nights feature a square dance or overnight pack trip for adults while children enjoy their own camp-out.

Fishing

Refer to Conejos River Area Fisheries Section for fishing information.

STEAMBOAT SPRINGS, COLORADO

Steamboat Springs Area Fisheries

Steamboat Springs is situated high in the Rocky Mountains of northwest Colorado in the center of vast ranching country. Like Aspen, Steamboat is more widely recognized as one of Colorado's premier ski resorts than as a summer playground. Only recently has the town been attracting large numbers of year-round recreationists.

The Elk and Yampa rivers along with their interconnecting high-mountain streams and lakes are the two primary drainages in the Steamboat vicinity.

Elk River Drainage

The Elk River is a fast, clear stream ranging from fifty to a hundred feet across. Usually low enough to wade from mid-July on, the Elk requires caution because of unusually slippery bottom rocks. The Elk's headwaters drain the northwest side of the Mount Zirkel Wilderness Area and eventually flow down to parallel County Road 129 between Clark and Steamboat Springs. This stretch consists primarily of posted private land; permission to fish it is required. The main branch sports a wide range of water from turbulent to slow moving and is rated good for ten-inch rainbow and a few brook and cutthroats. Some large browns are taken early in the season, with the best fishing found after the first of August.

Willow Creek Drainage

Willow Creek, the largest tributary of the main Elk, offers good fishing for nine-inch to twelve-inch rainbow, brook, and cutthroat trout. Big and Mad creeks, along with the Mad's north and south forks, are additional tributaries of the Elk with excellent fishing for brooks and a few cutthroat. Smaller feeder streams above Steamboat are rated fair to excellent for cutthroats between seven inches and ten inches in their higher reaches and brooks lower down.

North and South Forks of Elk River

The North Fork of the Elk is a small, brushy stream rated fair to good in its lower part for eight-inch rainbows and brooks and excellent for these species in its upper reaches. The Sanchez Lakes, fed by tributary streams of the North Fork, offer good fishing for twelve-inch cutthroats in the upper lake and rainbows and cutthroats averaging nine inches in the lower lake. The South Fork of the Elk, together with its tributary streams and headwater lakes, is rated fair to good for small rainbows and cutthroats to twelve inches.

Yampa River Drainage

The Yampa River has its headwaters in the Flat Tops Wilderness and drains the west side of the Mount Zirkel Wilderness Area and the Elkhead Mountains. In its upper reaches, the Yampa produces native and stocked ten-inch rainbow, cutthroat, brook, and brown trout from midsummer on. The lower stretch of the Yampa west of Steamboat Springs widens from fifty to an average of a hundred feet. Wadeable riffles and deep pools harbor northern pike weighing up to twenty pounds, and rainbows and browns as well as an unfortunate number of whitefish.

Productive Yampa patterns include large streamers such as muddlers and other sculpin patterns (#6–8) and stonefly nymphs (#6–8). Popular dry fly patterns include elk hair and goddard caddis, adams, and pale morning duns (#12–18).

Lake Fishing

Mountain lakes are rated good to excellent for browns and brooks and native rainbows and cutthroats averaging ten inches to fourteen inches. Interconnecting feeder streams carry fair to good fishing for smaller brooks and cutthroats in the six-inch to ten-inch range. The Mount Zirkel Wilderness Area has over forty named lakes above ten thousand feet that are restricted to access by foot or horseback travel only. The best months to fish these lakes are May and early June when the first ice melts occur. During warm summer months, the best fishing occurs in early morning with a slow midday pace which quickens in the late afternoon and evening.

Steamboat Lake is one of the most popular, and heavily fished of the local lakes, offering good fishing all summer long for eight-inch to seventeen-inch rainbows, browns, brooks, and a few cutthroat averaging ten inches. Native trout up to five pounds are netted occasionally. Every year the lake is stocked with three hundred fifty thousand to four hundred thousand fingerling rainbows, and several years ago a strain of Snake River cutthroat was planted and has prospered. Boat rentals and guide services are available at The Dock marina. Nearby, Pearl Lake receives less angling pressure, being restricted to the use of flies and lures only. This pristine mountain lake yields one-and-a-half-pound to six-pound cutthroats and a few large rainbows in the twenty-inch class.

Good alpine lake fishing is also found in the Flat Tops Mountain Range south of Steamboat Springs. Lakes within this drainage include Sheriff's Lake, Allen Basin, and the Yamcolo Reservoir—all of which are rated excellent for rainbow, cutthroat, and brook trout. Productive dry fly patterns (#14–16) that will work on any of these high lakes include the adams, mosquito, elk hair caddis, and royal wulff. In late August, blue damsels become active. Effective wet flies (#6–8) include muddlers and yellow zonkers and small (#14–18) nymph patterns such as the muskrat, grizzly shrimp, hare's ear, and adams. Float tubes are recommended.

Straightline's and Buggywhips Fish and Float Services are two guide services located in Steamboat Springs that cater primarily to fly fishers. Both sell licenses and carry an extensive selection of tackle and equipment.

Steamboat Springs Area Attractions

The town of Steamboat Springs is a great place to spend the day browsing through galleries, bookstores, and shops filled with every kind of western curio imaginable. The town also has several golf courses and tennis courts and maintains a number of natural mineral springs for bathers.

Square dances, street parties, music festivals, and western art exhibits are scheduled during Steamboat's busy summer season as part of the town's "The Way it Wuz" days. The Fourth of July Cowboy Round-up is a week-long celebration that includes a rodeo, parade, fireworks, concerts, and carnivals. In the evenings, visitors attend performances by the Steamboat Repertory Theatre and the Perry-Mansfield School of Dance; every Friday night during July and August the grandstands are filled at the Jackpot Rodeo. Dining is another pleasurable pastime in Steamboat Springs; many fine restaurants offer Continental, ethnic, and exotic cuisines.

Local sites reached within a three-hour radius from downtown Steamboat Springs include 283-foot high Fish Creek Falls, Steamboat and Pearl lakes, Rabbit Ears Pass (so named for its distinguishing rock formations), and Buffalo Pass, known as "the gateway to Mount Zirkel." The Buffalo Pass Road travels beyond Buffalo Pass to Hidden Lakes—a popular spot for picnicking, hiking, and fishing. Scenic flights, sailplane soaring, guided bicycle tours, river rafting, and hot air balloon and jeep trips are only a few ways to tour the local vicinity. A gondola ride up to the top of Mount Werner lends a spectacular panorama of the entire area.

Hikers and backpackers have access to miles of trails within Routt National Forest, the Mount Zirkel Wilderness, and the Flat Tops Primitive Area. The Flat Tops Primitive area, with its productive cutthroat fishery, Trapper's Lake, is reached via trailheads located south of Steamboat Springs near the town of Yampa. Gold Lake, Gilpin Lake, Three Island Lake, Dome Peak, and Mica Basin are but a few of the popular trails used for day hikes into the Mount Zirkel Wilderness. Many of these trails also lead to fine alpine lake and stream fishing. Little Red, Big Red, and Whiskey parks, located northwest of Steamboat Springs, are three natural areas with meadows to walk through and wildflowers to photograph.

DEL'S TRIANGLE 3 RANCH

Box 14, Steamboat Springs, CO 80477. Phone: (303) 879-1257. Contact: Delbert Heid, guide/outfitter. Total capacity: 5–10 on pack trips. Open July 4–September 30.

Accommodations: Vary according to pack trip: deluxe trips include 3 meals a day, sleeping tents, saddle and pack horses, guide, cook, and packer; standard trips include camp equipment, cooking and eating utensils, and cook.

Meals: N/A; see Accommodations.

Rates: Inexpensive. Fifty percent deposit required. Cash or check.

How to Get There: Follow Elk River Road north from Steamboat Springs through Clark; turn west on Road 62; follow signs to corrals.

Del's is recommended only to those who like roughing it. The Triangle 3 customizes small group pack trips along the Continental Divide area in the Mount Zirkel Wilderness. The ranch also maintains a string of horses for pack-in service to drop camps and offers scenic guided rides by the hour, half-day, and full day. Guests signed up for one of Del's deluxe or standard pack trips usually stay in lodging available in Steamboat Springs or Clark before and after their wilderness trek.

Fishing

Plenty of good fishing for brooks, browns, native cutts, and a few thirteen-inch to fifteen-inch rainbows is found within a two- to three-hour ride from any one of Del's semipermanent camps. Anglers should come equipped with a license and all the necessary fishing gear before leaving Steamboat Springs. A few last-minute items are available at the General Store in Clark.

GLEN EDEN GUEST RANCH

P.O. Box 867, Clark, CO 80428. Phone: (303) 879-3906. Contact: Dave Papini, general manager. Total capacity: 214. Open March 30 to December 20. Peak season: July 1–September 15. Low season: March 30–June 30 and September 4–December 20.

Accommodations: Two-bedroom housekeeping townhomes sleep up to 6; cabins with sleeping lofts and kitchen sleep up to 8. All units have 2 baths, fully equipped kitchen, rock fireplace, and sun porch with picnic table and grill. Fresh towels daily; clean linens after 5 days.

Meals: Three family-style meals daily on modified American Plan; a la carte also available. Evening steak rides can be arranged on request. Cocktails and wine list.

Rates: Moderate; daily rates; 3-night minimum July 1–September 11. Check, MasterCard, VISA, or American Express.

How to Get There: Located 18 miles north of Steamboat Springs on Highway 129. Steamboat Springs is an easy 3½-hour drive from Denver. Commuter flights and buses service Steamboat Springs from Denver. Free pick-up service from Steamboat Springs with advance notice. Rental car recommended for local travel.

The Glen Eden Guest Ranch is the center of historic Clark, Colorado. The main lodge and restaurant and thirty-two townhomes are situated in a meadow on the Elk River with magnificent views of Mount Zirkel, Hahn's Peak, and Sand Mountain. Families who prefer a little more freedom from the group-oriented activities that prevail at a guest ranch will appreciate the privacy that comes with renting an individual townhome at the Glen Eden Ranch. Natural cedar lends a rustic look to townhome exteriors while interiors are fully modern with contemporary furnishings.

Things to Do

Unstructured activities at Glen Eden center around several tennis courts, a heated swimming pool, and two hot tubs adjacent to the lodge. Badminton, volleyball, softball, and horseshoes are set up any time guests wish to play. Rock scrambling, hiking, and tubing on the Elk River are other favorite pastimes. Glen Eden wranglers are available for mountain horseback rides by the hour, half-day, and full-day. Whitewater rafting on the Colorado River is popular; advance notice is required for overnight pack trips. On weekend evenings, the Glen Eden becomes lively with entertainment and dancing in the open-beamed cedar Fireside Lounge; this draws a big crowd from neighboring guest ranches and from Steamboat Springs.

Fishing

Located on the banks of the Elk River, Glen Eden is only a short drive away from Steamboat, Pearl, and Hahn's Peak lakes. Many small streams and tributaries of the Elk are also easily reached from the ranch. Guides can be booked through sporting goods stores in Steamboat Springs or with the assistance of the Glen Eden staff.

THE HOME RANCH

P.O. Box 882, Clark, CO 80428. Phone (303) 879-1780. Contact: Ken Jones. Total capacity: 20. Open year round. Peak season: July and August. Reserve 6 months in advance. No pets.

Accommodations: Seven log cabins; 2 duplex units. All units have private bath, wood-burning stove, Jacuzzi installed on front porch.

Meals: Three family-style meals daily on American Plan; buffet-style selections available for pack lunch; gourmet dinners; outdoor barbecue twice a week. Beer, wine, and mixers; all other alcohol BYOB.

Rates: Expensive; weekly rates; daily summer rates. Seven-night minimum stay in July and August. Checks, MasterCard, VISA, or American Express.

How to Get There: Located 18 miles north of Steamboat Springs off County Road 129; look for sign just after Clark, CO. Steamboat Springs serviced by nonstop daily flights from Denver. Free pickup from Steamboat Springs airport.

The Home Ranch is a 650-acre resort and working cattle and horse ranch situated at the edge of the Routt National Forest. With its unique style and beautiful setting, it's easy to see why the Home Ranch has been featured in publications like the *Smithsonian*, the *New Yorker, Time, Esquire*, the Los Angeles *Times*, and *Sunset Magazine*. The Elk River tumbles down out of the Mount Zirkel Wilderness Area bordering the ranch on the north end. The surrounding meadows and aspen groves press against a picturesque Rocky Mountain background. Two of the region's most popular climbs, Sand Mountain and Hahn's Peak, are nearby. The first-class accommodations and four-star meals will certainly appeal to those who prefer elegance along with a country vacation.

Cabin interiors combine wood paneling and river rock walls; the decor features handmade furniture, antiques, and Indian rugs, and beds decked with handsome down comforters. The main lodge is a rambling log structure with nooks and crannies to explore and relax in. Located under one gigantic roof is a children's play loft, library, dining room, and one of the most impressive rock fireplaces found anywhere. Paned glass windows allow natural light to fill cathedral-ceilinged rooms. Oversize leather couches and lounge chairs throughout offer welcome respite to the saddle weary.

Things to Do

Activities are unstructured, so guests aren't pressured by schedules. All levels of western riding are taught, as well as roping and barrel-racing. In winter, during feeding time for the animals, guests climb aboard the haywagon and ride out to the pastures with a ranch hand. Ranch guides also accompany guests on sightseeing and fishing rides up to high mountain lakes. Inside the nearby Mount Zirkel Wilderness, Gold Creek and Gilpin lakes trails are favorite treks for riders, anglers, and hikers. Climbers can accomplish Hahn's Peak and Sand Mountain easily within a day. Someone is always available to identify wildflowers, wildlife, and geologic formations on guided nature hikes along trails groomed for cross-country skiing in winter.

The Home Ranch also offers an independent hiking program that uses llamas as pack animals

on back-country pack trips. The four- and five-day excursions are made available June through September by outfitter Peter Nichols; they operate out of a permanent base camp consisting of a large sleeping tent, cook tent, and solar shower.

During leisure hours, adults can enjoy a game of pool or Ping-Pong in the rec hall while a full-time babysitter keeps kids busy in the library or children's loft stocked full of toys. Evening events include a ranch rodeo and barbecue and a trip to Steamboat's Friday Night Jackpot Rodeo. A local band shows up one night a week to get things hopping, while guests are invited to join in with instruments from the Home Ranch collection.

Fishing

A stocked pond on the ranch is used primarily for casting and wading practice with the use of artificial flies, single, barbless hooks, and a general catch-and-release approach encouraged. Off-ranch fisheries include two private stretches on the Elk River totaling one and a half miles and on the tributaries of the Elk. Guided trips on the Encampment and Little Snake rivers and one- to three-day floats down the Colorado can also be arranged upon request. Steamboat and Hahn's Peak lakes are within easy driving distance and a number of high-mountain lakes can be reached with a comfortable day's hike.

The Home Ranch keeps extra pairs of stream cleats, waders, and rods on hand to lend; otherwise, anglers should come fully equipped. The ranch also stocks a limited supply of flies.

VISTA VERDE GUEST RANCH

Box 465, Steamboat Springs, CO 80477. Phone: (303) 879-3858. Contact: Frank and Winton Brophy, owners. Total capacity: 40. Open year round. Peak season: mid-June–Labor Day. Reserve 6 months in advance. No pets.

Accommodations: One- to 3-bedroom log cabins with full bath, fireplace, and front porch. Lodging available on American Plan only. Daily maid service.

Meals: Three family-style meals daily on American Plan; special meals include breakfast cookouts, barbecues, fish fries, and picnics. Ranch raises its own beef, poultry, and vegetables. Chef will prepare fresh-caught fish to preference.

Rates: Expensive: weekly and daily rates include lodging, meals, ranch activities, daily backpacking trips, admission to Steamboat Rodeo, fishing, and one-day float trip. Discount rates available first two weeks in June and in September. Three-day minimum stay. Special rates for children. Extra charges: fly-fishing school, two-day wilderness pack trip, ranch float trip, and round-trip pick-up from Steamboat Springs airport. Cash or checks only.

How to Get There: Located 25 miles north of Steamboat Springs, CO; follow County Road 129 north past Clark, CO; turn right onto Seedhouse Road (Highway 64) and follow it to the ranch.

The 1,600-acre Vista Verde Guest Ranch is a long-established western dude ranch and working cattle and horse operation. Bordered on one side by the Elk River and surrounded by the Routt National Forest and Mount Zirkel Wilderness Area, its setting is truly spectacular. Because guests are invited to pitch in and help with everyday ranch chores, the Vista Verde will appeal to those who want to really get a taste of what life is like on a western ranch.

Hand-hewn log cabins and several modern log homes sit on an aspen-covered hillside with views of hay meadows and Rocky Moutain peaks. A feeling of warm western hospitality is enhanced by fully carpeted interiors decorated with hooked rugs, calico curtains, and early American furnishings. The main lodge, built of native spruce logs, exudes the same cozy atmosphere as the cabins. A fire in the great stone fireplace crackles throughout the day and guests gather round to read and relax in comfortable antiques. The lodge also houses the main dining room, board-game parlor, and a stage for evening entertainment.

Things to Do

The Vista Verde's unstructured schedule allows guests to participate in ranch life or recreation whenever they want to. An extensive riding program pairs guests to horses and covers all aspects of western riding, grooming, and care of horses. Newfound saddle skills are tested in a weekly rodeo that also features apple-bobbing and egg-balancing contests. Kids and adults are welcome to join wranglers as they go about their daily chores: riding herd on two hundred head of cattle, checking fences, and haying or irrigating. At least once a week, a team of Belgian draft horses is hooked up for an old-fashioned hayride. All-day rides up the South Fork of the Elk River and overnight pack trips into primitive high-country areas are additional ways to improve equestrian skills as well as to sightsee.

Horses have Sunday off while guests take guided hikes up the Wyoming Trail to Mica Basin or Gilpin Lake. Gold panning, photography, and rockhounding entertain along the way. Jeep or hot air balloon trips are arranged on request. Whitewater rafting on the upper Colorado

River is usually part of every guest's itinerary. One day a week, an all-day excursion challenges a section of the Colorado River. The ranch also offers an exclusive two-day float trip for the more adventuresome. Other water sports such as sailing, waterskiing, and canoeing are found nearby on Steamboat Lake.

Between ranch activities, riding, and rafting excursions, guests play tennis at the nearby Glen Eden Guest Ranch. When the sun sets, the warm glow of the lodge draws guests to a mixed bag of weekly evening entertainment such as square dancing, western music, singalongs, and a staff show.

Fishing

Main angling attractions at the Vista Verde include the Elk River, the South Fork of the Elk, and Steamboat and Hahn's Peak lakes. Guided hikes, trail rides, and overnight pack trips up to lakes in the wilderness area can also be arranged.

See Steamboat Springs Area Fisheries for more detailed fishing information.

A fly-fishing clinic that covers everything from casting techniques, knots, and reading local waters to dry fly, nymph, and wet fly stream fishing is held at the ranch for an extra charge when a minimum of three guests express interest.

ASPEN, COLORADO

Aspen Area Fisheries

Aspen, the hub of the Fryingpan River area, located 180 miles west of Denver and 130 miles east of Grand Junction, is probably best known as Colorado's most popular winter ski resort. Publicity about Aspen's wealth of summertime activities dims in comparison to the attention it receives during the winter. Surprisingly, this area offers a multitude of summer vacation choices for families who have a variety of interests to pursue during their visit to the Rockies.

Besides the Fryingpan River, Aspen is centrally located to several other fisheries considered to be among Colorado's best: the Roaring Fork and Crystal rivers. Visitors are also within easy commuting distance to recreational and cultural attractions in the neighboring communities of Snowmass, Basalt, and Glenwood Springs.

The famous Fryingpan, Roaring Fork, and Crystal rivers, along with a number of secondary streams and wilderness lakes withn the White River National Forest, comprise the major sport fisheries in the Aspen area.

Fryingpan River Drainage

North and west of Aspen, in the town of Basalt, the Roaring Fork meets the Fryingpan River. The Fryingpan, designated a gold-medal trout stream between Basalt and Ruedi Reservoir Dam, offers easy access to public fishing and yields browns and rainbows averaging twelve to fourteen inches. Brooks and cutthroats up to eighteen inches populate its waters below the dam. Catch limits vary along this protected stretch of river, with some areas designated catch-and-release only. Fishing is with artificial flies and lures. These strict regulations help to maintain fish size and population along a stretch of water that would otherwise be devastated by fairly heavy fishing pressure during most of the year.

The Fryingpan is most noted for its green drake hatch occurring in the late summer and early fall. A majority of insects found along the river have a coloration ranging from ginger to rust to brown. Standard patterns that generally work well include stonefly nymphs, better known in these parts as the Fryingpan Special (#6–8); quill-winged caddis (#12–14); and the twenty-incher (#12–14), similar to an elk hair caddis with ginger-colored hackle and dark brown wing.

Between its origins along the Continental Divide in the Hunter-Fryingpan Wilderness and where it flows into the Ruedi Reservoir, the Fryingpan River, like the Roaring Fork, interconnects with many tributary streams, creeks, and high-altitude lakes that yield small brookies and cutthroats in the six-inch to seven-inch class. The Fryingpan's South Fork runs through a fairly rugged, hard-to-reach river canyon that is well worth the effort it takes to fish it. The South Fork not only offers solitude, but also has good fly fishing for rainbows and cutthroats in virtually every kind of trout habitat along its length.

Roaring Fork River Drainage

The headwaters of the Roaring Fork River lie within the Maroon Bells–Snowmass Wilderness. Its many smaller streams and creeks, beaver ponds, and glacier-carved lakes have fair to good fishing for rainbows, brooks, and cutthroats. Access to higher elevation areas is rugged and best suited to anglers in fit condition.

Fourteen miles of the Roaring Fork, between its confluence with the Crystal River and the Colorado River, is designated gold-medal trout water. Browns and rainbows up to twenty inches are not uncommon. Most access along this stretch is through private land and anglers must get permission to cross it. An eight-mile section between Aspen's Hollum Lake and the Woody Creek Bridge is classified as wild trout water and is restricted to use of artificial flies and lures only.

Downstream from Aspen, Snowmass Creek, a tributary of the Roaring Fork, and its headwaters at Snowmass Lake have good fishing for brooks in the creek with rainbows—some exceeding twenty inches—and smaller cutthroat in the lake.

Crystal River Drainage

The popular Crystal River, which joins the Roaring Fork thirty-two miles northwest of Aspen along Route 82, is a swift stream heavily stocked—and fished—with rainbow, brook, and cutthroat trout. Fish over thirteen inches are rare if anglers are not willing to hike to more out-of-the-way places that lie upstream from the towns of Marble and Crystal. The best fishing in the Crystal River drainage is in the Thompson Creeks, which flow into the river approximately five miles south of Carbondale.

Because of the tremendous difference in aquatic habitats and elevations from one drainage to the next, anglers should drop in on one of the professional fly shops in Aspen to find out what's working and what's not. Both Fothergill's and the Taylor Creek Fly Shop are staffed by professional guides with the latest fishing reports as well as a wide selection of equipment, accessories, and tackle. Taylor Creek also has an outlet in Basalt that caters especially to fly fishing on the Fryingpan River.

Aspen Area Attractions

Aspen is well known for its diverse number of outdoor recreational and sporting opportunities. Aerosports include ballooning and gliding, while water sports enthusiasts have kayaking, sailboarding, rafting, and sailing with any one of a number of reputable outfitters available to them. The White River National Forest encompasses the Aspen area and is laced with miles of trails for hikers and equestrians.

Aspen also has a number of worthwhile attractions of historical note. Guided tours are conducted daily through well-preserved Victorian mansions lining the streets of neighborhoods adjacent to the downtown area. The Aspen Center for Environmental Studies is a twenty-two-acre wildlife sanctuary that offers guided walks for naturalists and hosts regular evening lectures on wildlife, conservation, and the environment. In Redstone, an hour's drive away, the Redstone Castle is a twenty-three-room Tudor-style mansion built in 1903 by an associate of the Rockefellers. Just down the road from Redstone, in Marble, is the Yule Marble Quarry, which produced the stone for the tomb of the Unknown Soldier and the Lincoln Memorial. The silver-mining town of Ashcroft and the old mill town of Crystal City are two relics of the past that can be included in a fun day's itinerary.

Aspen is also home to a very cosmopolitan dining scene, with restaurants offering everything from Japanese, Swiss, and nouvelle California to Italian and Cantonese cuisines. Prices tend to be on the expensive side with a few of the trendier restaurants putting more emphasis on atmosphere than on food. But these spots are great for cocktails and peacock watching!

Local performing arts programs reach a peak during summer with the renowned Aspen Music Festival, established in 1949. Festivities include regular performances by internationally acclaimed musicians, workshops, and free concerts. Visitors may want to write ahead to the Music Festival for a listing of performances before scheduling a vacation.

The town also hosts one of the largest ballet festivals west of the Mississippi, which also draws an impressive number of theater-goers to drama, comedy, and musical performances by the American Theatre Company. Since 1978, the Aspen Playwright's Conference has entertained and educated the general public and aspiring authors by presenting readings of works-in-progress.

Aspen's visual arts enjoy as much popularity as its performing arts. The Aspen Center for the Visual Arts and the Anderson Ranch Arts Center are two institutions offering extensive cultural programs including exhibitions, workshops, and lectures. Visitors have a wide selection of fine galleries representing works from western, Native American, African, and Indian art to choose from.

AVALANCHE RANCH

12863 Highway 133, Carbondale, CO 81623.
Phone: (303) 963-2846. Contact: Jeff Bier, owner.
Total capacity: 58–66. Open beginning of May–beginning of October. Peak season: July–September.
Reserve 2–4 months in advance.

Accommodations: Housekeeping cabins with fully equipped kitchen, private bath, outdoor grill, and picnic table sleep 4–6; some with additional sleeping loft. One 3-bedroom house, Avalanche Creek Inn, reserved for groups of up to 8. Linens changed mid-week.

Meals: N/A

Rates: Inexpensive; daily rates for cabins and Inn. Children under 2, free. Check, travelers check, VISA, or MasterCard.

How to Get There: Located 25 miles south of Glenwood Springs. From Aspen, take Highway 82 north for 25 miles to Carbondale and Highway 133 south to ranch. Free pick-up from Glenwood Springs, CO, or Aspen, CO. Rental car recommended for local travel.

Avalanche Ranch, bordered on one side by the White River National Forest and on another side by one-quarter of a mile of the Crystal River, was originally a 160-acre homestead claimed in 1898 by a silver miner who built several of the cabins along with the main house. In 1958 five more cabins were moved onto the present 45-acre land tract as a result of a land swap. The guest ranch was purchased by its present owner, Jeff Bier, in 1976.

The cabins' original log exteriors remain intact, while interiors have been remodeled with pine-paneled walls, carpets, and comfortable, contemporary oak furnishings. Windows, skylights, and high ceilings give the rooms a light and airy feeling. Ranch facilities include a lawn area equipped for volleyball and horseshoes, barbecue pit and picnic tables, and a pond with rafts and a canoe.

Things to Do

Hiking, fishing, and walking field trips are pleasurable ways for the family to explore the ranch. Children can venture out along their very own Bear Cub Trail or play in a rustic tree house. A pond offers rafting and canoeing as well as fishing. Jeff Bier has lived in the area for over sixteen years and is happy to assist guests in making reservations for jeep tours, float trips on the Roaring Fork and Colorado rivers, and horseback riding excursions in Redstone and Marble. He'll also make arrangements with a number of local outfitters offering guided hikes, llama treks, and photography walks. Visitors interested in local lore will find shops in Redstone entertaining to browse through. Babysitters are available if Jeff is notified in advance.

Fishing

Children are welcome to fish in the ranch pond, while serious anglers have access to a private stretch of the Crystal River to fish and the Fryingpan and Roaring Fork rivers within easy commutes. Dinkle Lake yields rainbows ten inches to sixteen inches and brookies ten inches to twelve inches, while Thomas Lake has natives up to fourteen inches—both within a short drive from the ranch. Nearby Beaver Lake also offers anglers a unique experience.

For additional fishing information see the As-

pen Area Fisheries Section.

Taylor Creek Fly Shop, located in the City Market Shopping Center in Basalt, has a full line of angling equipment and accessories. Guided trips on the Fryingpan River are their specialty. Anglers should purchase a fishing license either in Glenwood Springs or Basalt before heading up to the ranch.

DIAMOND J GUEST RANCH

26604 Frying Pan Road, Meredith, CO 81642. Phone: (303) 927-3222. Contact: Bill and Martha Sims, owners. Total capacity: 72. Open year round. Peak season: July and August. Reserve 6 months in advance. No pets.

Accommodations: Nine private rooms in lodge share two bathrooms; 7 cabins with kitchen, fireplace or wood-burning stove, and bath sleep 5–6; 5 cabins with bath and fireplace or wood-burning stove sleep 2. Jacuzzi and hot tub available to guests. Linens changed on request.

Meals: Three family-style meals daily on American Plan; European Plan available May 21 to November 16. Hot lunch; gourmet dinner one night a week; weekly barbecues, with special barbecues for children one night a week. Mixers supplied; all alcohol is BYOB.

Rates: Moderate; weekly rates available for American Plan and European Plan. American Plan includes lodging, meals, and all ranch activities, horses, jeep trips, rafting, etc. European Plan includes lodging only; ranch activities and facilities extra. Family discounts available. Children under 3, free. Extra charges: climbing classes, overnight and backpack trips, pick-up from airport extra for guests staying less than a week. Cash, check, or travelers check.

How to Get There: Located 35 miles up Frying Pan Road where it intersects with Highway 82 in Basalt, CO. Free pick-up from Aspen airport or Glenwood Springs train or bus depot for guests staying 1 week. Rental car recommended for local travel.

The Diamond J Guest Ranch, although not wilderness remote, is farther removed from the hubbub of Aspen than either the T Lazy 7 or Avalanche Ranch. The four-season resort is surrounded by the White River National Forest and lies at the western base of the Continental Divide, a stone's throw away from the upper Fryingpan River.

The Sims family, owners of the ranch since 1982, add a special appeal to the Diamond J since dude ranching is more than a business to them—it is a life-style that turns strangers into friends.

Rooms are located in the lodge above the main dining room. A short walk through a meadow, past the stables and into a sheltering stand of pines, are several rustic log-sided cabins with wood-paneled walls, hardwood floors with area rugs, gingham curtains, and hurricane lamps. A few have claw-foot tubs and Indian blankets with intricate southwestern motifs.

Things to Do

Once you've learned how to stay in the saddle, exploring the surrounding mountains on horseback can be the highlight of your dude ranch vacation at the Diamond J. Short trail rides and longer jaunts by horseback are scheduled throughout the week; by Friday, guests are experienced enough to sign up for the Fun Rodeo. Four-wheel jeep tours into the high-mountain back country also leave from the ranch several times during the week depending on when guests want to go. Tuesdays are set aside for an all-day rafting trip. Fishing, gold panning, rock hopping, horseshoes, or just plain relaxing are additional activities guests can look forward to. Evenings are filled with slide shows, movies, and volleyball games; Fridays are reserved for entertainment provided by the staff, followed by an old-fashioned square dance.

The Diamond J has also combined forces with an outdoor/recreation program, "Inscape Venture," to provide guests with additional recreation. Three programs offered under this alliance include rock climbing; overnight and extended backpack trips; and nature walks, talks, and hikes.

Fishing

Diamond J lies in close proximity to the Fryingpan River and its many wilderness lakes and tributaries. Fishing on the Roaring Fork and Crystal rivers is also an easy commute on well-paved roads.

For additional fishing information, refer to the Aspen Area Fisheries Section.

Taylor Creek Fly Shop, at the junction of Highway 82 in Basalt, sells licenses, an excellent assortment of specialized flies, and has up-to-the-minute fishing information. A limited selection of tackle and equipment is available a short drive from the ranch in the small town of Meredith.

T LAZY 7 RANCH

Box 240, Aspen, CO 81612. Phone: (303) 925-7254. Contact: Lou or Rick Deane, owners/managers. Total capacity: 100–125. Open year round. Peak season: July 4–mid-September. Reserve 6–8 months in advance in peak season, 2–4 months rest of year. Pets allowed.

Accommodations: Five housekeeping "ranch houses" divided into 1- to 5-bedroom apartments sleeping 2–10; 3 large studio cabins sleep 6–8. All units have equipped kitchenettes, private bath, fireplace or woodburning stove, and balcony or sundeck. Towels changed daily; linens changed weekly.

Meals: N/A; breakfast, lunch and dinner rides cost extra. Hayrides and barbecues also extra.

Rates: Moderate; daily and weekly rates. Two-night minimum stay. Check or travelers checks.

How to Get There: Located 3½ miles from Aspen up the road to Maroon Bells and Maroon Lake. Free pick-up from Aspen airport. Rental car recommended for local travel.

The T Lazy 7 is a family-owned and operated guest ranch with traditions firmly rooted in western history. Joshua Deane arrived as an attorney for mining companies when Aspen was founded as a silver-mining town in the 1880s. He stayed on and served as Pitkin County judge for many years and married Lottie Cruikshank, an opera singer from Chicago. The Judge and Lottie's grandson, Had, also made a woman of celebrity status his leading lady when he married Lou Deane, a stage actress from Broadway. They moved to Aspen and bought the 500-acre ranch on Maroon Creek in the White River Wilderness that is the T Lazy 7 today.

In the past, the ranch's scenic Rocky Mountain vistas have appeared in such Hollywood films as *Red Stallion of the Rockies* and *Devil's Doorway* (starring Robert Taylor) and in western-theme advertising such as the Marlboro ads. The T Lazy 7 is a "family kind of place"; some families, many of whom are season regulars, stay from three to six weeks. The cabins overlook a beautiful forested glen abloom with flowers, which surrounds several trout ponds. Ranch offices are located in a lodge house with a recreation room and western bar open to guests only.

Things to Do

Three main walking trails on the ranch are mapped out: Old Stage Road, Maroon Creek trail, and the nature loop. Because T Lazy 7 is a designated game reserve, you'll find plenty of wildlife to observe. They even claim to have a pet mountain lion!

All guided and unguided horseback riding and activities offered by the T Lazy 7 stables are open to the public and available to guests at reduced rates. Guided pack trips into the Maroon Bells Wilderness are very popular and many visitors sign up for private lessons or riding by the hour. A hayride behind a pair of Belgium draft horses is a delightful way to see the stunning Maroon Creek Valley. For an easier ride, take the T Lazy 7's overland stagecoach to town for a tour of Aspen's historic Victorian houses.

Guest facilities include a heated pool, therapy whirlpool bath, sauna, and a volleyball court. Babysitters are available with plenty of advance notice.

ranch's peak guest season from July through the beginning of September. Fly fishing along three miles of T Lazy 7's privately owned and stocked stretch of Maroon Creek is reserved exclusively for guests. The stream has plenty of riffles and eddies that are designated fly-fishing-only for rainbows and a few brook trout. Willow Creek, which flows into Maroon Creek on ranch property, is also stocked and posted by the T Lazy 7. A good horse trail follows the creek nine miles up to its headwaters in Willow Lake, where there is good fishing for brook and cutthroat. Productive patterns to use on the slower stretches include western coachmans (#12), grizzly wulffs (#16), and adams (#16).

Pack trips to mountain lakes in the Maroon Bells–Snowmass Wilderness can be arranged through T Lazy 7's stables. Rides vary in elevation from seven thousand to eleven thousand feet and include fishing in East Maroon Lake, the headwaters of Maroon Creek, and Moon Lake (which has fair size cutthroat). One pack trip route drops through Conundrum Pass where saddle-weary anglers can relax in the natural pools of Conundrum Hot Springs.

Three trout ponds on the ranch are maintained for children under twelve years of age. Two are stocked with rainbows twelve to fourteen inches in length with a catch limit of two fish per day. Several nearby beaver ponds harbor native rainbows.

Fishing licenses and equipment can be purchased in a number of good fly shops in town.

Fishing

One of the great advantages of staying at the T Lazy 7 is that the prime fishing season, September through October, does not overlap with the

FORT COLLINS, COLORADO, & LARAMIE, WYOMING

RAWAH GUEST RANCH

Glendevey, Colorado Route, Jelm, WY 82063. Phone: (303) 435-5715. From November–May, write: P.O. Drawer K, Fort Collins, CO 80522. Phone: (303) 484-5585. Contact: Eric P. Jones, owner. Total capacity: 30. Open mid-June–Labor Day. Peak season: late July–mid-August. Reserve 1 year in advance. No pets.

Accommodations: Four single and multifamily cabins with bath sleep 2–8; 8 bedrooms in main lodge share 2 baths. Daily maid service.

Meals: Three family-style meals daily on American Plan; breakfast ride on Wednesdays, hot entree lunch, trail lunch on Fridays, dinner buffet on Saturday and Sunday. All alcohol is BYOB.

Rates: Moderate; daily and weekly rates include lodging, meals, and horses; add 10 percent for single person. Three-night minimum stay during July and August. Extra charges: Great Rocky Mountain Outfitters' three- to five-day pack trips, summer drop camps, and round-trip airport pick-up from Laramie, WY. Cash, check, or travelers checks.

How to Get There: Two-and-a-half hour drive from Fort Collins; take Highway 14 up Cache la Poudre River canyon to Chambers Lake; turn north at Woods Landing turnoff; follow gravel road 12 miles to ranch. One-and-a-half hour drive from Laramie, WY; take Highway 230 southwest to Woods Landing; then Wyoming State Road 10 south across the Colorado state line; road changes to gravel for last 20 miles to ranch. Regional airlines and AmTrak service Laramie, WY; rental cars can be arranged in Denver or Laramie.

Rawah Guest Ranch (pronounced RAY wah) is located in the Big Laramie River Valley in the northern Colorado Rockies. Surrounded on three sides by the Roosevelt National Forest, the 320-acre working ranch lies at the trailhead to the Rawah Wilderness Area. The ranch's relatively small size and emphasis on congeniality create a sense that all who come are part of an extended family. This is a relaxing hideaway for those seeking creature comforts in a remote mountain setting.

Accommodations in cabins and the lodge are comfortably furnished and feature knotty-pine or log-sided walls, hardwood floors, braided area rugs, and country-style curtains. Despite continual improvements, both the cabins and lodge rooms retain a wonderful rustic feeling. Western ranch decor is used throughout the main lodge, where dining and living rooms are embellished with walk-in size stone fireplaces and picture windows overlooking the banks of the Laramie River. A small rec hall equipped with a Ping-Pong table and the stables are located a short way from the main lodge.

Things to Do

Life at Rawah Ranch is unregimented. Horseback riding, hiking, and fishing are the primary activities. Individual riding abilities are assessed upon arrival and guests are matched to a friendly saddlehorse that remains theirs for the entire week. Wranglers accompany all rides to assist with equipment, provide instruction, and select trails to complement riders' interests in photography, fishing, or wildlife observation.

Hikers have immediate access to many miles of secluded trails in the Medicine Bow Range of the Roosevelt National Forest and the adjoining twenty-seven-thousand-acre Rawah Wilderness Area. Chambers Lake and Tunnel Campground are two main trailheads from which dozens of small footpaths originate. Popular trails in the nearby Poudre River Canyon include Greyrock, the Mount McConnell nature trail, and the South Fork route, which follows the South Fork of the Poudre River. Nearby Rocky Mountain National Park contains a vast hiking system; however, tourist pressure in the park is relatively intense when compared to the Rawah Wilderness.

An affiliate of the ranch, Great Rocky Mountain Outfitters, offers three- to five-day pack trips into the Rawah Wilderness. Guided hikes and fishing and sightseeing rides are led out of a comfortable base camp consisting of guest tents (including stove and cots) and a large cook tent that serves as the camp's social center.

Leisure time activities at the ranch include lawn sports, Ping-Pong, board games, and lounging. Car trips to local points of interest and into Laramie and Cheyenne are also arranged for guests. Both towns have a full roster of rodeos all summer long; the biggest tourist attraction is Cheyenne Frontier Days. This week-long celebration of the old West takes place during the last week of July.

Fishing

Some of Colorado's finest trout fishing is found on the Big Laramie River, which flows down out of the Roosevelt National Forest for nearly five miles before passing within a stone's throw of Rawah lodge. Feisty one-pound native browns averaging twelve inches to thirteen inches predominate in the main river, with rainbows, native cutthroats, and a few brooks found in nearby lakes and smaller feeder streams. One guest, who has been fishing the Laramie for sixty-five years, estimates that it's possible to catch (and release) twenty to fifty fish "in a couple hours—if the conditions are right."

The Laramie, along with its West Branch and tributary, Rawah Creek, are fairly shallow streams with gravel bars, intermittent pools, and overhanging banks. Hip boots will suffice in most instances; however, felt-soled shoes are recommended for extra traction and wading power. An 8- to 8½-foot, 5-6-weight rod will work for all the fishing found in this area.

Dry fly fishing starts in July with caddis, mayflies, rio grande kings, and royal wulffs (#12–14). There are also a few tan-bodied stoneflies (#4–6) on the water at this time as well as later on. Hoppers (#8–12) produce well all through August as do rio grande kings (#8–10) with a cutback wing or any dark hackle fly (#8–10) with black chenille body fished wet.

The Cache la Poudre and North Platte Rivers are secondary fisheries within a comfortable day's journey from Rawah. The average size of stocked rainbows in the Poudre—approximately 10 inches—is smaller than in other Colorado rivers due to the Poudre's cooler temperature. The river is plagued by a number of factors that hamper consistent quality fishing. Easy access from the Denver and Fort Collins metropolitan areas creates intense fishing pressure, and water consumption by agriculture and municipal and industrial interests causes extreme variations in stream flow. Fly-fishing purists will find the uppermost stretches of the Poudre more enjoyable because it is under wild trout management (no stocking). This section is restricted to the use of artificial flies and lures, and has special catch limits.

Great Rocky Mountain Outfitters also guides Rawah guests on fishing trips down the blue-ribbon trout fishery of the North Platte River. Situated in southeastern Wyoming, the North Platte is estimated to contain between 1,600 and 2,400 catchable rainbows, browns, and brooks per mile. The outfitters also guide overnight pack trips into the back country for brook, cutthroat, and brown trout found in streams, beaver ponds, and lakes. Blow fly and blue bottle fly imitations are productive high-mountain lake patterns.

Numerous lakes with fair to good fishing for diverse populations of eight-inch to fifteen-inch fish—kokanee, rainbow and cutthroat trout, grayling, and brooks—are found near the ranch. Popular lakes include Parvin, Dowdy, Bellaire, Chambers, Twin, Lost, and Hohnholz. Anglers should be aware that many of the small lakes and ponds in this area are on private property and permission from landowners is required.

The West Laramie Fly Store sells licenses and carries a complete line of fly-fishing gear and tackle. Anglers can also shop at numerous sporting goods stores in Fort Collins. Quite a few restaurants and lodges in the Poudre River Canyon sell licenses and limited selections of tackle.

CENTRAL NEW MEXICO

LOS PINOS GUEST RANCH

Box 8, Route 3, Tererro, NM 87573. Phone: (505) 757-6213. Winter phone (October–May 1): (505) 757-6679. Contact: Bill and Alice McSweeney. Total capacity: 16. Open Memorial Day weekend–first weekend in October. Peak season: mid-June–August. Reserve 4–6 months in advance. No pets; no children under 6.

Accommodations: Four 1- and 2-bedroom cottages sleep up to 4; all are nonhousekeeping units with bath. Daily maid service; laundry facility.

Meals: Three family-style meals daily on American Plan; hot and cold lunch as well as trail lunch, gourmet dinners. All alcohol is BYOB.

Rates: Moderate; daily and weekly rates. Children between 6–14 discounted. Extra charges: Guided horses, drives to local attractions, and pick-up at airport in Santa Fe or at train station in Lamy. Cash or check.

How to Get There: Located 45 miles east and north of Santa Fe, NM. Take highways 84 and 85 to Pecos, NM; follow paved road up canyon past Tererro to ranch. Closest airport serviced by commercial airlines is in Albuquerque; private planes can land at Santa Fe Municipal Airport. AmTrak services Lamy, NM. Pick-up from ranch in Lamy or Santa Fe. Rental car recommended for local travel.

Los Pinos Guest Ranch is a small guest ranch located within an hour's drive of the historic town of Sante Fe in north-central New Mexico. Nestled in an intimate canyon, it is surrounded by the thirteen-thousand-foot peaks of the Sangre de Cristo range. The Pecos Wilderness, out of which flows the Pecos River and its tributaries, is a short hike from the ranch.

Los Pinos has been in operation as a guest ranch for over sixty years. It is presently owned and operated by Bill and Alice McSweeney, whose hospitality comes in second to none. The ranch offers a great way to enjoy a relaxed, casual vacation while still taking in the cultural life that attracts so many tourists to the Santa Fe–Taos area.

The most memorable feature of Los Pinos' rustic guest cabins is their view across wild, grassy meadows dotted with stands of pine. Woven area rugs and homespun curtains add cheer. A turn-of-the-century log lodge houses the main dining and living rooms; comfortable ranchhouse furnishings are set off by Indian rugs, antiques, and overstuffed bookshelves. An adjoining screened-in porch allows guests to dine in an airy, outdoor setting.

Alice McSweeney prepares original dishes inspired by European and Irish cuisines. Their gourmet quality inspires local fame and she often takes reservations from outsiders who want to join guests at dinnertime. Her *Los Pinos Ranch Brand of Cooking* cookbook includes her own recipes.

Things to Do

Guests come and go as they please; the only planned event all summer long is the Los Pinos June Festival, when people come from miles around to take part in rodeos, weaving and craft demonstrations, and fly-fishing clinics, and to listen to some good old mountain fiddling. The rest of the summer is filled with horseback riding, hiking, and fishing in the Pecos Wilderness of the Santa Fe National Forest. Guided trail rides last an hour or two or can extend into all-day and overnight pack trips. The McSweeneys will help guests make all the necessary arrangements with local outfitters for longer wilderness treks and specialty fishing trips.

Besides being an ace cook and storyteller, Alice is an amenable and knowledgeable guide when it comes to off-ranch tours. She knows all of the historic gems in Santa Fe and Taos. Her favorite haunts lie off the beaten path; Los Pinos' guests visit ancient Indian ruins, modern-day pueblos, Spanish settlements, and old mining towns. Stops along the way include artists' studios, craft shops, museums, and quaint galleries. Lunch at an adobe hacienda is a traditional stop.

A notable local attraction is the renowned Santa Fe Opera, which performs June 15 through August 15. Attending one of their performances should definitely be included in an itinerary. Other unusual side trips include a visit to Ten Thousand Waves—a Japanese bathhouse located on Hyde Park Road outside of Santa Fe. It has indoor and outdoor hot tubs, cold plunges, and massage therapy in a unique Asian setting. A visit to the La Fonda Hotel in Taos to view its collection of unpublished Hemingway sketches and paintings is another interesting and worthwhile venture.

Fishing

The Pecos River flows through the ranch below its headwaters in the Pecos Wilderness. This sparkling river, characterized by swift riffles and deep pools, averages fifteen feet across and is generally wadeable with hip boots. A few stretches of water within a mile or two of Los Pinos have been set aside for fly fishing only. The Upper Pecos has native eight-inch to ten-inch cutthroats and is stocked with fingerling Rio

Grande cutthroats, browns, and rainbows that grow to an average seven inches to nine inches. Jacks, Winsor, Tanchuela, Cave, and Horsethief creeks are feeder streams with good angling for brooks up to nine inches and ten inches. A furious willow fly hatch in June is followed by predominately caddis and mayfly hatches throughout the rest of the season. Productive dry flies (#12–16) include black gnats, rio grande kings, adams, blue duns, humpies, gray wulffs, renegades, and mosquitos. Joe's hoppers (#8–12) are especially productive in August. Girdle bugs, woolly buggers, and hare's ears (#6–14) are popular wet flies.

Upper mountain lakes such as Spirit, Stewarts, and Baldy hold populations of seven-inch to nine-inch brown and brook trout. Huie Ley, a reputable local outfitter, guides custom fishing

trips into the Pecos Wilderness. His summer calendar begins to fill up by the end of February, so anglers should book their trips well in advance. Huie's shop, the Tererro General Store, carries an extensive assortment of flies tied to match local hatches. Licenses, terminal tackle, and a limited selection of gear can also be purchased at his store.

TELLURIDE, COLORADO

SKYLINE GUEST RANCH

Box 67, Telluride, CO 81435. Phone: (303) 728-3757. Contact: Dave and Sherry Farny. Total capacity: 35. Open: mid-June–mid-October. Peak season: July and August. Reserve 1 year in advance for cabins; 6–8 months for lodge. No pets.

Accommodations: Eleven rooms with private bath in lodge; 4 housekeeping cabins sleep 2–6, and have kitchen, bath, and porch, several with wood-burning stove or fireplace. Daily maid service; laundry facility.

Meals: Three family-style meals daily on American Plan for guests in lodge; modified American Plan also available to those in cabins. Breakfast daily and Friday chuckwagon breakfast after trail ride; trail lunches available; full dinner. All alcohol is BYOB.

Rates: Moderate; weekly rates for cabins and lodge. Groups of 4 or more discounted 15 percent. Cash, check, MasterCard, or VISA.

How to Get There: Located 340 miles southwest of Denver. Telluride airport is serviced by Mesa and Continental airlines; Hertz car rentals also available. Free ranch pick-up from Telluride airport. Regional airlines service Grand Junction and Durango. Telluride Transit offers limousine service to Montrose, Durango, and Grand Junction.

Cradled high in a valley ringed by the fourteen-thousand-foot peaks of the San Juan Mountains in southwestern Colorado is Skyline Guest Ranch. Originally a logging camp, the 160-acre parcel became a guest ranch in the 1950s. In 1968 the current owners—the Farny family—acquired Skyline as a base camp for their Telluride Mountaineering School. Skyline Ranch is surrounded on three sides by the Uncompaghre National Forest, which receives relatively little tourist pressure when compared to forest areas more conveniently located to the Denver metropolitan area.

Of the dozen or so regions that refer to themselves as the "little Switzerland of America," this remote and oft-forgotten corner of Colorado comes close to fitting the bill. Snow-capped peaks flanked by glaciated crevasses descend into wide alpine meadows splashed with wildflowers. The Farnys belong to a very special breed of outdoorsmen who indulge guests in activities and interests they find personally satisfying. Returning guests remark that a week spent at Skyline is similar to staying a week with close friends at a mountain home retreat.

Situated on hillsides that slope gently down to the main lodge, the cabins are quite comfortable and cozy. The lodge houses the main dining room and a large living room where guests have access to books, music, and the company of other guests and congenial staff. An informal western ranch setting is fashioned from a hodge-podge of comfortable couches and armchairs. Lamp fixtures make use of antique wagon wheels, and braided throw rugs adorn hardwood floors. Shared facilities include a rec room with a Ping-Pong table. An authentic sauna and adjoining wood-fired hot tub are located right on a gurgling creek that flows out of the ranch swimming lake.

Things to Do

The Farnys handpick their staff to include outgoing college students with diverse interests and specialized skills. Guests are paired with staff members who have similar interests and receive one-on-one instruction in backpacking, riding, rock climbing, and fly fishing; all the necessary equipment is provided by Skyline. Riding and hiking excursions into the Uncompaghre and San Juan National Forests leave the ranch daily; four-wheel drive vehicles are available for those who'd rather sightsee. Guests return to the ranch before dinner for a sauna and refreshing dip in the swimming lake. A pot-bellied stove and open fireplace in the main lodge become focal points for reading, conversing, and after-dinner sing-alongs.

Telluride is a handsomely preserved turn-of-the-century mining town protected by the National Historic Landmark Act. Victorian storefronts house unique curio stores, clothing shops, and smart cafes. For a town of its size, Telluride has an impressive roster of summertime events that includes an internationally recognized film festival, a mushroom festival, and chamber music, dance, and jazz festivals.

Easy day trips include a drive along Colorado's Highway 50 as it winds its way along the precipitous rim of the Black Canyon of the Gunnison or a drive along the Million Dollar Highway between Silverton and Ouray. While in Ouray, stop for a soak in naturally formed granite caves beneath the Wiesbaden Hot Springs and Spa. Another worthwhile excursion is a ride through the Animas River Canyon on the historic Durango to Silverton Narrow Gauge Railroad. Visits to the ancient Anasazi Indian cliff dwellings in Mesa Verde National Park and Hovenweep National Monument are as fascinating as they are educational.

A more unusual outing rock climbers will find appealing is a vertical trip up one of a battery of granite-sedimentary-volcanic walls just outside of Telluride. Ophir Wall, East Buttress, Cracked Canyon, Ames Wall, and the Telluride Cliffs lure hundreds of climbers each year who test their skills on nature.

Fishing

Skyline has two private ponds and one lake stocked with five-inch to six-inch fingerling Tas-

manian rainbows. These little fighters give novice fly fishers a chance to practice casting and to get used to the idea of catch-and-release in June and early July when snow runoff plagues the nearby Dolores and San Miguel rivers. High sediment content associated with heavy rainstorms can cause these rivers to muddy up quickly any time of year, but when they're running clear they can be hot!

Local fly-fishing aficionados claim that with the 1985 completion of the McPhee Dam on the Dolores, the river now has some of the best controlled water fishing for eighteen-inch to twenty-four-inch german browns found anywhere. The Dolores and its West Fork also produce rainbows averaging eight inches to twelve inches, with smaller feeder streams offering fair to good fishing for seven-inch to ten-inch native cutthroats and brooks.

The San Miguel is easy to get to because it flows along Colorado Highway 145 from Telluride to Norwood. Some of the San Miguel's best fishing is downstream from Norwood where the river turns away from the road and is joined by numerous, harder-to-reach feeder streams. This stretch is rewarding for rainbows up to twelve inches and browns up to twenty inches plus. The South and Lake forks of the San Miguel are small, brushy streams that offer more difficult fishing for eight-inch to twelve-inch rainbows, with a few brooks and cutthroats. Feeder streams have small brooks in their upper sections and rainbows and browns lower down.

Dry fly patterns (#14–16) used both on the Dolores and San Miguel include royal wulffs, male adams, mosquitos, ginger quills, elk hair caddis, hornbergs, and humpies. Gold-ribbed hare's ears are the most consistently productive nymph.

Skyline Ranch also runs fishing trips through the Black Canyon of the Gunnison. This section of the Gunnison is designated as gold-medal trout water restricted to the use of artificial flies and lures only; it is also virtually inaccessible except by floating. The canyon rim soars abruptly up from the river's edge 1,730 to 2,700 feet. Beautiful, fat, sixteen-inch to eighteen-inch rainbows and browns in prime condition are consistently caught in this stretch; fish over twenty inches are not uncommon. Arrangements for this trip must be made well in advance as it takes additional time and staff to put it together.

High-mountain lake fishing in this region is found in elevations averaging nine thousand five hundred feet. Many of the lakes suffer from winterkill or, sadly enough, from being fished out by overzealous backpackers. Rainbows average eight inches to twelve inches, with some brook and an occasional cutthroat and brown. Black ants (#16), shrimp, and scud patterns are good patterns to use on most of these high lakes. Fly-fishing purists are well advised to stick to the rivers and feeder streams.

Olympic Sports in Telluride sells licenses and a full line of equipment, tackle, and gear for anglers. Several clerks, who are also avid fly fishermen, are conversant with matching the hatch and locating hot spots at any given time.

ESTES PARK, COLORADO

C LAZY U GUEST RANCH

P.O. Box 3788, Granby, CO 80446. Phone: (303) 887-3344. Contact: John Fisher, manager; George and Virginia Mullin, hosts and owners. Total capacity: 80–110. Open June–October. Peak season: mid-July–Labor Day. Open to special groups for 15 or more from Labor Day through mid-October. Reserve 1 year in advance. No pets.

Accommodations: Thirty-nine nonhousekeeping cabins with private bath sleep 2–6; 22 of these cabins have stone fireplace. Bedrooms also available in lodge. Daily maid service; laundry facility.

Meals: Three family-style meals daily on American Plan; buffet lunches; gourmet dinners, as well as barbecues. Children eat an hour before adults. Beer and wine served with dinner; full-service bar.

Rates: Expensive; weekly rates. Rates vary according to cabin size. Daily rates available one week in June and first two weeks of September. Special rates available for parties of 2–6 people. Nonriding children under 6, half price. Extra charges: guided horseback rides and fishing trips, limousine service from Denver airport. Cash, check, or travelers checks.

How to Get There: Located 2-hour drive from Denver. Take I-70 west 7 miles past Idaho Springs; turn north on Highway 40 and follow it to Granby; 3 miles west of Granby, turn north on Highway 125 and drive 3½ miles to ranch. Pick-up available from Denver airport and bus depot in Steamboat Springs.

The C Lazy U has been dubbed the Rolls Royce of western dude ranches. Its emphasis on quality lodging and meals has earned it the highest ratings from both AAA and Mobil. This 2,500-acre working ranch in the Rockies just over the Continental Divide from Denver is one of the largest guest ranches in Colorado. A 55 percent ratio of return clientele attests to the efficiency of its large staff. The C Lazy U also offers one of the most competent, fully supervised "tots to teens" programs found anywhere. This vacation ranch mixes holiday luxury with old-fashioned informality.

C Lazy U has two lodges: a two-story main lodge and an auxiliary lodge. The centrally located main lodge contains the main lounge and dining room, bar, card room, library, and guest accommodations. Exposed-beam ceilings, log-and-mortar walls, and stone fireplaces are featured throughout. Small, immaculate social rooms are warmly furnished in a western motif—lantern chandeliers, Navajo rugs, and western landscape art. Huge art-book coffee tables complement oversized couches and lounging chairs.

Trail Peak Lodge, the auxiliary lodge, serves as the ranch's recreation center. It houses a glass-enclosed whirlpool, game room with a pool table and foosball, television room, and great hall where scheduled evening entertainment takes place. An outdoor heated swimming pool filled with Rocky Mountain spring water, saunas, and a bar and soda fountain are located nearby along with two competition-quality tennis courts and a racquetball court. C Lazy U's country store, down by the corrals, sells a full line of western wear, Indian jewelry, film, ranch cookbooks, souvenirs, and sundry drugstore items.

Things to Do

Horseback riding throughout forty square miles of Rocky Mountain terrain is the main activity at the C Lazy U. Equestrian skills can be practiced in class, improved upon on the trail, and demonstrated in a weekly Shodeo. Tots have their own riding program designed for their interests and abilities. Riding for the little ones is restricted to a pony ring where they are led around by a counselor. Other organized activities for children include swimming, picnicking, fishing, hayrides, and sports. The ranch also keeps equipment on hand for volleyball, soccer, and badminton.

Adults fill their leisure time with tennis, skeet shooting on the range, racquetball, and swimming. In the evenings, guests gather for square and country swing dancing, staff shows, and campfires.

The resort towns of Estes Park and Grand Lake, along with the Great Lakes of Colorado and surrounding national forests, parks, and recreation areas, are the biggest local tourist attractions. An aerial tramway in Estes Park is a thrilling way to get a panoramic view of Long's Peak, the ranges of the Continental Divide, and Rocky Mountain National Park. The town also

has several golf courses, a watertube, and the magnificent old Stanley Hotel, which hosts live entertainment in the evenings and ongoing arts and cultural events throughout the summer season.

Grand Lake, a charming small town where horses canter down the main street, still has board sidewalks, now lined with gift shops, galleries, and cafes. Summer events include barbecues, art and music festivals, and flea markets. The Players Company presents theater-in-the-round evenings June through September. Two eighteen-hole golf courses and the "Great Lakes of Colorado," at the western entrance to Rocky Mountain National Park, are nearby. The lakes offer 150 miles of recreational shoreline and marina services to accommodate a variety of water sports—windsurfing, waterskiing, sailing, and fishing. Yacht races and boat parades attract large crowds all summer long. Grand Lake Lodge is a great place to lunch while enjoying a bird's-eye view of the action.

The Arapahoe National Forest and Recreation Area, Rocky Mountain National Park, and the Roosevelt National Forest have numerous trails that offer hikers, backpackers, and anglers a variety of terrains to explore. A scenic drive along the well-publicized—and often very crowded—Trail Ridge Road, the highest continuous paved highway in North America, through Rocky Mountain National Park is a spectacular treat.

Fishing

Guests have exclusive access to one-and-a-half miles of Willow Creek that runs through the ranch. Twelve-inch stocked rainbows and browns up to two pounds are common. There's also a stocked pond for kids.

The Colorado River, its local tributaries the Blue and Fraser rivers, and the "Great Lakes of Colorado" are the main fisheries near the C Lazy U. The Colorado tumbles from its source on Mount Baldy and flows into the Great Lakes: Grand Lake, Shadow Mountain Lake, and Lake Granby, which hold populations of kokanee, salmon, rainbow, brook, mackinaw (up to thirty pounds), brown trout, and pike. Experienced anglers who explore less trodden paths along small feeder streams will find their efforts rewarded by action from bigger fish that have moved out of the lakes to spawn and feed. Farther downstream, more than twenty miles of the Colorado River and sections of the Blue River are classified gold-medal trout waters for large rainbows and browns. The brushy, willow-lined Fraser has sections designated wild trout water.

Super nymph fishing occurs in the main branch of the Colorado and its North Fork during the spring runoff in late March and continuing into early April. Brown stonefly nymphs (#6–8) and hare's ear nymphs (#6–12) sink beneath the roiling surface to feeding troughs of ten- to fourteen-inch rainbows and deeper down to browns averaging three-quarters to one pound. Fishing backs off in May when the snow runoff gets too muddy, and picks up again in June with an explosive willow fly hatch. Productive patterns (#14–20) include hornbergs, light and dark elk hair caddis, adams, royal wulffs, and light cahills. August and September are peak months for dry fly fishing—a good fisherman can expect to catch thirty ten- to thirteen-inch fish per day. Late afternoon and evening fishing for brown trout is unexcelled during September.

There's a lot of heavily posted water in this area not only on the Colorado but on the Fraser and Blue rivers. Guests at the C Lazy U have a special advantage over other nonresident anglers who come to fish on their own. The C Lazy U's fishing pro maintains a close association with local private landowners and, consequently, has access to many prime stretches of river that are otherwise closed to public access.

C Lazy U's pro also conducts guided trips on the more remote North Platte River from September 1 on. The North Platte has its headwaters in the Sierra Madre Mountains north of Granby near the Wyoming state border. This deep, wide river is a nationally renowned blue-ribbon trout fishery with portions designated wild trout waters. The Wyoming Game and Fish Department estimates a catchable 1,600 to 2,400 fish—browns, rainbows, and brooks—per mile. The best fly fishing occurs from midsummer after the spring runoff through fall.

Upper mountain streams and countless lakes above 9,500 feet within nearby national parks and forests have fair to good fishing for native cutthroats and stocked brooks and rainbows; browns are found in the lower elevations. This rugged Continental Divide terrain remains ice-bound into midsummer and does not produce particularly large fish; however, a few exceptions await saddle-bound anglers.

C Lazy U's country store carries a limited amount of tackle and inexpensive spinning rods. Serious anglers should come equipped with their own gear and chest waders. Nelson Fly and Tackle Shop in Tabernash and Fletchers in Granby carry a more complete line of gear and local flies.

CREEDE, COLORADO

Creede Area Fisheries

The small, western town of Creede, which serves as the lodging center for the Upper Rio Grande area, is located near the headwaters of the Rio Grande high in the San Juan Mountains in south-western Colorado. Once known as the state's "Silver Ribbed Treasure Trove" in its early days, Creede was one of the West's richest and wildest mining camps. Its boom town history began in 1889 when silver was discovered by Nicoloas Creede. By 1892 over a million dollars of silver per month were being shipped out of the area, and the population had swelled to ten thousand people strung out along Willow Creek Canyon. Many of the West's legendary characters—Bob Ford, killer of Jesse James; Jessie's brother Frank James; Bat Masterson; bunko artist Soapy Smith; and Poker Alice and her sidekick Calamity Jane—contributed to the town's colorful past. In the 1920s depressed silver prices caused many of the mines to close and the population dwindled. Lead and zinc mining renewed Creede's industry again in the 1930s and remain a chief source of revenue today, along with cattle ranching and tourism.

Creede is surrounded by the Gunnison, Rio Grande, and San Juan national forests. With the Rio Grande and its many tributaries, there are well over two-hundred miles of trout streams within an easy day's drive. Dozens of high-mountain lakes within the national forests teem with native german browns, rainbows, and brook trout. There are also plenty of trophy fish reservoirs to choose from: the Rio Grande, Road Canyon, Continental, Hondo, Big Meadow, and Beaver Creek.

Rio Grande Drainage

Prime fishing on the Rio Grande and its lower tributaries occurs late August through October, with the exception of the sensational mid-June willow fly hatch and the mid-July salmon fly hatch. Fishermen visiting this area in the fall do not have to compete with the summer crowds and can wade uninhibited through the autumn countryside. Even though 90 percent of the fish inhabiting the Rio Grande are wily german browns, nearly 90 percent of the fish caught are stocked rainbows. Competent fishermen can expect to catch both browns and rainbows in the fifteen-inch to nineteen-inch class.

A twenty-two-and-a-half-mile stretch of the Rio Grande is designated gold-medal trout waters from above the town of South Fork downstream to Del Norte. Portions of it are restricted to the use of artificial flies and lures only. Daily bag and possession limits for trout are two per day and all browns under sixteen inches must be returned. Coloradan anglers claim that some of the state's best fishing for large browns can be found in the Rio Grande between South Fork and Wagon Wheel Gap. Much of the Rio downstream from South Fork flows through private land holdings; public access is limited to leased areas.

Productive early season patterns (#10–14) include royal coachmans fished wet on a dropper, dark blue mayflies, orange-bellied goofus bugs, willow flies, elk hair caddis, and hair-winged rio grande kings. After the water clears in mid-July, trout will rise to a hair-winged variant such as the house and lot (#10–14), gunnison river specials, or flies with a peacock herl body such as renegades and half-back nymphs. A favorite local combo uses a ginger-quill gordon on a dropper with a dark mosquito as the end fly. Salmon fly imitations (#6–8) and stonefly nymphs work best during the mid-July salmon fly hatch. Black-and-orange doodle bugs (a bitch creek in reverse) and patterns resembling mosquito larvae are also reliable prior to summer's end when periodic hatches of virtually everything come to life. Later on in the season, dark brown patterns and gray hackle yellow or orange ashers become the trouts' preference. Big streamers cast upstream and allowed to free drift or stripped in will also take their share of big browns in the fall.

Secondary streams in the upper Rio Grande

drainage have fair fishing for cutthroat near their headwaters and fair to good fishing for brook, rainbow, and brown trout lower down. The upper meadows of Miners Creek, Rat Creek, and Shallow Creek—where fly fishing is at its best—are accessible by horseback. Many of these higher elevation creeks can also be reached by four-wheel drive. Creeks noted for some of the finer scenery and better fishing include Bear, Goose, Pole, Lost Trail, and West Lost Trail creeks. Closer to the town of South Fork, southeast of Creede, good fishing is found in Park and Beaver creeks.

Green drakes (#12–14) are productive from mid-July through September on these higher elevation streams and ponds; adams (#12–16) will also provoke action in streams. Blue quills (#14–16), midges (#8–10), matukas, short-haired olive-bodied woolly worms (#2), and crustacean patterns such as shrimp are the favored flies for alpine lake fishing.

A tourist brochure published by Creede's Chamber of Commerce and available on request is an invaluable aid to anglers. It has a map showing streams, creeks, and lakes in the area. The Ramble House, located on Main Street in Creede, is the major outlet for angling supplies in the area. Its owner, Alton Cole, is an avid fly fisherman and longtime local resident. His knowledge of the Rio Grande and back-country fishing is unsurpassed; he is always willing to answer any questions or make arrangements for guide services.

Creede Area Attractions

Creede's downtown consists of a main street lined with gift and curio shops housed in historic mining town buildings. Visitors can browse through shops filled with silver and turquoise jewelry, Indian artifacts, antiques, and handmade crafts or visit the Mineral County Museum, which houses an extensive collection of historical photographs and memorabilia from Creede's boomtown days. A pair of hiking shoes will come in handy for exploring the hillsides above town littered with abandoned mine sites.

Scenic drives along Colorado 149 lead to a number of interesting historical and educational points of interest. Wagon Wheel Gap Gallery, a

few miles downstream from Creede, is a Victorian train depot dating back to the days of the Denver and Rio Grande Railroad. It has been renovated into a fine arts gallery exhibiting American paintings, sculpture, and ceramics. Farther east, art buffs can visit the San Juan Art Center in La Garita, the Rio Grande County Museum in Del Norte, and the Rio Grande Arts Center in Alamosa. Bird-watchers and naturalists will enjoy a visit to the national wildlife refuges in Monte Vista and Alamosa.

South from Alamosa, on Colorado 285, Antonito serves as a depot for one of the last narrow-gauge coal-powered trains in the country, the Cumbres and Toltec Scenic Railroad. Visitors riding the train, which runs between Antonito and Chama, New Mexico, should plan on spending an entire day on the excursion.

Additional attractions include North Clear Creek Falls on the Lake City Highway northwest of Creede and the Wheeler Geologic Area set aside by Theodore Roosevelt as a national monument in 1908. Picnic meals and camping gear should accompany travelers to the geologic area since the trip takes six to seven hours by four-wheel drive. Scenic trips by jeep or raft can be contracted through any of the lodges mentioned. Hikers will enjoy miles of trails in the Rio Grande and Gunnison national forests and in the Weminuche Wilderness with its famed Rio Grande pyramid and window formations.

Annual events include the Rio Grande Raft Races in June, Creede's Fourth of July Celebration—the rip-roaring Days of '92—and the outfitters and guides July barbecue. The Creede Repertory Theatre, one of the finest theater companies in the country, also draws visitors to performances of dance, music, poetry, and drama from mid-June through August.

ANTLERS RANCH

HC 70, Creede, CO 81130. Phone: (303) 658-2423. Contact: Stanley and Zelda Meer McCrossen. Total capacity: 100. Open January–December. Peak season: July and August. Reserve 1 year in advance. One pet allowed free; extra charge for each additional pet.

Accommodations: Twenty-two riverside housekeeping units sleep 2–8; all have private bath, fully equipped kitchen, access to gas barbecues, and a centrally located pit barbecue. Laundry facility.

Meals: No meals served in lodge; groups can make arrangements for meals to be served on American Plan. Once a week, potluck fish fries take place for guests to get acquainted.

Rates: Inexpensive; weekly and daily rates. Special 20 percent discount in spring and fall (3-night minimum). Extra charges: airport pick-up from Gunnison or Alamosa. Cash or check only.

How to Get There: Located 5 miles southwest of Creede, CO, on State Highway 149. Rental car recommended for local travel; available at Gunnison and Alamosa airports.

Stanley and Zelda Meer McCrossen want to "give people the experience of a low key, casual and comfortable vacation." The McCrossens bought the 70-acre ranch in 1983 after spending several summers in Creede attending performances of the widely acclaimed Creede Repertory Theatre. They ended up falling in love with the grander stage of the town's remote Rocky Mountain setting.

Twenty-two housekeeping units stretch out along a half mile of the Rio Grande. Guests have access to gas barbecues scattered around the cabins as well as to a centrally located open-pit barbecue with picnic tables and benches. The lodge houses a game room with a pool table, board games, books and magazines, and a sitting room with a fireplace for comfort on crisp evenings. A country store stocks a limited selection of groceries, some fishing tackle, and miscellaneous items. Fishing licenses are sold but guests will have to head to Alton Cole's Ramble House in Creede for most fly-fishing supplies.

Things to Do

As is true for most visitors to the Creede area, fishing the Rio Grande and its many tributaries is the number one priority. In between casts, anglers can join in a game of Ping-Pong, horseshoes, volleyball, pool, or badminton. Hiking trails, abandoned mines, and the town of Creede are all within an easy commute from the ranch.

For additional fishing information, refer to the Creede Area Fisheries section.

BIG RIVER GUEST RANCH

Creede, Co 81130. Phone: (303) 658-2259. Contact: Don or Loraine Seastone, managers. Total capacity: 50 cabin guests plus trailer spaces. Open May 26–Labor Day. Peak season: July–mid-August. Reserve 6 months in advance, large family groups especially. No pets.

Accommodations: Light-housekeeping cabins sleep 2–6; all have private bath and kitchen. Barbecues available for outdoor cooking.

Meals: No meals served in lodge. Meals available across the river at Blue Creek Lodge and at several restaurants in Creede.

Rates: Inexpensive; weekly and daily rates. Full hook-up available for trailers. Cash or check only.

How to Get There: Located 12 miles northwest of South Fork on State Highway 149. Follow 149 south 10 miles from Creede to ranch. Rental car recommended for local travel; available at Gunnison and Alamosa airports.

Big River Guest Ranch's lodge house was originally an old stagecoach stop in Wagon Wheel Gap on the way to Antelope Springs. When tracks for the Denver and Rio Grande Railroad were laid through town, the lodge, along with several cabins, was moved down to the present-day riverside location and incorporated into a family homestead. Big River has been operating as a guest ranch for over fifty years, with families of three generations returning to these fifty acres of spruce, aspen, and cottonwood. Not much has changed, and the guests like it that way.

Many of the rustic cabins still have their original log-and-mortar exteriors, while interiors have been modernized with electricity and plumbing. Furnishings are simple, yet comfortable, accented by pine paneling, braided throw rugs, and cafe curtains. The lodge is open to guests for playing cards by a large stone fireplace, a session at the piano, or simply for visiting. Snack foods, a few fishing items, and licenses are also sold in the lodge.

Things to Do

National forest land contiguous to the Big River ranch offers spectacular terrain for hiking, picnicking, and horseback riding. Public stables with horses for hire by the hour or day are located a short distance away. Big River will also arrange jeep tours and suggest locations where rock hounds can have a field day.

Fishing

Big River has a long stretch of land along the Rio Grande within walking distance of the cabins. This easy access makes angling any time of day possible. South and west of the ranch, fishermen will find rainbows and browns in the South Fork of the Rio Grande, Park and Beaver creeks, as well as in Big Meadow and Beaver Creek reservoirs. Many smaller streams and lakes near the old mining towns of Platoro and Summitville are found farther south.

For additional fishing information, see the Creede Area Fisheries section.

The selection of tackle sold in the lodge is geared primarily to bait-and-spin fishermen. Fly-fishing anglers will have to take a trip into Creede for supplies.

BROKEN ARROW RANCH

Creede, CO 81130. Phone: (303) 658-2484. Contact: Jerry and Kristy Dennis. Total capacity: 42 cabin guests plus trailer spaces. Open Memorial Day–mid-September. Peak season: June–August. Reserve 2–6 months in advance. Pets must be leashed.

Accommodations: Six rustic housekeeping cabins have private bath; 5 cabins share central toilet and separate showers for men and women. All have hot plate, wood-burning stove, and refrigerator; bedding, linen, and utensils provided. Daily maid service available for an extra charge to guests staying more than 1 week.

Meals: N/A. Several restaurants in area offer food.

Rates: Inexpensive; daily rates include fishing privileges on two private lakes. One night free per week for guests staying longer than 1 week. Extra charges: maid service for guests staying more than 1 week, four-wheel drive, and pack trips. Cash, check, or money order.

How to Get There: Located 12 miles southwest of Creede on State Highway 149. Rental car recommended for local travel; available at Gunnison and Alamosa airports.

Broken Arrow is a kicked-back, low-key fishing retreat unhampered by the modern conveniences of television and telephones. The original 160-acre cattle ranch was turned into a farming operation in 1936 by Thomas Powell and his wife Josephine. They built their own house first, then the lodge, and added one or two cabins a year until there were eleven. Josephine worked side-by-side with her husband pounding nails, hauling lumber, and sewing curtains. Eventually, outhouses and pumps were added. Pack trips into upper regions of the National Forest where the ranch had range rights were developed later on. The original ledger lists the first guest's arrival in August 1940. The Powells willed their land to nephews whose families are still involved in Broken Arrow's upkeep and daily operations today.

Even though Broken Arrow has some of the most rustic cabin facilities in the area, they prove to be very popular with fishermen. Housekeeping cabins are situated in an open field within a short walking distance from one another. Cabins all have a wood stove, gas or electric hot plate, and refrigerator, and are very basic: linoleum floors, paneled walls, and overhead lighting.

Things to Do

Guests have use of an archery range and horseshoe pit anytime they're not fishing, which is what most guests at the Broken Arrow prefer to do. Four-wheel drive pack trips up to high mountain lakes are arranged by request.

Fishing

Two private spring- and creek-fed lakes located on Broken Arrow Ranch are within easy walking distance from the cabins. Guests take advantage of fishing here during the early-morning and late-evening hatches when it doesn't interfere with their angling time on the Rio Grande and its tributaries. Seepage Creek feeds these lakes after it flows out of the Santa Maria Reservoir and picks up warm water from Antelope Hot Springs on its six-mile journey to the lakes. This makes the average temperature of the water much warmer than in other lakes at this elevation, which provides a longer growing season for trout and natural vegetation alike. The upper lake is known for its big brookies and the lower lake for

its eighteen- to nineteen-inch german browns and rainbows.

Medium-sized (#6–10) leech patterns such as woolly worms and woolly buggers work well on the ranch. The best fishing occurs in June, although most anglers hook up with trout all summer long. The lakes are fairly shallow and can be waded with hip boots. Colorado catch limits apply and a state license is required.

The ranch also has rights to fish in several lakes closed to public access. These lakes can only be reached by four-wheel drive, which limits intrusions by pedestrian anglers and creates a very special opportunity for fly fishers at Broken Arrow Ranch.

For additional fishing information, see Creede Area Fisheries section.

4UR GUEST RANCH

P.O. Box 340, Creede, CO 81130. Phone: (303) 658-2202. Contact: Katus and Joe Walton, managers. Total capacity: 50. Open June–October. Peak season: July–August. Reserve 1 year in advance; reservations for less than 1 week not accepted in July and August. No pets.

Accommodations: Three buildings house guest rooms with private bath; one log cottage with fireplace and porch also available. Full maid service daily.

Meals: Three family-style meals daily on American Plan. A la carte breakfast menu, chuckwagon breakfast once a week; full lunch and elegant gourmet dinners; fish fry once a week; a cocktail party for guests to get acquainted. Complete wine list and selection of alcohol available.

Rates: Expensive; daily rates include lodging, meals, fishing, riding, and use of all ranch facilities. Reduced rates for children 4–12; children under 3, free. Extra charges: jeep trips, day trip to Lost Lakes, overnight trip to Lost Lakes, skeet range, round-trip airport pick-up. Cash, check, MasterCard, VISA, American Express.

How to Get There: Located southwest of Creede, CO, off State Highway 149. Private planes have use of 4UR hangar at Creede's airstrip. Rental car recommended for local travel; available at Gunnison and Alamosa airports.

Many guests have returned to the 4UR ranch for more than forty years to indulge in some of the most gracious western hospitality found in Colorado. The 4UR is definitely the place for anglers and their families who want to disengage from the rest of the world while enjoying incredible fishing on a private stretch of the Rio Grande reserved for guests' use only.

Log cabins and lodges are elegantly furnished with old world and western accents. In the evenings, guests return to their rooms to find that their beds have already been turned down. The main lodge houses an intimate dining room, card room, cozy cocktail parlor, and library. The exquisite decor features exotic trophy mounts and an art collection gathered from around the world. Large picture windows look out over a grand view of the surrounding ranch lands and guest facilities. A spa, swimming pool, tennis courts, and stables are located a short walk away. Dinners are a sit-down gourmet affair at the 4UR and guests tend to dress up a little: women wear long skirts or pantsuits while men don casual sports coats and slacks.

Things to Do

Activities are posted on a bulletin board every morning and guests partake in any or none at all—as they wish. For those who desire total relaxation, there's a pool warmed by natural hot springs and a sunning deck. Nearby are hot sulphur spring baths and a sauna. Muscles that have gone unused for too long will be rejuvenated by a vigorous workout in the health spa. Guests can also play tennis or sign up for a guided horseback trip for the day. Full-time counselors supervise an extensive children's program that includes hikes, hay rides, and other outdoor fun. Llama rides are reserved for children under five.

The 4,000-acre ranch is surrounded by the Rio Grande National Forest. This country will delight no matter how you choose to see it: by four-wheel drive, riding, or hiking. It offers magnificent scenery for the photographer, artist, and wildlife observer alike. Hunting for Indian artifacts and searching for ore specimens are also favorite pastimes in these hills.

Fishing

Anglers should not let the roster of activities offered sway their decision about whether or not the ranch is the place for them. The 4UR is a serious fishing retreat. In fact, 4UR offers some of the area's finest private access to fly fishing for browns, rainbows, and cutthroats. More than nine miles of streams, designated fly fishing only, are within easy reach from the lodge. The Rio Grande and Goose Creek are divided into half-mile stations that are the exclusive domain of in-dividual anglers. Stations can be drawn the night before for morning posts; afternoons revert to first-come, first-served basis. Novices can perfect their casts on the ranch's small, well-stocked lake.

For additional fishing information, see Creede Area Fisheries section.

A real convenience is the fact that anglers don't have to go anywhere if they run out of fishing supplies. The ranch store sells licenses, gear, and locally productive flies.

WASON RANCH

Box 220, Creede, CO 81130. Phone: (303) 658-2413. Contact: Rod and Marilyn Wintz, managers. Total capacity: 100. Seven riverside cottages open all year; cabins available May–November 15. Peak season: July and August. Reserve 1 year in advance for peak season; for May, June, and September, reserve 5–6 months in advance. No pets.

Accommodations: Housekeeping log cabins with kitchenette and private bath sleep up to 6; 7 riverside cottages with complete modern kitchen sleep 6. Eight-person maximum in cottages. Linens provided for all accommodations.

Meals: No meals served in lodge; managers will recommend places to dine in town.

Rates: Inexpensive; daily, monthly, and seasonal rates. Discounts for stays of 7 days or longer. Three-day minimum stay in cabins; 5-day minimum in cottages. Extra charges: float trips, jeep trip to Lost Lakes. Cash or check only.

How to Get There: Located 2 miles southeast of Creede on State Highway 149. Rental car recommended for local travel; available at Gunnison and Alamosa airports.

Wason Ranch lies in the southeastern end of the wide Creede valley. Originally a homestead, the ranch grew into a large horse-raising operation that supplied the U.S. Army until shortly after World War I. Nowadays the ranch is run as a popular guest resort with a high percentage of repeat clientele. Wason will be of particular interest to anglers as it is the only guest ranch in Creede that boasts four private miles on the famed Rio Grande. Families and anglers looking for a relaxed vacation with all the amenities will find the ranch very comfortable.

Housekeeping log cabins with kitchenettes include a dining area and are equipped with electric ranges, refrigerators, and basic cooking and eating utensils. Interiors are a blend of log-and-mortar and pine paneling. Cabins are arranged neatly along the edge of a common area used for lawn games and barbecues. Other shared facilities include a basketball court and recreation hall with a Ping-Pong table and plenty of room to sit and visit in.

Across the highway from these units, Wason Ranch maintains seven riverside cottages that resemble modern tract homes. Unlike their urban counterparts, these accommodations are perched on the banks of the Rio Grande with a view of the San Juan Mountains.

Things to Do

Guests at Wason Ranch come and go as they please. Those not out fishing can tour Creede's historic sites or hike and horseback ride in the surrounding national forests (see information in Creede Area Attractions).

Fishing

The 1,700-acre Wason Ranch meanders along four private miles of prime fishing water on the Rio Grande. The ranch is the only outfitter licensed to guide float trips on the upper Rio Grande. Ninety percent of the fish caught are german browns. Wason's stream management program, coordinated by a fish biologist, designates half of this stretch of water for catch-and-release fly fishing only. The ranch stocks 10,000 fingerling browns each year and permits guests to keep two browns twelve inches and under; rainbows of any size caught outside the fly-fishing area can also be kept. A small lake on the property is stocked to give beginning fly fishers a place to wet their lines before attempting the big river. The ranch can also arrange jeep trips up to high lakes with native rainbows and brooks. There is very little fishing pressure on these lakes because permission is required to use them. Rod Wintz, avid fly fisherman and ranch manager for

over twenty years, is very amenable to helping those who request it.

For additional fishing information, see Creede Area Fisheries section.

Anglers should stop in Creede or South Fork to purchase fishing licenses and supplies since the ranch does not sell any.

RATON, NEW MEXICO

VERMEJO PARK RANCH

P.O. Drawer E, Raton, NM 87740. Phone: (505) 445-3097/5028. Contact: Jim Charlesworth, general manager. Total capacity: 85. Open early June–mid-September. Peak season: July and August. Reserve 3–5 months in advance. No pets.

Accommodations: Six cottages sleep up to 6; dormitory-style lodging also available. Additional lodges in Sangre de Cristo Mountains accommodate up to 30 guests. Daily maid service; laundry facility.

Meals: Three family-style meals daily on American Plan; breakfasts cooked to order, sit-down and trail lunches, full dinners, barbecue every Saturday night. Beer and wine available, pay as you go full-service bar.

Rates: Expensive; daily rate includes lodging and meals. Family plan available. Extra charges: rod fee, guides, horses, airport pick-up, four-wheel drive rental. Cash or check only.

How to Get There: Located 225 miles north of Albuquerque, 220 miles west of Amarillo, TX, 100 miles south of Pueblo, CO, and 220 miles south of Denver. Take State Road 555 for 40 miles west of Raton to ranch. Commercial airlines service airports in Albuquerque, Amarillo, Pueblo, and Denver. Rental car recommended for local travel; available at local airports. Charter flights into Raton's Crews Field can be arranged through Eagle Tail Aviation in Raton.

Located on the eastern slope of the Sangre de Cristo range in northeastern New Mexico, Vermejo Park Ranch operates as a working ranch and as a managed wildlife and game reserve. Consisting of 392,000 acres, the ranch is one of the largest blocks of privately owned land in the United States. It covers varied terrains from piñon, juniper, and oakbrush lowlands to tundra-sided snow-capped mountains with elevations between six thousand and thirteen thousand feet.

Fields and streams at Vermejo are carefully managed by a full-time wildlife biologist and his staff, guaranteeing quality yields of game and fish. Home to New Mexico's largest elk herd, Vermejo Park embraces twenty lakes and nearly twenty-five miles of trout-filled streams, access to which is reserved for guests. A staff of professional guides sees that guests get the most out of their daily excursions. With its impressive size and specialized staff, it's no surprise that Vermejo is one of the most exclusive guest ranches in the West. Visitors to Vermejo are generally accustomed to traveling first class and prefer the option of highly personalized care.

Most guests stay in the complex of lodges and spacious cottages known as Headquarters. These impressive stone buildings with red-tiled roofs are clustered together on twelve acres of beautifully landscaped grounds. Casa Grande, one of the lodges, serves more as a museum housing antiques and period pieces collected by previous Vermejo proprietors than as a guest house. Nearby Casa Minor houses all of Headquarters' dining and lounge facilities as well as a full-service bar and a fishing tackle and souvenir shop.

Cresmer and Costilla, two outlying lodges, are located fifteen and twenty-eight miles away at elevations of 8,800 and 9,960 feet respectively. Cresmer Lodge lies deep in the heart of Vermejo's lake country while Costilla Lodge is located high in the Sangre de Cristo Mountains in a remote wilderness region with trout-filled waters of the Costilla creeks nearby. Both are rustic cabins constructed of native logs and are warmed by large stone fireplaces.

Things to Do

Activities at Vermejo focus on exploring the diverse terrain encompassed by ranch boundaries. Staff guides lead trail rides, hikes, sightseeing, photography sessions, and four-wheel drive tours; however, there are no set schedules. A skeet and silhouette range is available to those wishing to sharpen their shooting skills; shotguns are provided, rifles are not. The most popular off-ranch venture is a visit to the La Mesa Park Racetrack in nearby Raton, reputed to have some of the finest quarter-horse racing in the country. Daytime trips to Taos allow guests to taste the interesting culture and history of the area.

Fishing

Fishing is by far and away the most popular summertime activity at Vermejo Park. There are so many private lakes and miles of streams on the ranch that guests can spend an entire month at the ranch and never cast to the same water twice. Vermejo's professional guides can be extremely useful the first day or two in helping anglers decipher the lay of the land.

Icy, gin-clear streams have native populations of eight- to fourteen-inch cutthroats, brooks, and rainbows. The Vermejo River averages approximately fifteen to twenty feet in width and contains the native Rio Grande cutthroat. The two Costilla creeks are somewhat smaller and are populated with a mixture of rainbows, brooks, and cutthroats. Due to the increased popularity of fly fishing, one entire stream has been set aside for the exclusive use of fly fishers.

Only dry and wet flies are permitted on the scenic glacial lakes and beaver ponds at elevations up to 11,500 feet. Native twelve- to thirteen-inch rainbow and cutthroat predominate, with a few brooks in these high-altitude lakes—most of which are accessible by four-wheel drive vehicles. Stocked one- to one-and-a-half-pound rainbows in the ranch's lower lakes average fourteen to fifteen inches with a few record-size brookies of three to four and a half pounds. The stickleback brook trout—endangered in New Mexico—is a highly revered inhabitant in one of the lakes. Bait fishing is limited to two of the lower lakes; the remainder are reserved for the use of artificial flies and lures only.

A good selection of dry and wet flies (#10–14) to use on Vermejo's streams and lakes includes joe's hoppers, rio grande kings, irresistibles, adams, black gnats, elk hair caddis, royal wulffs, hornbergs, and humpies. Productive nymph patterns (#10–14) are gold-ribbed hare's ears, tellico nymphs, zug bugs, and damsel flies on the lakes.

Flat-bottomed johnboats equipped with oars (motors are optional) are used on a first-come, first-served basis on all lakes. In an effort to maintain quality control on both stream and lake fisheries, guests are asked to sort their catch according to the particular fishery and to record essential data with the fish biologist at the Fish House. This is also where fish are cleaned, frozen, and stored for guests until they leave.

Intensive three-day fly-fishing clinics are offered during the course of the summer. Sessions cover equipment, knot tying, fly presentation, trout ecology, and feeding behavior for beginners and advanced anglers alike. One entire session is devoted specifically to fly tying. Vermejo's Tackle Shop sells licenses and carries a full line of Dan Bailey flies, lures, and a full selection of other fishing tackle. A New Mexico state fishing license is not required except on certain streams and lakes.

MEEKER, COLORADO

White River Area Fisheries

Located in the northwestern corner of Colorado, the town of Meeker is known to sportsmen and recreationists as the "gateway to the White River Valley." The valley stretches east from town into the White River National Forest and its northern neighbor, the Routt National Forest.

The White River, its north and south forks, and their tributary streams are the area's most popular waterways. Easy access to the larger rivers via paved and gravel roadways subject them to the brunt of local angling pressure, whereas countless harder-to-reach lakes and streams within the two national forests produce spectacular, undisturbed sportfishing in altitudes between eight thousand to twelve thousand feet. Serious fly fishers bound for the higher climes are well advised to enlist the services of a local guide/outfitter as the terrain is rugged and weather unpredictable.

White River Drainage

The White River and its north and south forks clear in mid-July and remain productive through late fall. The main branch and the South Fork of the White River offer challenging fishing for the experienced fly fisher. There are twenty-six miles of the South Fork to fish from the South Fork Campground back up to the highway, with numerous feeder streams along the way. Average and beginner fly fishers will find fishing on the North Fork of the White River a little easier. The North Fork branches off the main river and flows north to Marvine, Ute, and Lost creeks above the town of Buford. These are small brushy streams best suited for anglers adept at noodle fishing for selective, small fish. The lower stretch of the North Fork is mostly private; however, within the public access domain of the White River National Forest there are miles of feeder streams with fishing for brooks and rainbows.

Productive fly patterns vary depending on cloud cover, temperatures, the angler's location on the river, and natural hatch activity. The season starts with a mid-July willow fly hatch. Muddler minnows and hornbergs can be used then. Productive all-season patterns include gray hackle, red and yellow mayflies, and small dark flies (#14–16) such as mosquitos, black gnats, and black flies. Chest waders and cleats are recommended since river boulders are slick. A 7½- to 8½-foot, 5-weight rod is adequate for most situations; a slightly heavier rod can be used as a backup on windy afternoons.

High-country lakes open up in late July, with the peak of angling occurring from mid-August to September. Native brooks and rainbows in these timberline lakes are selective feeders but patience and timing can produce some vigorous beauties ranging from one-half to six pounds. Popular hike-in lakes include the Marvine and Baily lakes groups, Lake of the Woods, and Big Fish. Mirror Lake, which has a few good-sized twelve- to fifteen-inch rainbows and lots of small brooks, is a perfect lake for novices, while Sable Lake with its trophy-sized wily cutthroats is for more experienced anglers. Dry fly favorites (#12–16) include the adams, royal coachmans, renegades, blue duns, and small dark patterns such as black gnats and mosquitos. Popular wet flies are tricolor browns, hornbergs, stonefly nymphs, and hare's ears.

Lake Avery is a man-made reservoir that offers good fishing for brooks, browns, cutthroats, and twelve-inch, half-pound rainbows. Crustacean patterns such as shrimp and crawdads have produced a few deep-bellied rainbows weighing over five pounds from the lake. Trappers Lake, a large wilderness lake with natural reproducing twelve- to fifteen-inch cutthroats, forms the headwaters of the White River. It produces excellent fishing in June and July when the cutts are spawning. Effective early-season fly patterns include old faithfuls, the trappers lake special, and orange ashers (#14). Brighter fly patterns and spinning lures, such as mepps and daredevils, work better later on. Special restrictions limit fishing to artificial flies and lures only. Buford's Hunting and Fishing Lodge is the nearest outlet for a wide assortment of local flies, licenses, and a limited selection of gear. Millers Ace Hardware in Meeker and the Roaring Fork Angler in Glenwood Springs also sell licenses and carry tackle and equipment.

White River Area Attractions

Meeker's White River Museum has one of the finest collections of western artifacts in existence. The log building housing the museum was used as officers quarters for federal troops after the Meeker Massacre in 1879. The museum is a fascinating showpiece of Americana that should not be missed.

Other historical sites of interest include the oil shale on Piceance Creek and the Rock House—a one-room schoolhouse in continuous use since the turn of the century. The old Meeker Hotel boarded Teddy Roosevelt when he came to hunt and Eleanor Roosevelt when she used to visit her son Elliot at nearby Bar Bell Ranch.

Scenic drives include Route 13 south from Meeker to Rifle Falls and Rifle Reservoir. From Rifle, visitors have easy access to raft trips and a variety of water sports on the Colorado River and to Glenwood Springs—the world's largest natural hot mineral baths. Glenwood also has a number of tennis courts and golf courses.

The biggest event of the summer is Meeker's annual Fourth of July celebration, the Range Call Rodeo, reputed to be one of Colorado's oldest celebrations of its kind.

"BUDGES" WHITE RIVER RESORT

June 10–October: Box 1107, Eagle, CO 81631. Phone: (303) 328-7447. Year round, write: 21679 East Otero Place, Aurora, CO 80016. Phone: (303) 690-6627. Contact: Jack and Elaine Harrison. Total capacity: 33. Open July 1–November 15. Peak season: August–September. Reserve 2 months in advance. No pets.

Accommodations: Seven log cabins with wood-burning stove sleep 4–6; they share a common bathhouse and have no electricity. Daily maid service; laundry facility.

Meals: Three family-style meals daily on American Plan; breakfast, hot lunch or trail lunch, full dinners. Beer and wine available at meals; snacks sold in lodge store.

Rates: Moderate; daily rate includes lodging and meals. Special group and family rates depend on number of people and days requested. Extra charges: riding and packhorse rentals, wilderness pack trip, summer drop camps. Cash, check, travelers checks, or money order.

How to Get There: Located 75 miles northwest of Vail, CO, and 60 miles northeast of Glenwood Springs. Take Dotsero exit off I-70 just west of Gypsum; follow it north along the Colorado River 1 mile to Coffee Pot Springs Road; turn left and follow road to Deep Lake (mile 31); lodge is 8 miles farther down the road. "Budges" is 40 miles from nearest paved road; although 2-wheel drive vehicles can make it, 4-wheel drive is recommended. Closest commercial airport located in Avon.

"Budges" White River Resort is located on the southern boundary of the 235,000-acre Flat Tops Wilderness Area in the White River National Forest. It is quite remote—nearly forty miles from the nearest paved road. The dusty ride across the Flat Tops plateau to "Budges" is an awesome one visitors are not likely to forget: a carpet of wildflowers covers gentle alpine meadows stretching to the horizon, Basque sheepherders herd their flocks from meadow to meadow through thick glades of aspen, and precipitous gorges hold streams dwarfed by the surrounding canyons.

Although "Budges" offers comfortable lodging and delicious meals, the resort touts itself as a wilderness camp rather than a guest ranch. Visitors make their way here knowing the lodge and cabins remain the last bastion of comfort in this wilderness section of the Colorado Rockies. "Budges" will appeal to those who like to hike, horseback ride, and fish in unpolluted splendor far away from the noise of cities and highways. Pack-in services to drop camps and extended back-country pack trips are also offered.

Construction on the White River Resort began in 1928 when the present-day bunkhouse was built. The lodge was built in the early thirties, and seven cabins have been added on over the years. Except for the addition of plumbed bathrooms, the log-and-mortar cabins remain as they were originally built. Although interiors are furnished with only the bare essentials, these rustic accommodations are charming nonetheless: throw rugs, homespun curtains, and beds decorated with patterned quilts are warmed by the glow of kerosene lamps at night. The main lodge is the only building at the resort with electricity. It houses the dining room and board-game parlor where a massive bull elk trophy is mounted over the fireplace. Cabinets and wall shelves display a variety of western artifacts and interesting relics from the lodge's past.

Things to Do

Guests can do as they please in the unstructured atmosphere of "Budges." Hiking, horseback riding, and fishing are pastimes planned at each individual's discretion. Trails lead to high meadows with wildflowers and dark timber areas populated by deer and elk. All-day trail rides into the Flat Top Wilderness Area are scheduled by request.

Overnight and extended back-country trips are accompanied by a wrangler, an experienced guide, and cook. Authentic western barbecues at the end of the day are set against some of the most impressive scenery in the Rockies. While the sun sinks in the west, peaks such as Trapper's, Shingle, and Marvine, which surround the base camp, become immense shadows against a glorious star-filled sky.

Fishing

The South Fork of the White River runs within casting distance of your cabin door. Thirteen miles of river below the resort and six miles above are in the designated wilderness. Brooks and rainbows, stocked every three to four years, and native cutthroats growing to eighteen to twenty-two inches can weigh as much as three to five pounds.

"Budges" White River Resort has access to some of the finer wilderness fly fishing found in the lower forty-eight. Unsophisticated trout inhabiting the waters of this remote region, restricted to foot and horseback travel only, seldom see a fly or a lure. Although cutthroats, rainbows, and brook trout averaging ten to fifteen inches predominate, a few small, nondescript alpine lakes have produced monsters in the four- to five-pound range. Nearby Deep Lake yielded the state record mackinaw one year. Fall offers the absolute best dry fly fishing of the entire season. "Budges" wranglers are knowledgeable anglers and are willing to customize rides and hikes to suit individual preferences and abilities.

Nymphs are productive early in the season while all-season dry fly favorites include adams, irresistibles, and gray hackle yellows. The lodge sells fishing licenses along with a good selection of flies; a few extra pairs of waders are kept on hand to lend and rods to rent. Sporting goods stores in Glenwood Springs and Vail also sell an assortment of high-mountain fishing tackle and gear. Anglers should come completely outfitted since it requires a full day's drive to and from the ranch to reach the nearest town.

FRITZLAN'S OUTFITTERS

1891 County Road #12, Meeker, CO 81641. Phone: (303) 878-4845. Contact: Cal and Arlene Fritzlan. Open June–November 15. Peak season: September. Reserve 1 year in advance.

Accommodations: Lodge and 3 cabins house guests before and after back-country trips. Two permanent camps for groups up to 15; moving camps for groups up to 8.

Meals: A la carte meals served in lodge; bar and restaurant open to public.

Rates: Inexpensive. Special rates for drop camps, Marvine Lakes camp, overnight camp, cross-country pack trips. Pick-up from airport charged extra. Cash, check, VISA, or MasterCard.

How to Get There: Located 30 miles east of Meeker, CO. Pack trip guests arriving by commercial airline or private plane will be met at Grand Junction or Meeker airports.

Fritzlan's offers excellent outfitter services for fishing, hunting, and camping vacations into the Marvine Lakes region of the Flat Tops Wilderness. The Fritzlan family has been in the business since the 1930s when Arlene's uncle guided Hollywood celebrities out of Palm Springs, eventually returning to Meeker to manage other lodging and guide services. Today, three generations of Fritzlans work together managing their own wrangling operation, reputed to be one of the oldest and best in the valley.

Guests are packed into one of two permanent summer camps maintained by the Fritzlans on the Marvine Lakes, an easy six-mile horseback ride through scenic Colorado high country. Each camp accommodates up to fifteen people in sturdy canvas-sided tents. Fly fishers have access to rubber rafts kept at the lakes; knowledgeable wranglers lead the way to productive stream fishing for cutthroats, brooks, and rainbows. Guests supply their own personal gear and fishing equipment.

Three meals a day are served in a large cook/dining tent. Guests are expected to supply their own flies and fishing gear on all pack trips. Buford's Hunting and Fishing Lodge, nine miles west of Fritzlan's, is the nearest place to purchase a license along with a wide selection of local flies. Millers Ace Hardware in Meeker and the Roaring Fork Angler in Glenwood Springs also carry sporting goods supplies.

RIPPLE CREEK LODGE

39020 County Road 8, Meeker, CO 81641. Phone: (303) 878-4725. Contact: Ken Jett, outfitter/guide. Open June–September. Peak season: July and August. Reserve 2–4 months in advance.

Accommodations: Eight light housekeeping cabins have kitchen and private bath (3 cabins share a central bath); most with fireplace. Moving and stationary camps for groups up to 8.

Meals: Notify lodge in advance for fixed price meals; trail lunches can also be arranged.

Rates: Inexpensive; daily rates. Vacation plan includes lodging, meals, and horse. Special packages include pack trips, drop camps, Ripple Creek weekender. Extra charges: meals, horse rental and trailering, and round-trip airport pick-up. Cash or check.

How to Get There: Located 39 miles east of Meeker, CO, and 200 miles west of Denver. Airport pick-up available for guests arriving in Steamboat Springs. Rental cars available but not necessary for wilderness trekkers.

Ripple Creek Lodge has been used as a hunting and fishing lodge since the 1930s. Building of the lodge in 1943 completed the facilities, most of which remain the same today. Ripple Creek's owner, Ken Jett, has built up his packing business by guiding expeditions of geologists out of Craig since the early sixties. A majority of his business comes from hunters, although fishing clientele has increased in the last few years. Guided pack trips and packhorse rentals into the Flat Tops Wilderness of the White River National Forest are his specialty.

Rustic cabins are simply furnished and are more likely to appeal to hard-core fishing and hunting parties than to families expecting modern accommodations.

Ripple Creek's log lodge, which houses a central dining room, sits atop a hill overlooking the cabins. Its kitchen adjoins a large, sheltered barbecue patio that serves as a favorite gathering spot for the BYOB cocktail hour each evening.

A variety of riding, fishing, and hiking excursions are available. Guests supply their own sleeping bag, personal gear, and fishing equipment.

Fishing

Ken and his wranglers know this country like the backs of their hands. Numerous no-name lakes as well as some prime charted waters producing big cutthroats lie within their concessioned domain. We promised we wouldn't tell where, but Ken claims that a twenty-three inch, five-pound cutthroat was pulled from one of his favorite spots in 1984. Brook trout averaging eighteen to nineteen inches and weighing up to four pounds are found in another lake that remains a well-kept secret.

SEVEN LAKES RANCH

738 County Road 59, Meeker, CO 81641. Phone: (303) 878-4772. Contact: Rocky or Joan Rockwell. Total capacity: 16–24. Open Memorial Day–November. Peak season: July–September. Reserve 6 months in advance; or call on a chance. No pets.

Accommodations: Six modern cabins with private bath and fireplace sleep 2–6. Daily maid service; laundry facility.

Meals: Three family-style meals daily on American Plan: breakfast, hot lunch, snacks, and full dinners.

Rates: Moderate; daily rates include lodging, meals, and private lake fishing; special 5-day rates. Two-day minimum stay. Reduced rates for children. Extra charge for pick-up from Meeker airport. Cash, check, VISA, or MasterCard.

How to Get There: Ranch will send directions when reservations are confirmed. Commercial airlines service Grand Junction; private planes can fly into Meeker.

Seven Lakes Ranch began as a fish farm at the turn of the century and developed into a guest operation purely by happenstance during the 1930s. A couple of travelers, stranded on this isolated stretch of road because their car had broken down, hiked to the nearest farmhouse to get help. They became immediate friends with the farmer and his family, fell in love with the area, and returned for many years as ranch guests. The ranch gradually added more regular visitors to its guest roster.

Norm and Steb Sherwood, former owners of Seven Lakes, rebuilt the ranch from the ground up. It remains a family-run operation offering very comfortable, upscale accommodations and delicious country-style meals. It's a perfect retreat for families and couples looking for a more than an ordinary vacation.

Cabins are widely scattered amidst groves of aspen. The cabins' knotty-pine paneling, fireplaces, and comfortable furnishings accented with area rugs, homespun curtains, and western art all work together to create a homey feeling. The main lodge of log-and-mortar construction resembles a small ranch house. It is located a short walk from the cabins. A wide front porch overlooks a landscaped garden with a view of the White River valley beyond. Oversized couches and chairs in the main living room are the kind you can get lost in. The warm, inviting decor features hurricane lamps, bird decoys, wildlife pictures, and a prominent stone fireplace. Bookshelves are stuffed with an extensive collection of books on western life, Indian folklore, travel, and wildlife, which guests are welcome to read at their leisure. An intimate dining room lying off to the side is cheerfully decorated with red-and-white checked tablecloths and western artifacts.

Things to Do

Recreation and leisure time are informal and unstructured. Horseback riding, fishing, and hiking are fun ways for families to spend the day together exploring the scenic White River valley. Guided nature walks and tours to places of local interest are often highlights of a Seven Lakes vacation.

Fishing

Lake fishing for trout averaging one to three pounds in the ranch's private lakes is the main angling attraction at Seven Lakes. The ranch stocks the lakes from its own private hatcheries where native species of cutthroat, brook, brown, and rainbow trout are raised. Fishing for brooks and rainbows peaks early in the season, with browns and cutthroats becoming more active later in summer. Rowboats and canoes enable guests to cover the entire lake; angling is restricted to fly fishing or single-hook lures. State licenses are not required on the ranch.

Seven Lakes guests also have access to seven-and-a-half miles of private fishing on the White River, which requires a guide. The manager is a crack fly fisherman and well qualified to take anglers on the White, Fryingpan, Roaring Fork, and Crystal rivers—all within an hour-and-a-half drive of the ranch. He also conducts informal how-to clinics for the benefit of novices. A nominal fee is charged for all off-ranch fishing to cover the cost of transportation and guide services. Overnight and extended back-country fishing trips into the Flat Tops Wilderness can also be arranged.

Buford's Hunting and Fishing Lodge, located a short drive away, has fishing licenses for anglers planning to fish in streams, rivers, and lakes off ranch property; it is also the nearest outlet that stocks a wide selection of flies.

TRAPPERS LAKE LODGE

7700 Trappers Lake Road, Meeker, CO 81641. Phone: (303) 878-5510. Contact: Dale and Sheri Hopwood or Bill Greene, owners/managers. Total capacity: 60. Open June 15–September 15. No pets.

Accommodations: Ten guest cabins sleep 4–6; central bathhouse, kerosene lamps, and coal and wood stoves. Linens and bedding supplied.

Meals: A la carte meals available in ranch restaurant; three ranch-style meals daily on modified American Plan by special request only. Beer is sold in lodge store; all other alcohol is BYOB.

Rates: Inexpensive; weekly and daily rates. Discounts for children; children under 6, free. Extra charges: meals, horse rental, rowboats and canoes, and guided trail rides and fishing trips into Flat Tops Wilderness. Cash, travelers check, or money order.

How to Get There: Lodge reached by traveling 20–50 (depending on direction) miles of gravel road that climbs from 8,000 to 10,000 feet. From Meeker, follow RBC-8 east to Buford; continue east along North Fork of the White River; follow signs to lodge.

Built in 1917 as a wilderness oasis for hunters, fishermen, and hikers, Trappers Lake Lodge and its rustic guest cabins are situated at the end of the road overlooking 320-acre Trappers Lake. Trappers Lodge is the sole concession on this wilderness lake in the White River National Forest and is a great place for anglers who enjoy alpine lake fishing and don't mind roughing it a bit for accommodations.

Cabins—without plumbing and with very simple furnishings—are sprinkled across a hillside above the lodge and Trappers Lake. Trappers Lake Lodge houses a restaurant and a small store that stocks basic food items; fishing tackle (lures and flies); and a limited selection of spinning rods, reels, and leaders. The restaurant is open to the public. Both ranchers and employees of the U.S. Forest Service and the Colorado Division of Wildlife often join the Hopwoods and their guests in the restaurant. This is the only eatery for miles around and mealtimes are a good occasion to get to know these locals and find out where the fishing's hot.

Things to Do

Guests socialize in the lodge, which houses, in addition to the restaurant, a small library and lounge area where impromptu card and board games are usually in session in front of a big fireplace. Rowboats and canoes are for rent on the lake and horses are for hire by the day or by the hour down at the stables. Overnight pack trips can also be arranged through the lodge. Trappers provides food for overnight trail rides while guests provide their own bedroll and personal gear. Hikers and backpackers have miles of trails to explore and a good chance of finding remnants of horns, bones, and Indian arrowheads in a land once used as hunting grounds by the Ute Indians.

Fishing

The majority of Trappers Lake Lodge guests come to fish Trappers Lake and the headwaters of the North Fork of the White River. Fed by the Flat Tops Wilderness drainage and Frasier Creek, the lake measures one-and-a-quarter miles long and a half-mile wide. In places it plunges to a depth of two hundred feet. Naturally reproducing cutthroats average fourteen to fifteen inches.

The lake's wilderness designation prohibits the use of motors, and tackle is limited to the use of artificial flies and lures. Special catch restrictions apply.

Being a licensed guide, Dale Hopwood knows of numerous small lakes where angling pressure is not as intense as it gets at times on Trappers Lake. Back-country fishing trips cost extra and guests must provide their own personal gear and bedroll.

IDAHO

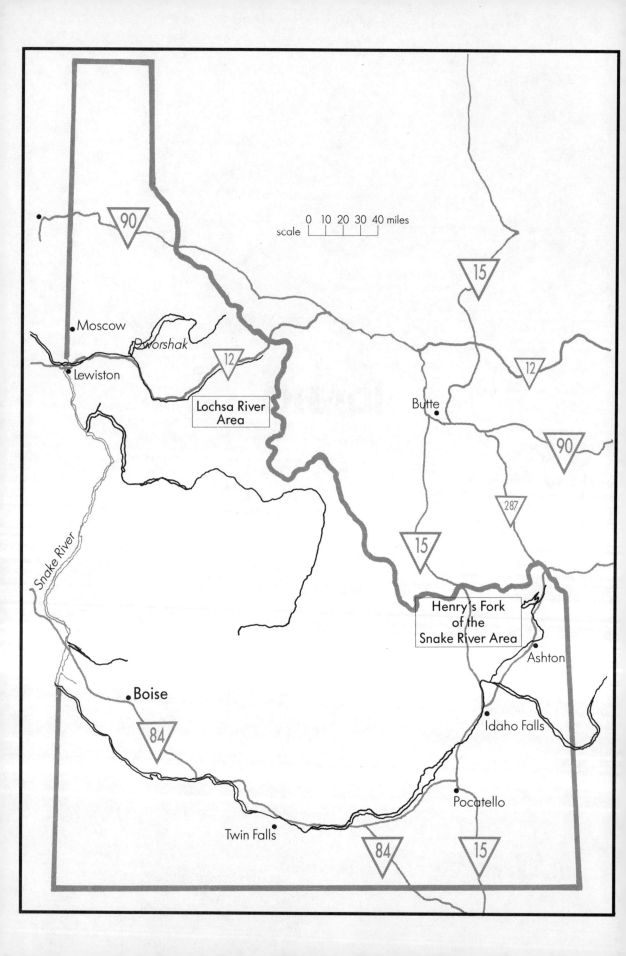

scale   0 10 20 30 40 miles

90

15

Moscow

Dworshak

12

Lewiston

Butte

12

Lochsa River
Area

90

287

15

Snake River

Henry's Fork
of the
Snake River Area

Ashton

Boise

84

Idaho Falls

Pocatello

Twin Falls

84

15

ASHTON

THREE RIVERS RANCH

Box 866, Warm River, Ashton, ID 83420. Phone: (208) 652-7819. Contact: Don and Julie Simmons, managers. Total capacity: 10. Open late May to mid-October. Peak season: August–September; best fishing in June and October. Reserve 9 months in advance; 3 months in June and October. Minimum age, 12 years. No pets.

Accommodations: Five remodeled log cabins sleep 2 each; electric heat, private shower, covered porch. Facilities available for seminars and groups of 12 in separate lodge; with private baths, common dining area.

Meals: Three family-style meals daily on American Plan; breakfast, streamside lunch, and full gourmet dinners, complimentary cocktails and hors d'oeuvres and barbecue served once a week. Alcohol available in nearby Ashton.

Rates: Expensive; weekly rates include lodging, meals, complimentary cocktails and wine, round-trip transportation to airport, daily transportation, and 5 days of guided fishing. Extra charges: Two-day campout on river, gratuities expected. Fifty percent deposit required. Cash or check.

How to Get There: Located midway between West Yellowstone, MT, and Idaho Falls, ID, both of which service regional airlines. From Idaho Falls, take Route 91 north to Ashton; turn east on Highway 47 to ranch. Rental car not needed as ranch supplies all transportation.

Three Rivers Ranch is nestled up in a small valley formed by the confluence of the Henry's Fork of the Snake and Warm rivers and Robinson Creek. This 800-acre ranch has operated as a guest facility for over sixty years, luring people back year after year to sample some of the finest hospitality and fishing found in the West. Numerous articles have been written about this classy operation, and the high marks it has received are well deserved.

The ranch caters to no more than ten guests at the main facility at any one time. A high staff-to-client ratio ensures that every guest enjoys a unique experience. The primary emphasis is on catch-and-release fly fishing, which places this small ranch in the class of a destination fishing resort. For ardent fly fishers looking for the opportunity to hook into some big trout, this ranch is the logical choice: everything about Three Rivers is top-notch, making it one of the premier fly-fishing resorts in the West.

The rustic exteriors of recently remodeled cabins tucked into the trees on the edge of Robinson Creek belie the creature comforts found within. Furnishings include antique dressers and chairs and homespun curtains; paneled walls and covered porches with chairs and racks for hanging rods and waders round out the comfortable effect. Constructed of rough-hewn logs, the main lodge has been remodeled into an intimate and rustically elegant building. Hardwood floors are covered with oriental rugs and the living room is replete with oversized couches, leather chairs, and antique chandeliers. The lounge area is equipped with a solid mahogany bar. The elegant touches continue in the small, cozy dining room with large picture windows overlooking the river, where dinners are served on fine bone china and tables are set with sterling silver and crystal glasses and wine goblets. Fishermen who wish to fish the during the evening hatches will have their cocktails, meals, and wine awaiting them when they return no matter how late the hour. As the manager states, "If anglers are out late, it's because the fishing is good. We worry when they come in two hours early."

Things to Do

A limited number of extracurricular activities are offered to nonfishing guests. The ranch, however, will arrange for a staff member to take guests on tours of Yellowstone Park or to nearby Harriman State Park, where horseback riding is available.

Fishing

In addition to having several miles of private fishing water on the Warm River and Robinson Creek, the ranch has access to the Teton, Falls, and Buffalo rivers — all tributaries of Henry's Fork of the Snake — and the South Fork of the Snake River. Three Rivers also has excellent access to the main Henry's Fork and fisheries in Yellowstone Park. Refer to Yellowstone Park Area Fisheries for a description of these drainages.

The Warm River and Robinson Creek are two beautiful freestone creeks averaging forty to one hundred feet in width. Both are wadeable and easily fished with little hindrance to backcasts. Both streams have sizable populations of brooks, cutthroats, rainbows, and browns. Whereas the average size of fish in the Warm River is somewhat smaller than in Robinson Creek (ten inches versus thirteen inches), catch rates of forty fish per day are not uncommon on either. Furthermore, Robinson Creek — reserved exclusively for ranch guests — can produce good-sized fish up to seventeen to eighteen inches.

The Falls, Teton, and South Fork of the Snake rivers are located to the south of the ranch, while the Buffalo River feeds into Henry's Fork about a half-hour's drive to the north. All are freestone mountain streams with consistently swift water flow and good populations of rainbows and cutthroats going to eighteen inches and up. The South Fork is a little larger than the rest of the tributaries; its tremendous salmon fly hatch occurs in early July. Like the Henry's Fork, all of these streams are primarily fished from McKenzie drift boats. Experienced guides put guests over plenty of big fish using these boats.

Every two guests are assigned a guide for the duration of their stay. Three Rivers' guides are among the most competent anglers found anywhere and they are extremely cognizant of the skills and tolerance levels of each fisherman. They gladly impart their knowledge of local waters to their clients and will not hesitate, if requested, to assist with any aspect of fly angling a guest might be having problems with. More important, guides emphasize quality fishing. As Don Simmons puts it, "Why should we take guests over to the Ranch [the famed Railroad Ranch on the Henry's Fork] during the green drake hatch and have them go clbow to elbow with other fishermen when we can put them on a half-dozen other spots where they can catch as many fish and maybe not see another fisherman all day?"

Typical western flies include royal wulffs, humpies, and adams (#10–20). Wets and streamers include woolly buggers, matukas (#6–8), and gold-ribbed hare's ears (#10–14). This list only scratches the surface of the prolific number of locally productive patterns. Three Rivers has a complete Orvis Shop on the premises that sells everything from licenses to rod-and-reel outfits. Both the shop and the guides carry a complete selection of flies tied specifically to match local hatches; guests wanting to tie their own are supplied with a complete list of hatches upon request.

Although many guests bring two or more rods to handle the various water and weather conditions, a stout 8½- to 9½-foot, 6–8 weight rod equipped with both a floating line and sink-tip line will suffice for this area. Guests who are new to fly fishing can rent a rod from the shop. Chest waders with traction devices such as stream cleats and a wading staff are recommended as many streams are swift and slick-bottomed.

SOUTHERN IDAHO PANHANDLE

LOCHSA LODGE

Powell Ranger Station, Lolo, MT 59847. Phone: (208) 942-3405. Contact: Gus and Gerry Denton, owners. Total capacity: 40. Open year round. Peak season: July and August. Reserve 2 weeks to 1 month in advance. No pets preferred.

Accommodations: Seven log cabins with electricity and wood-burning stove sleep 1–6; 6 units share central bathhouse. Five motel units sleep 4–6; private bath. Daily maid service.

Meals: Meals served a la carte from reasonably priced menu. Selection of beers, wines, and premixed cocktails available in tavern.

Rates: Inexpensive; daily rate. Extra charges: nominal fee for pick-up from Missoula airport. Cash, check, travelers checks, MasterCard, or VISA.

How to Get There: Located a few miles east of Powell Ranger Station on Highway 12. Lodge will meet guests at Missoula, MT airport 57 miles east. Rental cars available at airport.

The Lochsa Lodge is located deep in the heart of the Clearwater National Forest at the southeastern edge of the Idaho panhandle. This remote area receives relatively little tourist pressure yet is easily accessible by car from either Missoula, Montana, or Lewiston, Idaho. Anglers, families, and groups come here each year to enjoy the spectacular alpine scenery, fishing, and the rustic comfort of the lodge.

Lochsa Lodge, located at river's edge, has been run continuously as a guest operation since 1929 when the original resort was built. Since the Dentons purchased it in 1984, they have extensively remodeled the older structures and have added a few creature comforts. For people looking for an inexpensive hideaway with access to fabulous fishing, the Lochsa Lodge is a good place to start.

Cabins spaced throughout the towering pines that abound in the Lochsa valley are rustic, though very clean, and equipped with electricity and wood-burning stove (complimentary wood provided). The main lodge is a handsome log structure housing the dining room and tavern. The dining room has a large fireplace where a fire is lit every evening and on cold days. The adjacent tavern room has a pool table and is chock full of western memorabilia. Located nearby, a well-stocked country store sells everything from gasoline to fishing equipment to groceries.

Things to Do

Hiking in the adjacent forest is the principal activity for those who are not fishing or relaxing. Good trails lead out into the various tributary stream canyons just a short walk from the lodge. Abundant wildlife and magnificent scenery await those in good physical condition. If guests prefer horseback riding, the lodge can arrange for a local outfitter to take them out for the day.

The lodge has a nicely equipped playground, including swings, set up for children. Guests can play horseshoes or lounge on the lawn in front of the river. A barbecue pit is located at the river's edge for guests to use.

Fishing

The main stem of the Lochsa River forms about a quarter of a mile upstream from the cabins. Here the Crooked Fork of the Lochsa and White Sands and Squaw creeks join to form a fast-running, gin-clear mountain river. The main stem averages fifty to more than a hundred feet in width. Punctuated by huge boulders, riffles, and pocket water, the deceptively swift current makes chest waders with traction devices essential.

A large population of cutthroats, rainbows, and whitefish forms the principal fishery in the main stem as well as in the tributaries. After the river clears—usually around mid-June—continual hatches of insects such as early-season stoneflies,

mayflies, caddis, and late-summer grasshoppers keep these fish on the bite well into late September. A good angler can almost expect forty-plus days with fish averaging twelve to fourteen inches and plenty in the sixteen- to twenty-inch class. Steelhead and salmon also make their way up the river; however, the upper Lochsa is considered to be prime spawning habitat so fishing for these species is strictly prohibited.

The main stem is restricted to barbless hook, catch-and-release fishing only, whereas the tributaries have no restrictions other than a daily creel limit. Standard western patterns such as stoneflies (#8), elk hair caddis, adams, royal wulffs, and humpies (all in #12–16) will all take fish. In August, a good hopper pattern (#8–10) is very productive from midday through the afternoon. The lodge store sells licenses, flies, and leaders.

MONTANA

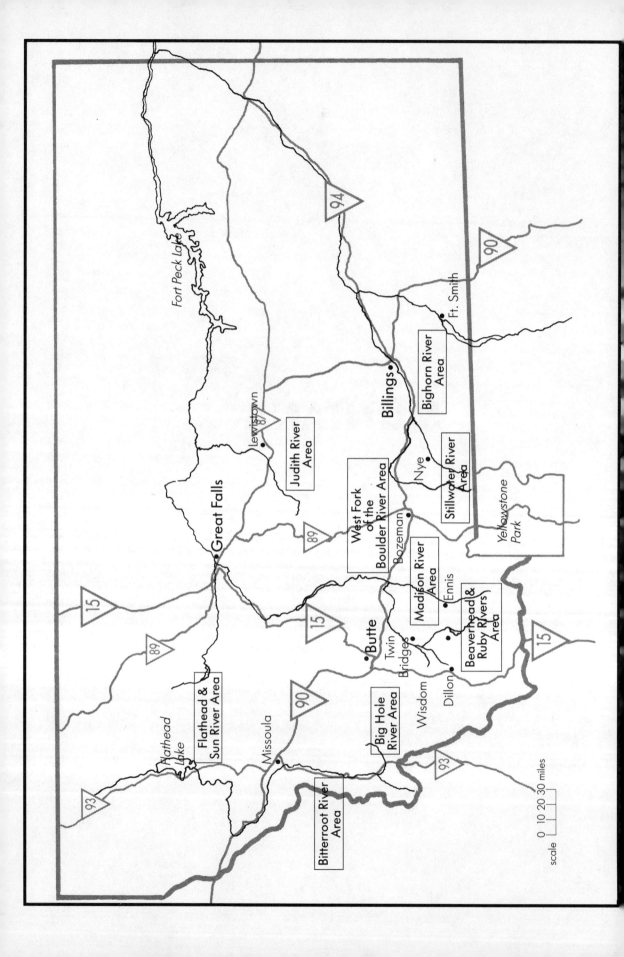

DILLON & TWIN BRIDGES

TOBACCO ROOT GUEST RANCH

374 Mill Creek Road, Sheridan, MT 59749. Phone: (406) 842-5655. Contact: John and Kristin Naisbitt. Total capacity: 24. Open year round. Peak season: July 1–September 15. Reserve 3 months in advance. No pets.

Accommodations: Six units housed in 3 duplex cabins; wood-burning stove, private bath, porch, electric heat. Daily maid service.

Meals: Three family-style meals daily on American Plan; breakfast in lodge, sack lunches, full country-style gourmet dinner. Beer and wine; all other alcohol is BYOB.

Rates: Moderate; weekly and daily rates include lodging, meals, horseback riding, ranch activities, and local tours. Reduced rates for children. Extra charges: guided float fishing trips, tours of Yellowstone Park. Cash or check.

How to Get There: Located east on Highway 287, 60 miles southeast of Butte. From Butte, take Highway 10 southeast; follow Highway 41 south to Twin Bridges; take Highway 287 southeast to Sheridan, where ranch is. Free pick-up and delivery from airport and train station in Butte or Bozeman. Rental car recommended for local travel.

The Tobacco Root Guest Ranch, nestled up in the Ruby River drainage about forty miles northeast of the town of Dillon, is a first-class resort. Open year around, Tobacco Root Guest Ranch offers the ideal spot for a family summer vacation as well as for the serious angler who wishes to fish a number of blue-ribbon fisheries, with the Big Hole, Madison, Beaverhead, Jefferson, and Ruby rivers all located within an hour's drive.

Duplex cabins are comfortably furnished and have wood-burning stoves. A small porch outside the entrance to each unit has stacked wood for the stove. The main lodge—a beautiful log building with high, vaulted ceilings—contains the main dining room warmed by a large stone fireplace, a cozy reading room with library, and a recreation room complete with Ping-Pong, pool tables, and a piano. Large windows impart a cheery, airy feeling and, though built approximately fifteen years ago, the lodge looks and feels like new. Dinner at the ranch is a country gourmet affair and locals, by advance reservation only, often join guests at suppertime.

Things to Do

In addition to the superb and varied fishing, Tobacco Root Ranch has a range of activities that appeals to the entire family. Daily guided horseback rides and tours to local points of interest are included in the ranch package. Riding and hiking trails with beautiful alpine vistas and pine forests that stretch forever lead up into the Tobacco Root Mountains above the ranch.

This region of Montana has a strong mining heritage, and abandoned mines and old boomtowns dot the landscape. Local folklore is steeped in stories of miners, panhandlers, and other colorful characters. The nearby settlements of Nevada City and Virginia City reconstruct what were once the two main Gold Rush towns in

Montana's mining heyday. Museums, old storefronts, and nightly performances of melodramas are included in tours provided by the ranch. Tours of Yellowstone Park can also be arranged.

Guests wanting to relax at the ranch can play pool or put together a game of volleyball, horseshoes, or Ping-Pong. Or they can just sit back with a good book on the porch or in the library. A hot tub relaxes saddle-sore muscles.

Fishing

Centrally located with excellent access to five main fisheries, the Ruby, Beaverhead, Jefferson, Madison, and Big Hole rivers, the ranch offers guided float trips in conjunction with a local fishing company, Four Rivers Fishing Company. Due to the number of streams the guides have to choose from, guests can almost always count on finding a hot spot with the kind of fishing that matches their skills.

Running through ranch property is a one-mile stretch of Mill Creek, a tributary of the Ruby River. Unlike the Ruby, Mill Creek is small and brushy with prime habitat for small rainbow and brook trout that average about twelve inches. The main Ruby River clears about mid-June and from then on it can be an excellent fishery for eight- to sixteen-inch brook and rainbow in the upper section and brown trout up to twenty inches or more in the lower river. The ranch has access to nearly two and a half miles of private fishing on the upper Ruby (a nominal fee is charged) where catch-and-release activity can be amazing. It's a good place for beginners as the casting is easy and the fish, though small, are abundant. Small elk hair caddis (#12–16) and streamers such as mickey finns (#8–12) will be all that's needed.

The Beaverhead has gained the reputation of being one of Montana's premier trophy trout streams. An abundance of insect life coupled with a relatively stable and cool stream flow account for the highest trout growth rate in the lower forty-eight. This is primarily a brown trout fishery with the average size fish exceeding seventeen inches and two pounds. Now and then an angler will hook into large rainbows that run up to five pounds. Any fisherman contemplating

a trip over to the Beaverhead should think twice, as these fish are not easily caught. Despite the good caddis and cranefly hatches, the preferred tackle consists of large (#2–6) weighted streamers including yuk bugs, girdle bugs, and bitch creeks. These big ungainly flies need to be slapped in right next to the bank underneath the willows that overhang long stretches of the river. This type of fishing can be very frustrating for anglers unaccustomed to pinpoint casting with heavily weighted flies. For the accomplished fisherman, however, the potential trophy of a lifetime awaits.

The Jefferson River is one of the most unpredictable trout fisheries in Montana. Water fluctuation and the return of cloudy irrigation water can cause this river to go off-color for weeks at a time. Clear water and a cloudy day, on the other hand, can produce a day of fishing never to be forgotten. Like the Beaverhead, the predominate species is the brown trout which can grow to a prodigious size of seven to nine pounds. Dry flies (#10–16) include royal wulffs, humpies, and elk hair caddis, and, during August, grasshoppers (#8–10). Favorite streamers and wets are girdle bugs, yuk bugs, and bitch creeks, along with muddlers (#4–8).

For further information on the Madison and Big Hole rivers, refer to the Yellowstone Park Area Fisheries section and Alta Ranch.

Licenses can be purchased in Sheridan or Twin Bridges; for a larger selection of tackle and gear, it's a good idea to stop at one of the numerous fly shops in Butte, Bozeman, or Dillon.

WISDOM

SUNDANCE LODGE

Wise River, MT 59762. Phone: (406) 689-3611. Contact: Lee and Jan Davis, owners. Total capacity: 20–40. Open year round. Peak season: mid-June–August. Reserve 1 month in advance. No pets.

Accommodations: Three cabins and 5 lodge rooms; one cabin has kitchen, all have bath. Daily maid service.

Meals: Meals available on European Plan.

Rates: Inexpensive; weekly and daily rates do not include meals. Extra charges: horseback riding, pack trips, llama trek, airport pick-up. Cash, check, travelers check, MasterCard, or VISA.

How to Get There: Located 55 miles from Butte, a 1-hour drive. From Butte, take I-90 west to I-15 south; go west on Highway 43 through Divide and Wise River; turn right on La Marche Creek Road and follow it to the ranch. Commercial airlines and buses service Butte; rental cars available at airport.

The Sundance Lodge is located in the northern end of the Big Hole Valley in southwestern Montana. Originally homesteaded around the turn of the century, this picturesque 260-acre ranch has been transformed over the years into a very comfortable retreat for families and groups of anglers.

Surrounded on the north and south by the Beaverhead National Forest, this part of Montana receives much milder summer weather than other parts of the state. As a result, the lower part of the valley is intensively farmed, creating a beautiful green patina contrasting with the rugged beauty of the nearby mountains. Nestled up against the forest, Sundance Lodge offers the best of both worlds: excellent access to the famed Big Hole River coupled with all the amenities nonfishing family members will be looking for.

The lodge's original homestead cabin is located near the entrance to the lodge. Although very rustic, this hand-hewn structure is as authentic as they come. Not surprisingly, it is in high demand by small, repeat groups and families. The lodge itself is a beautiful log structure that serves as the central spot for social gatherings. Downstairs, a spacious living and dining room has a large stone fireplace fronted by an immense couch. Spread around the perimeter, small four- and two-person dining tables allow guests to enjoy the crackling fire and camaraderie while they eat. Adjacent, a quaint, full-service bar accommodates guests relaxing with an evening cocktail. A large recreation room upstairs off the central hallway contains two pool tables, a Ping-Pong table, and shuffleboard.

Things to Do

Morning, afternoon, and all-day rides into the surrounding forest are the principal organized activity for those who aren't fishing. Within three miles of the lodge is the beautiful Anaconda Pintlar Wilderness which encompasses some spectacular though rugged terrain. In addition to day trips, Sundance can arrange for extended pack trips into the wilderness.

The lodge has large lawn areas where guests

can play a variety of outdoor games such as croquet, horseshoes, and badminton. Guests can also
soak away their tired muscles in a Jacuzzi housed
in one of the older homestead buildings. Children will enjoy the large herd of domesticated
llamas that the Davises raise for sale to backpacking outfitters. Sundance also keeps a sailing din-
ghy on a small pond near the main lodge and an
Avon raft for guests who want to take an unguided float on the Big Hole River.

Fishing

The Big Hole River is the main angling attraction
at Sundance. The ranch also has access to a number of fine, smaller fisheries. A little over one mile
of La Marche Creek, teeming with small eight-
to twelve-inch brook trout, runs through the
property. La Marche is fishable for over five miles
upstream; the higher up you go, the more native
cutthroats are encountered. Several alpine lakes
also offer good fishing; the best way to enjoy
them is by pack trip as the terrain is rugged and
the going slow. The lodge pond—full of brook
trout that have come in from La Marche Creek—
is a good spot to practice casting and is perfect
for teaching youngsters how to fish.

The nearby Big Hole River is a favorite among
Montana fly fishers. After spring runoff, the river
is mostly wadeable. Abundant riffle and pocket
water fosters good numbers of large rainbows in
the upper section and browns in the lower river,
principally from the town of Divide on downstream. The Big Hole is known as having perhaps the best salmon fly hatch found in the

United States. Anglers who don't enjoy crowds
should consider fishing another river during this
hatch, which lasts from around mid-June to early
July, as the river becomes very popular. This
hatch is also very weather sensitive. Catch rates
from July through October can be just as good
and anglers often find themselves in complete
solitude. An interesting feature of this river is
that, while fish average twelve to seventeen
inches, an impressive number of fish exceed five
pounds.

Les will gladly make the arrangements for
guests interested in contracting the services of a
number of reputable fishing guides in the area.
Anglers should bear in mind that guides book up
early for the salmon fly hatch. Fishing licenses
are sold in both Wise River and Wisdom in the
town saloons. Flies, tackle, and gear can be purchased in Butte, prior to arrival, or at Frank Stan-
chfield's Troutfitters, in Wise River.

FORT SMITH

BIGHORN ANGLER

Fort Smith, MT 59035. Phone: (406) 666-2233. Contact: Mike Craig and Holly Brooks, owners. Total capacity: 20-25. Open March-November. Peak season: July 10-September 15. Reserve 3 months in advance; 4-6 months for August. No pets.

Accommodations: Nine motel rooms with private bath; one cabin with bath, kitchen, and cable television reserved for groups of up to 5. Daily maid service for motel guests; laundry facility.

Meals: Kitchen available for food preparation. Polly's Cafe across street from motel serves 3 meals daily. All alcohol is BYOB.

Rates: Inexpensive; daily rates include lodging and use of kitchen facilities. Extra charges: guide service, boat rental, shuttle service. Cash, check, or travelers checks.

How to Get There: Located 90 miles southeast of Billings, MT. From Billings, follow U.S. 90 east to Hardin; take Route 313 south to Fort Smith where ranch is located. Commercial airlines service Billings airport; private planes can fly into strip at Fort Smith. Rental car recommended for local travel.

Located southeast of Billings, deep in the heart of the Crow Indian Reservation, is the Bighorn River. The twelve-mile stretch of water that originates at the spillway of the Yellowtail Dam is fast becoming known as *the* mecca for trophy brown trout fishing. There is perhaps no other river in the world that will consistently produce more large browns — eighteen-plus inches — per day than this outstanding fishery. This area will definitely appeal to diehard anglers who want some truly spectacular fishing.

The Bighorn Angler is the oldest and most reputable guide service, with comfortable lodging and a complete fly shop located minutes from the river. Co-owners Mike Craig and Holly Brooks moved to Fort Smith in 1982, shortly after the river was reopened by a U.S. Supreme Court ruling. They have teamed together to build a thriving outfitters and motel service to handle the many anglers descending on the Bighorn each year. Fly-fishing fanatics return annually to sample the warm hospitality and superior river knowledge that characterize the Bighorn Angler.

Bighorn Angler's motel complex houses guests in a wood-paneled building with nine modestly furnished bedrooms. There is also a separate facility for a small group or family. The Angler's motel complex offers a living room equipped with fireplace, cable television, a guest refrigerator, and comfortable easy chairs and sofas. Guests gather here each evening to share the day's fishing exploits, watch fishing tapes on the VCR, and get pumped up for another day on the glorious Bighorn. A pool table and fly-tying area are located in the communal kitchen behind the guest quarters. Guests are also sent to Polly's Cafe across the street for inexpensive to moderately priced fare.

Fishing

The notoriety the Bighorn River has gained since it re-opened in 1981 has not come about without problems. Fishing pressure has increased dramatically, and it is not uncommon to have as many as fifty boats per day working the twelve-mile

stretch below the dam during the peak months of May, August, and September. The river receives substantially less pressure, with as few as ten boats per day, at other times. This, coupled with the lack of trophy trout fishing restrictions, has led to a rapid decline in the rainbow population. Whereas in 1982 catch rates for large rainbows and browns were almost equal, nowadays the browns caught outnumber the rainbows by a nine-to-one margin. Additionally, it appears that the number of fish in the five-pounds-plus class is starting to wane.

In spite of these problems, this resilient fishery has not shown any material decline in either the number of fish per mile or average size of fifteen-plus inches. The reason for this is that, due to the river being a tailwater fishery, stream flow and water temperature remain fairly constant. According to Mike Craig, the Bighorn is in reality "a huge spring creek with great aquatic insect life and fantastic trout growth of five inches per year." A staggering statistic — compiled by electro-shocking the river — reveals that the Bighorn pos-

sibly has more fish larger than eighteen inches per mile than the Madison has *total* fish per mile.

The Bighorn, with an average stream flow of about 3,000 CFS, averages a little over 200 feet in width. Although the river is mostly wadeable, with the exception of deep runs and midstream glides, the preferred method of angling is by boat as more water can be covered. Fishing the entire twelve-mile stretch in a day will only allow an angler to sample some of the more productive runs, as this river is slower flowing than most Montana streams. Boats must keep on the move to complete the drift by nightfall.

While there can be excellent fishing almost year round, the insect activity peaks from late July through September. Profuse hatches of black caddis, blue-winged olives, and golden stoneflies accompany terrific midday hopper activity. As the shadows lengthen in late afternoon, the large fish abandon deep water and begin to forage along the shallow channels and moss-laden flats in search of food. Clouds of emerging and spent insects often blanket the water, driving the fish into spectacular feeding frenzies. Many anglers feel that there is no finer dry fly fishing found anywhere else than on a late summer's evening on the Bighorn.

All-around dry flies for summer hatches include adams, yellow humpies, and dark elk hair caddis (all #16), hoppers (#6), and royal wulffs (#12–14). Wets and nymphs such as shrimps (#10), pheasant tails (#16), and hare's ear and caddis emergers (both in #14) will take good fish when there is no surface feeding.

Standard equipment includes a 8- to 9-foot, 5–7 weight rod, single-action reel with a floating line, and at least 100 yards of backing. Chest waders with felt soles and thermal underwear worn underneath to prevent hypothermia are recommended.

The Bighorn Angler Fly Shop carries a wide variety of tackle and equipment while licenses and conservation stamps can be purchased at the Yellowtail Market across the street.

MISSOULA

ALTA RANCH

West Fork Stage, Darby, MT 59829. Phone: (406) 349-2363. Contact: Don and Mary Winters, managers. Total capacity: 12–20. Open June–October. Peak season: July and August. Reserve 2 months in advance. House-trained pets only.

Accommodations: Three rustic housekeeping cabins with private bath and kitchen; one has washer/dryer. Linen available; ranch staff will do laundry.

Meals: N/A; groceries available in Missoula and Hamilton. Special meals can be arranged with ranch staff well in advance.

Rates: Inexpensive; weekly rates. Extra charges: daily trail rides, float trips by angler Doug Swisher. Cash or check.

How to Get There: Take Highway 93 south from Missoula, MT, to 3 miles south of Darby; take Route 473 west; take left fork past Painted Rocks Lake to ranch. Rental car recommended for local travel; rentals available at Missoula airport.

The 120-acre Alta Ranch is located high in a pristine mountain valley through which flows one of the principal headwater streams of the Bitterroot, the West Fork. Nestled against the Continental Divide and adjoining the Selway-Bitterroot Wilderness, the region is among the most picturesque found in Montana, with pine-covered peaks and valleys dotted with streams and lakes.

Since Alta Ranch was purchased in the seventies by its present owner, Charles Rogler, three beautiful log cabins serving as guest quarters have been added. In addition to being far off the beaten track, the ranch is near a variety of blue-ribbon trout streams, making it a favorite of serious fly fishers, as well as of families who prefer a more self-reliant vacation in a secluded setting.

Rustic, hand-hewn log cabins are spread over a tree-covered slope overlooking a meadow and stream. Their rustic exteriors belie the creature comforts found within and a feeling of warmth and western luxury. Bedrooms are decorated with colorful throw rugs and homespun curtains while dining and living areas are furnished with large, family-style dining tables and comfortable lounge chairs and sofas in front of fireplaces. A series of framed paintings and lithographs adds a final touch of class to each cabin.

Things to Do

While most guests at Alta come for the good local fishing, there is also plenty of hiking to be done on miles of scenic trails throughout the Bitterroot National Forest. Reached either on foot or by horseback, alpine vistas and meadows covered with wildflowers await the adventuresome guest. Ranch owners also have arrangements with a neighboring ranch, operated by a licensed outfitter and guide, to provide trail rides.

For a more laid-back day of lounging, the ranch is a perfect spot to settle back with a good book. The ranch does not provide babysitting; families with infants or small children who require constant supervision should consider staying at one of the larger guest ranches offering "kiddie programs."

Fishing

A one-third mile stretch of the West Fork of the Bitterroot flows through the ranch. The West Fork—one of the better brook and cutthroat fisheries in the area—is a small alpine stream that usually clears up after the runoff in late June. Good hatches of insects from July through early September often accompany impressive catch (and release) rates for these beautiful fish averaging eight to thirteen inches. A few miles below the ranch at Painted Rocks Lake, the West Fork's pace picks up and the stream becomes populated primarily by cutthroat, rainbow, and an occasional brown trout. Sheer numbers decline somewhat on the lower river but the fish are larger, averaging eleven to sixteen inches.

The Bitterroot River joins the West Fork at the bottom of the canyon leading up to the ranch. From this point down to Hamilton, the Bitterroot is a slow flood-plain valley stream, especially during the peak irrigation months of July and August. In spite of the low flow and clear blue water, this section of the Bitterroot harbors enough riffle water, logjams, and tree-shaded undercut banks to protect an outstanding fishery. Large numbers of rainbow, cutthroats, and some browns inhabit this easily accessed stretch. Good early summer caddis and continual mayfly hatches provide abundant food for trout averaging twelve to sixteen inches, with good numbers of fish in the eighteen-plus inch class.

Two secondary fisheries located within an hour-and-a-half drive from the ranch are the Big Hole and Selway rivers. Big Hole is located to the east on the opposite side of the Continental Divide in a wide farming valley. (Refer to Sundance Lodge entry for a description of the Big Hole fishery.) Just across the border in Idaho, the Selway River starts high in the Selway-Bitterroot Wilderness west of the ranch. While very different, both rivers offer outstanding fishing.

The Selway River, reached by taking Route 473 over the Nez Percé Pass into Idaho, is one of the last remaining wilderness streams found in the lower forty-eight. With the exception of the upper stream access granted by Forest Service roads, this stream flows for miles with almost no human contact. Lightly fished, the Selway is fast gaining the reputation of being one of the very best catch-and-release cutthroat streams found anywhere. The Selway is characterized by rugged terrain, steep embankments and canyons, swift water, and difficult wading at times. Additionally, slower stretches are lined with grass- and reed-covered banks that offer just the right amount of shade that the many rattlesnakes found here enjoy. In spite of these problems, the Selway can yield fantastic catch rates—fifty-plus fish per day—to the good fly fisher. Yet it is quality, not quantity, that makes the Selway so outstanding: only a select group of anglers are in good enough shape to fish this beautiful stream where fish average ten to twelve inches and cutthroats in the fifteen- to seventeen-inch class are not uncommon.

Standard equipment for this area includes two rods. A light 7- to 7½-foot, 4–5 weight rod is best for working the small brushy creeks near the ranch, while 8½- to 9- foot, 6–7 weight rods will be needed for the larger rivers. Hip waders with felt soles and wading staffs are also recommended, especially on the Selway. Productive dry fly patterns (#10–14) include adams, royal wulffs, humpies, mosquitos, elk hair caddis, salmon flies (#4), and hoppers (#6–10). Nymphs and wets include hare's ears, pheasant tail (both in #10–12), muddler minnows, stoneflies, and bitch creeks (all in #4–8). Small stream and creek patterns include the dry flies already mentioned but in smaller sizes (#16–20). The ranch does not sell licenses so these must be purchased prior to arrival.

Float trips are guided by noted angler and author, Doug Swisher, who accepts catch-and-release parties only. Reservations should be made with him as soon as possible as he books up early. Call him direct at (406) 363-2878.

LIVINGSTON

BURNT LEATHER RANCH

McLeod, MT 59052. Phone: (406) 222-6785/ 932-6155. Contact: Chuck and Shell Reid. Total capacity: 6–8. Open mid-May–September. Peak season: mid-July–October. Reserve 4–6 months in advance. No pets.

Accommodations: Three rustic log cabins with wood-burning stove; 2 cabins share a bath, 1 has private bath. Daily maid service.

Meals: Three family-style meals daily on American Plan; breakfast, hot lunch, cocktail hour with hors d'oeuvres, full ranch dinner. All alcohol is BYOB.

Rates: Expensive; weekly rates include lodging, meals, ranch activities, pack trips, and free airport pick-up. Cash, check, or travelers checks.

How to Get There: Directions provided on booking.

The Burnt Leather Ranch is located at road's end, high in the West Boulder River Valley twenty-five miles southeast of Livingston, Montana. In spite of the area's proximity to some of Montana's larger cities, it receives relatively little tourist or angling pressure due to few public campgrounds or access points. With the Gallatin National Forest at the ranch's backdoor, Burnt Leather is an ideal spot for those looking for a quiet, undisturbed vacation.

One of the most unique features of the ranch is its size. Though there are accommodations for ten guests, the maximum group size totals only eight at any one time. Burnt Leather's "intimate size" coupled with a high staff-to-guest ratio, gives the ranch a feeling of western hospitality seldom found in a guest ranch setting. Small groups of friends and families can occupy the entire facility, enjoying the run of the place.

Rustic, turn-of-the-century log cabins are spread over a small, sloping meadow above the lodge. Each is comfortably furnished with country curtains and wood-burning stove. The cook shack housing the kitchen and a small dining room is located a short walk away from the cabins. The dining area is cheerfully decorated with trophy mounts and western memorabilia. One small guest table sits near a wood-burning stove that warms the entire room and enhances a feeling of camaraderie.

A lodge equipped with pool, Ping-Pong, and card tables sits uphill from the cook shack in a meadow. A bar, western library, stone fireplace, and comfortable lounge chairs and sofas make the lodge the primary place to gather in the evenings. Outside, a porch with a barbecue and additional chairs offers a haven to guests who want to sit back and take in the commanding view.

Things to Do

Activities are low-key at Burnt Leather. Recreation centers around horseback riding and hiking through the six main trails branching out into the Gallatin National Forest from the ranch. This section of the Rockies contains some spectacularly rugged terrain. Sheer mountain peaks and cirques tower above intermountain valleys laced with streams and sparkling lakes. Abundant wildlife provides back-country trekkers with numerous photographic opportunities. Saddle sores go along with the territory but the rewards are worth it.

Fishing

Nearly four miles of the West Fork of the Boulder River run through the ranch. The West Fork is a brushy, gin-clear mountain stream after the spring runoff. It harbors an abundant population of cutthroat and brown trout averaging twelve to fifteen inches, with some fish going over twenty-four inches in the stretch on ranch property. Farther upstream, where the ranch maintains a semi-permanent fishing camp, the river's principal inhabitant becomes the cutthroat. Although the size of fish diminishes, catch-and-release rates can be fabulous. Below the ranch, brown trout predominate with a few rainbows interspersed. The lower West Fork receives quite a few of the large spawners, up to three to four pounds, that come up out of the main Boulder River. The chance to catch a trophy trout awaits.

Literally hundreds of lakes and streams higher up in the West Fork drainage are teeming with rainbows, cutthroats, and brooks. Chuck knows of some lakes that produce fish averaging two to three pounds. Customized trips into more remote

areas of the Gallatin National Forest and Yellowstone Park are designed according to anglers' individual endurance levels and riding skills. The fishing in this upper plateau can be just about as good as any place shy of Alaska in terms of catch-and-release rates.

Hip waders will suffice in most of the streams in this region, with an 8-foot, 6 weight rod and dry line handling most situations on these smaller fisheries. Dry flies (#12–16) include humpies, irresistibles, adams, and elk hair caddis, with hopper imitations (#8–10) working best in August. Productive wets and streamers include small stoneflies, weighted muddlers (#6–10), and hare's ears (#12). Licenses, tackle, and equipment can be purchased at a number of stores in Livingston.

BOB MARSHALL WILDERNESS AREA

Bob Marshall Wilderness Area Fisheries

The Bob Marshall Wilderness area actually consists of three contiguous wildernesses: the Bob Marshall, Great Bear, and the Scapegoat. The Bob Marshall Wilderness was created and named for one of the true champions of the American wildlands shortly after his untimely death in the early forties. Since then, the Great Bear and Scapegoat parcels have been added to form a vast wilderness region comprised of over one million acres, known to locals simply as the Bob.

Encompassing some of the most rugged and imposing back country in the Rocky Mountain chain, the Bob contains numerous deep valleys dotted with alpine lakes and streams surrounded by massive upthrust mountain peaks. Each year the lucky few who pack into the Bob, either by foot or on horseback, gaze in awe at such wonders as the Chinese Wall, Prairie Reef, and Gateway Gorge. One of the last large wilderness areas, the Bob receives relatively little pressure when compared to its southern counterparts, the Wind River Range and the Thoroughfare region of Yellowstone Park.

There are three principal river drainages originating in the Bob: the Sun River to the east, the Middle Fork of the Flathead River to the north, and the South Fork of the Flathead to the southwest. All three of these river systems enjoy the reputation of being world-class fisheries. Countless feeder streams alive with native westslope cutthroat, rainbow, and brook trout also contribute to the angling appeal of these drainages. There are also several lakes that contain trophy trout in the two- to nine-pound range; outfitters are glad to share the names and whereabouts of these lakes, provided anglers respect an oath of secrecy.

Sun River Drainage

There is little evidence of a native fishery existing in the Sun River above man-made Gibson Lake. Numerous plantings of brook, cutthroat, and rainbows have taken hold, however, producing good to excellent fishing in the Sun's drainage. As befits their individual natures, cutthroats have established themselves in higher elevation fisheries while a large number of brooks inhabit quieter pastureland streams and ponds. Fish in smaller alpine streams and lakes, many of which seldom see any angling action at all, run between eight to fifteen inches. Larger rainbows averaging between fourteen to twenty-two inches predominate in the larger North and South Forks of the Sun, causing them to endure the greatest amount of fishing pressure.

Both the South and North Forks of the Sun River are similar to but smaller than the South Fork of the Flathead. The water generally clears up in mid-July and remains gin clear through September, when hunters start trekking into the Bob. Pebble-strewn bottoms interspersed with boulder riffles, pocket water, and logjams make for prime trout habitat. This is primarily mayfly and terrestrial water but for the most part fish are obligingly unselective. Small black gnat, mosquito, and ant or beetle patterns (#10–16) and the ubiquitous standard western patterns (#12–18) such as royal wulffs, pale morning duns, and adams will all take their share of fish. Nymphs (#12–16) such as muskrats, pheasant tail, and light-colored mayflies work well on more selective feeders.

Flathead River Drainage

Both the Middle and South Fork of the Flathead lie on the west side of the Divide—which receives considerably more rainfall than the eastern side. Forests are more densely populated with evergreen fir and spruce, and wildlife is more apparent; elk and deer are common, with occasional glimpses of mountain goats and golden eagles.

The star inhabitant of these rivers is the beautiful native west-slope cutthroat, sometimes referred to as the blue back or flat. These fish, with their distinctive red lower jaw slashes, share the river with smaller numbers of spawning bull trout weighing up to twenty pounds that make their way up the river from Hungry Horse Reservoir (in the case of the South Fork) or from Flathead Lake (in the case of the Middle Fork). A few rainbows and brookies are also found throughout both drainages though not in the quantities found east of the Divide.

Both forks of the Flathead offer some of the finest wilderness cutthroat fishing found in the country. The good fly fisher can expect thirty-fish days once the water clears in July and on into fall. Trout average fourteen inches with larger cutthroats up to twenty inches not uncommon. Local Fish and Game personnel theorize that vast numbers of "eighteen-plus" cutthroats migrate upriver to spawn, then mingle with the smaller resident population for the summer.

Excellent hatches of mayflies and mosquitos and small hatches of caddis provide an abundant food source. West-slope trout, like their east-of-the-Divide counterparts, also tend to be relatively unselective of pattern and color. They do seem to show a preference for size, however, and any attempt to match that of the natural hatches will invariably bring better results. Standard western patterns such as wulffs, house and lots, humpies, and renegades work well most of the

time. It's also wise to take along a good selection of (#12–18) mosquitos, pale morning duns, comparduns, and elk hair caddis. When nothing else is working, various terrestrials (#10–14) such as black ants and small cricket and beetle patterns can bring up a monster.

The choice of gear for the Bob presents an interesting problem. For those traveling by foot, weight and bulk are obvious factors to consider. In this instance, a multiple section 8-foot, 5–6 weight rod and reel combination (such as Cortland makes) would be the logical way to go. Anglers being packed in by an outfitter should, by all means, bring a good 8- to 9-foot, 6 weight rod and reel with at least seventy-five yards of backing. A medium-stiff two-section rod offers far greater control and feel (especially in the wind) than a multiple-section backpacking rod. Sink tip lines and some gaudy, brightly colored flies (#4–6) such as the purple peril or mack's canyon steelhead patterns will come in handy for anglers after big bull trout. These big flies will bring the most rewards if fished on a dead drift to get the fly on the bottom, then allowed to swing slowly in front of a watchful bull trout's holding position.

AVERILL'S FLATHEAD LAKE LODGE

Box 248, Bigfork, MT 59911. Phone (406) 837-4391. Contact: Doug Averill, manager. Total capacity: 100. Open mid-May–September 30. Peak season: July and August. Book 6 months to 1 year in advance.

Accommodations: Bedrooms with adjoining living rooms in two lodges; 2- and 3-bedroom cottages for larger groups. South Lodge available for large groups. Front decks offer view of Flathead Lake. Daily maid service; laundry facility.

Meals: Three meals served daily on American Plan; breakfast cooked to order, breakfast trail rides, sack lunch or informal picnic lunch, full dinner, separate seatings for children at dinner; once a week dinner trail ride.

Rates: Moderate; weekly rates include lodging, meals, horseback riding, ranch activities, special children's programs, and use of all facilities. Pack trips and fly-in fishing trips extra, depending on size of party. Cash, check, or travelers checks.

How to Get There: Route 93 south from Kalispell to Somers; east on Route 82; south on Route 35 past Bigfork, MT; turn right a few miles south of Bigfork at ranch sign. Airline service daily into Kalispell; AmTrak services Whitefish. Free pick-up from airport and train station.

Averill's Flathead Lake Lodge is nestled on 2,000 timber-covered acres on the northeastern shore of one of the most scenic large lakes in the West, Flathead Lake. This resort, which has one of the most comprehensive activity schedules of *any*, is an authentic guest ranch that has been in the Averill family since 1945. Quite simply, the Averills have created one of the finest privately owned family vacation resorts in the United States.

All lodgings are comfortably furnished with wooden furniture, reading lamps, and woven area rugs. Bedrooms adjoin a living room with sofas and cozy lounge chairs, and roomy front decks await guests who just want to relax and enjoy the spectacular view of Flathead Lake visible from most of the cabins.

The main lodge and the smaller South Lodge were built in the early thirties. The main lodge, a massive building, serves as dining room and gathering place. An immense stone fireplace with lounging area imparts a cheery, casual atmosphere to the spacious room. Large picture windows on either side of the fireplace overlook the front porch and the lake beyond. The two-story South Lodge has a lovely stone fireplace fronted by inviting sofas and huge coffee tables.

Tennis courts, a swimming pool, corral, and riding arena are just a few minutes' walk from the cabins. Across a wide expanse of tree-shaded lawn, in front of the lodge, is a beach and marina where canoes, fishing, sailboats, and waterskiing await.

Things to Do

So many activities are scheduled at Averill's that guests easily forget that vacations are often the best time to relax and do nothing at all. Daily trail rides, whitewater raft trips, and excursions to nearby attractions and fishing spots are all included in the package plan. Children are so exhausted after a busy day that they won't even notice the absence of televisions. In spite of the variety of activities offered, those seeking solitude will find plenty of quiet nooks to prop their feet up and read or snooze.

A full-time recreational director is in charge of a highly structured and diversified program for children that includes arts and crafts, horseback riding and instruction, overnight campouts, evening bonfires on the beach, and hiking. Babysitters are available for youngsters too young (under six years) to ride. Adult guests sign up after dinner for the following day's activities that require special transportation or food preparation, such as all-day float/fishing trips and excursions to Glacier National Park.

Horseback riding is the principal activity at Averill's. Trail rides through the surrounding mountains depart every morning and afternoon. Breakfast, dinner, and evening rides and all-day rides with chuckwagon lunch are also options. Riding instruction is available for all guests over six years of age. Wranglers are also old hands at teaching dudes the ways of calf roping and ranch chores. A weekly gymkhana is the climax of a fun week of horsemanship.

The nearby town of Bigfork is a quaint town with unique gift shops, cafes, and galleries representing the work of locals and nationally recognized artists and craftspeople. It also has a very good summer playhouse. Adults can spend the evening dancing in one of the local saloons in Bigfork. Spectacular Glacier National Park and a number of good golf courses are also within an hour's drive from the ranch. Every bit as awesome as Yellowstone Park, Glacier National Park has the advantage of being far less crowded. A day's drive along the park's east-west highway, the "Going to the Sun Road," is a must-see.

Fishing

Averill's guided excursions leave the ranch daily for a variety of streams, rivers, and lakes. Competent staff guides will also custom-design trips for anglers looking for more remote fishing in wilderness regions.

Flathead Lake is a logical choice for anglers who like to troll for large bull trout, a land-locked species of dolly vardin, or mackinaw that occasionally reach monstrous proportions. While there are some rainbow and cutthroat in the lake, the chance of hooking a trophy mackinaw or bull trout lures most anglers to Flathead Lake. Other lakes easily reached by road include Swan Lake, Lake Mary Ronan, and Lake Koocanusa, which abounds with kokanee, a land-locked species of silver salmon. Large northern pike are also found

in a number of lakes, most notably Echo Lake, close to the ranch.

Hundreds of small feeder streams flow into the three main forks of the Flathead and the Swan rivers, the two primary river fisheries in the vicinity of the lodge. The ranch offers daily raft trips down the Swan in large twelve-man rafts. These trips are limited to four anglers to ensure that everyone has plenty of casting room. The Swan is one of the most picturesque rivers in the Flathead Valley and the fishing can be spectacular. Brookies and cutthroats in the eight- to fourteen-inch range predominate. The preferred standard western attractor patterns (#12–16) include royal wulffs, adams, and humpies.

For anglers who want something a bit more exotic, the ranch has a number of trips available for an additional charge. The South Fork of the Flathead River offers superb fishing as it winds its way out of the Bob Marshall Wilderness; Averill's can arrange a plane to take up to three anglers into the back country to fish it. The plane drops people off at Meadow Creek, where a raft awaits for a twenty-mile drift down to Spotted Bear Creek. Rainbows, native cutthroats, and occasional bull trout inhabiting this pristine stretch of water go after (#14–18) royal wulffs, adams, and humpies. Anglers intent on catching a few of the bigger bull trout on their spawning runs up river will find it useful to pack a spinning outfit along with some brightly colored spoons as these fish (like kokanee) can be extremely difficult to catch on flies.

Averill's ranch also keeps a canoe on Saint Mary's Lake in Glacier National Park. An early departure gets anglers there in time to paddle across the lake and hike into a smaller lake filled with two- to five-pound rainbows. Tackle boxes should include a wide assortment of streamers and wet flies (#6–12), such as spruce flies, marabou streamers, and carey specials.

Finally, should guests tire of local fisheries, the ranch can arrange for a plane to fly guests south to Ennis where they can spend a half-day floating the famed Madison River. The plane leaves from Bigfork right after breakfast and returns shortly before the cocktail hour.

Fishing licenses, tackle, and gear are not sold on the ranch but are readily available from a number of sporting goods stores in Kalispell.

BEAR CREEK GUEST RANCH

P.O. Box 151, East Glacier Park, MT 59434. Phone: (406) 226-4489 (Bear Creek #1). Contact: Bill Beck. Total capacity: 16. Open June 1–September 10. Peak season: mid-June–mid-August. Reserve 2–4 months in advance. Pets allowed.

Accommodations: Four log cabins sleep 4–6; private bath, electric heating. Daily maid service; fresh linens supplied on request.

Meals: Three family-style meals daily on American Plan; breakfast, light lunch and sack lunch, full dinner. Chef will prepare fresh-caught fish to order. Mealtimes are flexible.

Rates: Expensive; weekly rates include lodging, meals, and horseback riding. Reduced rates for children under 10; discounts for each additional child. Cash, checks, or travelers checks.

How to Get There: Located just off Highway 2; 17 miles west of East Glacier Park and 70 miles east of Glacier International Airport in Kalispell. Free pick-up from Kalispell airport. Rental car recommended for local travel.

Bear Creek Guest Ranch abuts the southern edge of Glacier National Park about midway between the towns of West Glacier and East Glacier Park. The ranch lies just off the highway, tucked into the Lewis and Clark National Forest. While the ranch serves as a family resort during the summer months, the primary emphasis is on day horseback trips into the surrounding wilderness. Because of owner Bill Beck's guiding and fishing expertise, this ranch will definitely appeal to the aggressive outdoorsman who would gladly trade saddle sores for the opportunity to get in some fabulous alpine fishing.

Comfortably furnished log cabins are wood-paneled. The main lodge, located at the entrance to the ranch, is a two-story log structure with an additional four bedrooms, and a dining room, living room, and small game room. The living room serves as a gathering spot after dinner as it is chock full of large chairs and sofas fronting a stone fireplace.

Things to Do

Daily horseback rides are tailored to guests' riding ability and endurance. Hundreds of miles of riding and hiking trails branch out from the ranch, so everyone from the tenderfoot to the aggressive outdoorsman will find something to their liking.

For guests who want to take a break from the saddle, the ranch provides float trips down the Middle Fork of the Flathead, tours through Glacier National Park, trips to local museums, and guided nature and wildlife walks. Those who simply want to relax at the ranch have use of a library, pool and Ping-Pong tables, swimming hole, and fish pond. Babysitting is available with advance notice.

Fishing

The Middle Fork of the Flathead, which originates in the Great Bear Wilderness to the south of the ranch, is the principal river fishery. With a one- to three-hour ride, guests are deep in the wilderness where twelve- to sixteen-inch cutthroats abound. This river, like the South Fork, is home to the native west-slope cutthroat and the spawning bull trout.

Bill, however, does not emphasize the angling on the Middle Fork as it's his experience that better fishing is regularly found in nearby lakes. Ole Lake, a two-and-a-half-hour ride into the park, offers "unbelievable" fishing for eight- to fourteen-inch cutthroats along with excellent opportunities to view wildlife. West of the ranch, in the Great Bear Wilderness, Almeda Lake is literally teeming with small cutthroat. South in the Great Bear, five-pound cutthroats cruise through the clear waters of Tranquil Lake. In addition to these larger lakes, there are dozens of hidden gems that Bill introduces guests to. He knows the area well and is an accomplished fly fisherman who loves to teach people the sport. Productive western flies (#10–16) to use include humpies, adams, irresistibles, royal wulffs, and gold-ribbed hare's ear nymphs.

Having long, light leaders—no more than two-pound test—is perhaps the biggest key to catching fish in this region. Anglers can purchase licenses, tackle, and gear in a number of fly shops and sporting goods stores in Kalispell. The nearest location to purchase licenses is at the general store in East Glacier Park. The ranch carries a good supply of terminal tackle including flies and can equip anglers with rental rods and reels.

CIRCLE 8 RANCH

Box 729, Choteau, MT 59422. Phone: (406) 466-5564. Contact: Al and Sally Haas. Total capacity: 20. Open June 1–September 15. Peak season: August. Reserve 2 months in advance. No pets.

Accommodations: Seven 1- and 2-bedroom cabins with private bath, fireplace, and free supply of firewood restocked daily.

Meals: Three family-style meals daily on American Plan; breakfast cooked to order, buffet style sandwich lunch with sack lunch once a week on all-day ride, full dinners. All alcohol is BYOB.

Rates: Moderate; weekly rates include lodging, meals, horseback riding, and all ranch activities. One-week minimum. Special rates for children under 12. Extra charges: pack trips, airport pick-up. Cash, check, or travelers checks.

How to Get There: Take Highway 89 from Great Falls 45 miles northwest to Choteau; continue west towards Teton Pass ski area and look for ranch sign. Regional airlines service Great Falls; a small plane strip is located in Choteau.

The Circle 8 Ranch is one of the oldest guest ranches in the Bob Marshall Wilderness region, having been in continuous operation since 1930. The original owners, Ken and Alice Gleason, sold the ranch to the Nature Conservancy in 1979, thus ensuring that this beautiful 3,000-acre ranch nestled in the forest at the foot of the Bob will remain as is forever.

The current operators, Al and Sally Haas, worked for the Gleasons for ten years prior to the ranch's sale and have continued on to manage it for the Conservancy. They maintain the fine western tradition of offering genuine hospitality in a guest ranch setting. In addition, Al and his wranglers customize pack trips into the Bob for ardent fishermen who return year after year for the fabulous wilderness fishing.

Guest cabins are widely spread over a tree-shaded meadow; bedrooms are decorated with throw rugs, chairs, a sofa, and a stone fireplace.

Things to Do

Activities on the ranch center around horseback riding. All guests are assigned a horse from a string of beautiful quarter, Morgan, and Tennessee walking horses. Rides leave the ranch every morning and afternoon; the variety of trails is such that everyone from the novice to expert horseman will enjoy themselves. With the ranch being located so close to the Bob Marshall Wilderness, three- to five-hour rides can put guests into parts of the wilderness where others seldom venture.

On-ranch activities include swimming and sunbathing by a large, heated pool a short walk away from the lodge. A cozy rec room has Ping-Pong and pool tables and is also a relaxing place to gather for a card game. Popular late-afternoon and evening pastimes are horseshoe pitching, volleyball, and badminton. Guests also find the main lodge to be a wonderful place to curl up with a good book in front of a roaring fire.

As noted earlier, Al Haas is an experienced packer who specializes in taking guests into the back country. He prefers to travel through the northeast quadrant of the wilderness as it receives perhaps the least pressure.

Fishing

Two small streams, the North and South forks of the Teton River, border the ranch property. These streams, like the beaver ponds located a short horseback ride away, contain brookies and cut-throats averaging ten to eleven inches with an occasional lunker up to eighteen inches. Like the rivers in the Bob Marshall Wilderness, these streams are receptive to standard western patterns (#10–16) such as royal wulffs, grasshoppers, and the ubiquitous elk hair caddis.

Refer to Bob Marshall Wilderness Area Fisheries for more fishing information.

JJJ WILDERNESS RANCH

P.O. Box 310, Augusta, MT 59410. Phone: (406) 562-3653. Contact: Max, Ann, and Ernie Barker, owners. Total capacity: 20; pack trips limited to 6–10 people. Open early July through August. Peak season: August. Reserve 3–6 months in advance for ranch; 6 months–1 year for pack trips.

Accommodations: Five cabins sleep up to 6; electricity, wood or gas stove for heat. Three cabins have private bath; 2 share bathhouse.

Meals: Three family-style meals daily on American Plan; hot breakfast, light lunch, full dinner, cookout and barbecues planned regularly. Pack trips provide same fresh fare as lodge.

Rates: Moderate for ranch stay (weekly rates include lodging, meals, horseback riding, and fishing in ranch pond) and pack trip (rates include horses, guides, pack animals, and all meals). Cash, check, or money order.

How to Get There: Located 80 miles west of Great Falls and 25 miles west of Augusta. From Augusta, go west past Forest Service Information Station; road turns to gravel; continue on 3 miles to a fork; bear right and continue 17 miles through Sun River Canyon; cross concrete bridge (ignore steel bridge) and climb switchback to top; ranch driveway is marked on right-hand side.

The JJJ Wilderness Ranch has been operated as a rustic guest ranch and departure point for pack trips into the Bob Marshall Wilderness since the Barker family purchased it in 1976. A good deal of their time has been spent refurbishing some of the older log structures. About 50 percent of their clientele use the ranch as a guest facility, branching out to sightsee, hike, fish, or horseback ride in the Bob Marshall Wilderness of the Lewis and Clark National Forest which surrounds the ranch. The remainder of the clientele consists of back-country trekkers who use JJJ's outfitting services to portage them and their gear on customized, extended trips into the wilderness.

Guest cabins are comfortable, though rustic. A small centrally located lodge houses a cozy dining room and informal living room furnished with comfortable lounge chairs and a small western library.

Things to Do

Ranch guests will enjoy a very informal schedule that includes relaxing outdoor recreation, primarily on the trail. The Barkers are available for guided horseback rides into the Lewis and Clark National Forest. They share their knowledge of the indigenous plants and wildlife with riders and with those who prefer to admire the scenery at a more leisurely hiking pace. Customized pack trips into the Bob meet the specific needs of individual parties.

Fishing

The nearby lower Sun River offers good fishing for rainbow and brown trout and is easily reached by car. Because its easy access attracts a lot of locals, the Barkers prefer to take guests up to the North Fork of the Sun River, reached only by boat or on horseback.

Refer to Bob Marshall Wilderness Area Fisheries for more fishing information.

All equipment and licenses must be purchased prior to arrival either locally in Augusta or, preferably, in Great Falls or Helena where there's a greater selection of tackle.

7 LAZY P GUEST RANCH

P.O. Box 178, Choteau, MT 59422. Phone: (406) 466-2044. Contact: Chuck and Sharon Blixrud, owners. Total capacity: ranch, 25–30; pack trips, 6–10. Open July–mid-September. Peak season: August. Reserve 4–6 months in advance.

Accommodations: Six cabins sleep 4–6; 5 with private bath, 2 with fireplace. Daily maid service; laundry facility.

Meals: Three family-style meals daily on American Plan; hot breakfast, hot lunch or sack lunch available, full dinner. Pack trip meals offer simpler fare than meals at lodge.

Rates: Moderate for ranch stay (daily rates include lodging, meals, horseback riding, and ranch activities) and pack trip (rates include tents, horses, guides, pack animals, and meals). Extra charges: round-trip pick-up to Great Falls. Cash, check, or travelers check.

How to Get There: Located outside Choteau on road leading to Teton Pass ski area. Directions will be given on making reservations.

The 7 Lazy P Guest Ranch is a family-run guest ranch and outfitter located on the valley floor of the North Fork of the Teton River, twenty-eight miles northwest of Choteau, Montana. The nearby Bob Marshall Wilderness is a major attraction, evidenced by the fact that 50 percent of 7 Lazy P's clientele opt for back-country pack trips.

The Blixruds have operated the ranch for over twenty-five years and Chuck is one of the better-known local wilderness guides. In recent years, the ranch has gained a reputation as a small guest resort and for being a perfect retreat for small seminars. Even so, Chuck and Sharon love sharing the back country so much they tend to emphasize family pack trips.

Guest cabins are comfortably furnished. The main lodge, a combination log and flatboard structure with picture windows overlooking the ranch, houses the main dining room, a lounge area with a large stone fireplace, and, in a separate wing, a lovely solarium with Jacuzzi.

Things to Do

The Blixruds design custom trips to meet the preferences of individual parties. They love to explore the wilderness as much as anyone and there is always new country to see. Several package trips for people interested in discovering the Bob include the Chinese Wall Trip (ten to twelve days) which offers a combination of fishing, sightseeing, and photography on several river systems and in numerous alpine lakes within the rugged Bob Marshall Wilderness; the Sun River Trip, designed primarily for fishermen who have five to six days to spend in the wilderness; the South Chinese Wall Trip, an extension of the Sun River trip designed for those who have five to six more days to spend; and the Middle Fork of the Flathead Trip, a ten- to twelve-day trip that starts at Schafer Ranger station on the Middle Fork of the Flathead and includes some of the most expansive vistas found in the Bob.

The ranch will send a complete list of necessary equipment for pack trips when reservations are confirmed. Fishing licenses, tackle, and gear must be purchased in either Great Falls or Helena prior to arrival at the ranch.

LEWISTOWN

SOUTH FORK LODGE

Utica, MT 59452. Phone: (406) 374-2356. Radio phone: (406) 423-5451. Contact: Ben Steel, owner. Total capacity: 10. Open year round. Peak season: July and August. Reserve 4 months in advance. No pets.

Accommodations: Four guest rooms in lodge share 2 baths.

Meals: Three family-style meals daily on American Plan; hot breakfast, hot lunch or sack lunch, traditional western dinner. Dinner ride with steak and fish fry twice a week. All alcohol is BYOB.

Rates: Moderate; weekly rates include lodging, meals, horseback riding, jeep trips, and excursion. Special rates for children. Extra charges: trout fishing trips, airport pick-up in Great Falls or Lewistown. Cash, check, or travelers checks.

How to Get There: Take Highway 87 from Great Falls southeast past Windham; follow Highway 289 south to Utica; road goes about 23 miles before signs for lodge are posted. From Lewistown, take Highway 87 west to Hobson; then highway 239 to Utica; follow directions above to get to lodge. Regional airlines service Great Falls and Lewistown. Rental car recommended for local travel.

The South Fork Lodge, located in the Little Belt mountains of west-central Montana, is an ideal spot for those looking to explore a little-known area of the state. Charlie Russell first settled here upon coming out West; many of his paintings memorialize this part of Montana. With the closest small city of Lewistown being over sixty miles away, the lodge is remote and secluded and offers good car access to a number of underrated and underutilized fisheries.

The majority of guests are repeat clientele who enjoy both the camaraderie of a small ranch and the fact that the lodge lies far off the beaten path. In addition to providing week-long family vacation and fishing packages, the lodge also offers pack trips into the surrounding Lewis and Clark National Forest. This flexibility, combined with the owner's knowledge of the surrounding area—Ben was born and raised just south of Utica—makes the South Fork Lodge an appealing alternative to the hoopla of Montana's more tourist-oriented locations.

The main lodge, constructed of logs in 1977, serves as headquarters for the 300-acre ranch and houses guest rooms and a combination dining and recreation room. The dining area is partially separated from the rec room by a large double-sided stone fireplace so that guests can enjoy a crackling fire both while they are eating and afterward. Western art, wagon-wheel chandeliers, attractive throw rugs, and trophy mounts combine to enhance the casual ambience of the lodge. Outside the rec room, a large deck with lounge chairs overlooks a meadow dotted with beaver ponds.

Things to Do

As with most western guest ranches, the principal activity is horseback riding. South Fork maintains a string of gentle trail horses; scenic rides into the surrounding forest can be arranged depending on individual desires and abilities. The lodge can also arrange for pack trips into remote areas of the Little Belt mountains where both scenery and fishing are spectacular.

Jeep rides through the Little Belt region offer a change of pace for those tired of fishing or trail riding. Abandoned homesteads, ranches, and mining sites dot the area, providing good photographic opportunities as well as the chance to find memorabilia from Montana's frontier past. On hot days, guests are packed off to Martinsdale Reservoir by way of ranch vehicle for an afternoon of boating, swimming, and water skiing.

Fishing

Within a little over an hour's drive, the lodge has access to three principal river drainages: the Judith, Smith, and Musselshell, and two lakes: Sutherlin and Martinsdale Reservoir. The three river fisheries flow, for the most part, through private property and are limited access for most anglers. Ben knows many of the ranchers personally, so he can take guests into stretches of these rivers that seldom see any hooks.

The closest river to the lodge is the Judith, with its south fork running just below lodge headquarters. Although not recognized as a blue-ribbon trout stream, the upper reaches of the various forks of the Judith are a fair to good fishery for small eight- to thirteen-inch cutthroat and rainbow. The main fork has some larger fish and is predominately a rainbow brook and brown trout fishery. Angling on these small streams can be frustrating as they are quite brushy and the water is clear enough that the fish are easily spooked. Careful stalking and wading techniques coupled with a fair amount of patience will yield good results.

The Smith River, located west of the lodge, is a world-class trout fishery and, in its lower section, one of the most popular floating rivers in the state. Lodge guides tend to focus on the upper section along with the two forks of the Smith that join near the town of White Sulphur Springs. The forks have incredible quantities of pan-sized rainbow and brooks and are easily fished—a good combination for the novice fisherman. The main stem of the upper Smith has very good fishing, without a lot of angling pressure, for larger ten- to twenty-inch rainbows and brooks.

The Musselshell River offers good fishing for rainbow, brook, and brown trout, especially in the section above the town of Twodot. Farther upstream, near the town of Martinsdale, the two forks of the Musselshell join to form the main river. It is to these two forks that Ben likes to go, as they receive little fishing pressure. Average fish in this drainage run from twelve to sixteen inches and there is always the opportunity to hook fish eighteen inches and over. The upper Musselshell is probably one of the more underrated fisheries in the state.

Both Martinsdale Reservoir and Lake Sutherlin have good fishing for large rainbow, brook, and brown trout averaging one and a half to two pounds. Lunkers up to eleven pounds are hooked occasionally. The lodge has boats on both lakes and will gladly shuttle guests there on request.

Guests planning on a "strictly fishing" vacation should consider signing up for South Fork's trout fishing trips. For a nominal extra fee, guests are teamed up with local guides who will put them onto the best water each day. Equipment to bring includes two rods: an 8- to 8½-foot, 6–7 weight rod for the larger rivers and a 7- to 7½-foot, 4–5 weight rod for the small, brushy streams. Hip waders will suffice as most of the rivers and streams are quite shallow. Standard western fly patterns (#10–18) such as royal wulffs, adams, irresistibles, ginger quills, and elk hair caddis will all take fish. August sees some great hopper action (#6–12). Licenses and equipment can be purchased in either Lewistown or Great Falls prior to arrival.

ENNIS

C-B RANCH

Box 604, Cameron, MT 59720. Phone: (406) 682-4954. Contact: Cynthia Boomhower, owner. Total capacity: 18. Open June 23–September 15. Peak season: July 15–September 1. Reserve 9 months in advance. No pets.

Accommodations: Three duplex log cabins with private entrance, private bath, fireplace or wood-burning stove, electric heat. Daily maid service.

Meals: Three family-style meals daily on American Plan; breakfast cooked to order, hot lunch or trail lunches, full western dinners. All alcohol is BYOB.

Rates: Moderate; weekly rates include lodging, meals, horse, guided rides, and use of ranch facilities. Daily rates also available. Extra charges: pickup at airport or train station. Cash, check, or travelers checks.

How to Get There: Take Highway 84 west from Bozeman to Norris; turn south on Highway 287 through Cameron; watch for ranch sign on left. Rental car recommended for local travel.

The C-B Ranch is a 6,000-acre ranch headquartered in a beautiful mountain valley on the west side of the Madison Range. The ranch was a working cattle ranch until 1971, when a guest operation began. Today the ranch still maintains ties to its ranching past with the breeding of a small herd of Charlais cattle.

The current owner, Mrs. Boomhower, has built all of the current guest facilities. Her love for the West is evident throughout the ranch buildings in her special attention to quality and detail. Fishermen, couples, and families with grown children will all enjoy the intimate feeling of the C-B Ranch.

Throw rugs and western paintings lend a casual elegance to the guest cabin interiors. A beautifully constructed log main lodge lies just downslope from the guest cabins and houses the dining room, living room, and recreation hall. A bright, cheery dining room has one long table where guests sit down to family-style meals. A stone fireplace in the living room is surrounded by oversize chairs and a sofa. The recreation room has a wet bar and pool table.

Things to Do

Guests are assigned their own horse for the duration of their stay. The ranch offers guided trail rides into the adjacent Madison Range of the Beaverhead National Forest. C-B also leases 14,000 acres in the Lee Metcalf Wilderness, so the variety of trails and alpine scenery is virtually unlimited, as is the opportunity to see wildlife such as deer, elk, or antelope in their natural habitat.

Other activities center around fishing and touring the local attractions, including Yellowstone Park. This is not to say, however, that guests aren't free to take the day off to relax, go for a leisurely hike, or curl up with a good book in front of the fireplace in the main lodge.

Fishing

In addition to the lower Madison and all of the Yellowstone Park fisheries, C-B has approximately five miles of private fishing on Indian Creek, which flows through ranch property. This little stream produces some nice rainbows and a few cutthroats averaging ten inches, with a fair number running up to fifteen to sixteen inches. The ranch also leases a quarter-mile stretch of O'dell Creek, which flows into the Madison near Ennis. This meandering meadow stream is reminiscent of the Yellowstone spring creeks with its gin-clear water, small insects, and big rainbows averaging fifteen inches and going to twenty-plus inches. Unlike Indian Creek, which is easily

fished with standard attractors such as royal wulffs and humpies (#12–16), O'dell Creek can be fickle and challenging, requiring anglers to sample a variety of patterns in different sizes to figure out what the trout are hungry for. Fly shop personnel in Ennis can help with this puzzle.

Refer to Yellowstone Park Area Fisheries for further information.

Licenses, tackle, and equipment can be purchased in a number of fly shops in Ennis or West Yellowstone.

T LAZY B RANCH

532 Jack Creek Road, Ennis, MT 59729. Phone: (406) 682-7288. Contact: Bob and Theo Walker, owners. Total capacity: 8. Open June 1–October 31. Peak season: August. Reserve 4 months in advance. Well-behaved pets allowed.

Accommodations: Two small lodgepole pine cabins and one log-sided cabin sleep 2–3 each; electricity, no running water, central bathhouse. One guest bedroom in lodge. Daily maid service.

Meals: Three family-style meals daily on American Plan; hot breakfast, streamside sack lunch, full dinners. Mealtimes flexible to accommodate anglers. All alcohol is BYOB.

Rates: Moderate; daily rates include lodging and meals. Special rates for children. Extra charges: guided float trips and hunt trips. Cash, check, or travelers checks.

How to Get There: From Bozeman, take Highway 84 west to Norris; follow Highway 287 south through Ennis; turn east on Jack Creek Road and follow it 9 miles to ranch. Free pick-up and delivery to Bozeman or West Yellowstone airports. Rental car recommended for local travel.

Located a few miles outside of Ennis, the T Lazy B is a small guest ranch that caters to fly fishers. Its access to the lower Madison and other fisheries including those in Yellowstone Park makes for a high number of repeat clientele. Owner Bob Walker is one of the better-known fishing guides in the area; his expertise ensures that guests will have the opportunity to hook up with some trophy trout.

The main lodge and several small cabins are nestled into a small glen formed by Jack Creek Canyon. The cabins are simply furnished and comfortable, though there is no running water in them. The main lodge contains the dining room and a lounge area with a small stone fireplace.

Things to Do

Most off-ranch activities consist of touring local attractions. Yellowstone Park is only an hour's drive to the north. Ennis offers quaint shops and western art galleries that are fun to browse through. About fifteen miles west of Ennis on Highway 287 are the old restored Gold Rush towns of Nevada City and Virginia City.

While there are good hiking trails in the Madison Range to the east of the ranch, the principal outdoor activity other than fishing is upland bird hunting. The season for upland game such as Hungarian partridge and sharptail, and blue and ruffed grouse starts in September, which coincides with some of the best fishing on the Madison and other nearby rivers. The ranch provides dogs and guides for those guests who want to have a crack at these beautiful birds.

Fishing

In addition to having good access to the lower Madison, the ranch has a half-mile stretch of Jack Creek which flows through the property. A small, brushy, pocket water stream, Jack Creek has a lot of rainbows with some browns and brooks. Fish average from nine- to twelve-inches, with a fair number of fish up to fifteen inches. Small attractor patterns (#12–16) such as royal wulffs and adams work well on this stream.

See Yellowstone Park Area Fisheries for more information.

Fishing licenses, tackle, and gear can all be purchased in a number of fly shops located in Ennis.

NYE

STILLWATER VALLEY RANCH

Nye, MT 59061. Phone: (406) 328-6222. Contact: Carolynn or John Mouat. Total capacity: 25. Open May 15–October 15. Peak season: July and August. Reserve 3–4 months in advance. No pets.

Accommodations: Two cabins serve larger groups and families; private bath, fireplace, and outdoor patio a few feet from the river. Two lodges, one with suites with private bath and one with bedrooms with private bath. Daily maid service.

Meals: Three family-style meals daily on American Plan; hot breakfast cooked to order, hot lunch, BYOB cocktail hour, full dinner. Hot plate dinners held for late anglers.

Rates: Moderate; weekly rates include lodging, meals, horse, and transportation. One-week minimum stay. Special rates for children under 14. Special packages include scenic pack trips, fishing pack trips, and float trips on Yellowstone, Big Horn, and Stillwater rivers. Extra charges: guide services, half-day casting lessons, airport pick-up from Billings, MT. Cash, check, or travelers check.

How to Get There: Located 100 miles southwest of Billings, MT. Take I-90 west from Billings to Columbus; follow Highway 78 to Absaroka; take Highway 419 south through Nye up Stillwater Valley to ranch; look for ranch signs on left.

The Stillwater Valley Ranch is located on the banks of the Stillwater River, just north of Yellowstone Park. This valley is among the most spectacular in Montana. The rugged peaks of the Absaroka-Beartooth Wilderness jut skyward a few miles to the south and the lower valley reaches are covered with aspen and evergreen. Guests wanting to sample some of the famed Montana big sky will find a perfect headquarters in this guest ranch.

Stillwater Valley Ranch also operates under the name Montana Wild West Adventures and provides one of the largest selections of fishing, packing, and ranching vacations found anywhere. If the options listed in their brochure are not enough, the ranch will gladly customize trips to assure that never-to-be-forgotten vacation.

Lodge bedrooms and riverside cabins are attractively furnished with wall-to-wall carpeting and oversized chairs and sofas. Guests choosing to venture on an extended float fishing trip, back-country pack trip, or combination float-pack trip are provided with full accommodation camps each night. Large, walk-in tents afford rustic comfort in the great outdoors.

Things to Do

In addition to the variety of trips and off-ranch vacations the ranch offers, a standard dude ranch package is also quite popular. Horsemanship skills are carefully nurtured throughout the week with a series of gymkhanas and trail rides into the breathtaking Absaroka-Beartooth Wilderness. The week's events culminate each Saturday in a rodeo where guests and wranglers alike showcase their equestrian skills.

Several scenic pack trips take in a remote part of the American West that has remained virtually unchanged over the years. The ranch's Beartooth Rendevous takes guests high into the wilderness to recreate the legendary "Mountain Man Rendevous," complete with great fishing, black-powder and long-rifle demonstrations, and other exciting events.

Fishing

The ranch works in concert with the Montana School of Fly Fishing operated by sons Steve and Mike Mouat. Staff guides concentrate on four principal fisheries located near the ranch: the Stillwater, Yellowstone, and Bighorn rivers, and alpine streams and lakes within the Absaroka-Beartooth Wilderness. All guides are avid fly fishers who gladly share their knowledge of casting, wading, and reading the water techniques.

The Stillwater River is anything but still. Originating high in the mountains to the south of the ranch, the river is a sixty-mile stretch of boulder-studded swift glides, riffles, and waterfalls interspersed with an occasional deep pool or back eddy. Tough wading makes chest waders with traction devices and wading staff essential on the Stillwater.

Above the ranch, the river has good populations of brook and rainbows averaging ten to fourteen inches. The section of river between the ranch and the town of Absaroka contains mostly rainbows in the twelve- to eighteen-inch range with some lunkers going over twenty inches. From Absaroka down to the confluence of the Yellowstone River, browns and rainbows average fourteen inches with good numbers of fish over eighteen inches.

The ranch itself has a beautiful stretch of fly-fishing water flowing through its boundaries.

Though much of the rest of the river passes through private property, the Mouats have been granted permission by other landholders to fish many miles of otherwise inaccessible stretches of the Stillwater that seldom see fishermen.

The river usually begins to clear in early July and the fishing continues to be good through October. Standard dry fly patterns (#10–18) include elk hair caddis, comparaduns, royal wulffs, adams, and humpies. Wets and streamers include gold-ribbed hare's ear and pheasant tails (#10–14), black matukas, stoneflies, and muddlers (#6–8).

Pack-in fisheries located in the adjacent wilderness offer some of the most spectacular alpine fishing in the country. Dozens of lakes and small streams provide a variety of fishing for cutthroat, rainbow, brook, and the rare golden trout. Catch-and-release rates can often be tremendous, depending on the angler's skill; however, it is the quality of fishing that makes these back-country waters truly amazing. Several lakes have fish averaging eighteen to twenty-four inches and catch rates of thirty-plus fish per day are not uncommon.

For a description of the Yellowstone and Bighorn rivers, refer to the Yellowstone Park Area Fisheries section and to the write-up of the Bighorn Angler.

The Montana School of Fly Fishing stocks a complete supply of angling supplies needed for fishing local waters. Staff members also conduct private casting and fishing clinics for ranch guests at a nominal fee.

YELLOWSTONE PARK

Yellowstone Park Area Fisheries

Just mentioning the word *Yellowstone* is enough to whet the appetite of anyone who enjoys the outdoors. The park has been a wilderness mecca to millions of visitors who have marveled at the interplay of untamed wildlife and geologic grandeur. The overwhelming size of the park coupled with the number of scenic attractions and hiking trails make Yellowstone a destination vacation area for families, couples, and anglers.

While there is lodging available inside the park, the lodges and guest ranches we have selected to cover this large area are all located outside the park itself. The reason for this is simple: *quality of experience*. From the Fourth of July through Labor Day, Yellowstone is packed solid with visitors and the park's concession-run hotels take on a frenzied level of activity reminiscent of the Super Bowl and a large convention combined. On the other hand, the facilities outside of the park enjoy a tranquil atmosphere more conducive to a family or fly-fishing vacation. All are located less than an hour's drive from the park, so guests can admire Yellowstone by day and escape the multitudes by night.

"Seventy-five percent of the blue-ribbon trout waters found in the lower forty-eight states lie within 100 miles of Yellowstone National Park." While we don't know who first said this, we do know that it is probably true. Quite simply, there is no other spot in the country with as many renowned fisheries in as small an area as Yellowstone. Major blue-ribbon rivers originating in the park include the Yellowstone, Gardiner, Lamar, Gallatin, Gibbon, Madison, Firehole, Bechler, Falls, Lewis, and Snake rivers. Famous and sometimes uncrowded park creeks include Soda Butte, Slough, Cache, Pelican, and Indian creeks. Lake fisheries include Sylvan, Yellowstone, Heart, and Riddle lakes.

It should be noted that this is, by no means, an exhaustive list of the park's fisheries. Any of the competent guides who work the park will know of dozens of other fisheries, some of which seldom see hooks and can provide *unbelievable* catch rates when hot. The sheer volume of fisheries located in and adjacent to Yellowstone precludes any attempt to individually assess them. However, five principal fisheries receive over 80 percent of the total fishing pressure: Yellowstone Lake, Yellowstone River, Madison River, Firehole River, and Slough Creek.

Yellowstone Lake

Yellowstone Lake sits in the middle of the park at an elevation of 7,731 feet. The size of the lake—nearly 130 square miles—can be intimidating to the uninitiated angler at first glance, but the fishing is more often than not spectacular. In 1975 special regulations were posted to restrict daily creel limits to two fish per day under thirteen inches. The policy has worked so well that some local guides contend that it is difficult to locate an area on the lake where the fish are small enough for their clients to keep. Standard attractor patterns, such as wulffs, adams, and humpies all work when cast to rising fish. Medium-sized streamers such as mickey finns and bucktail streamers work when there is no apparent surface feeding.

Yellowstone River Drainage

The section of the Yellowstone River that flows within the confines of the park is, perhaps, the most renowned strictly native fishery in the world. The native Yellowstone cutthroat have attracted hundreds of thousands of anglers over the years to this stretch of water, dubbed "the Yankee Stadium of Fly Fishing" by local guide Ray Hurley. The section that has some of the best fishing and, consequently, the most intense fishing pressure is between Fishing Bridge and the Sulphur Cauldron. The other easily accessed portion of the river is from just below Alum Creek down to the falls just below Cascade Creek. With the exception of these two sections, the park-bound Yellowstone lies either in the wilderness above Yellowstone Lake or below the Grand Canyon of the Yellowstone. These two latter sections have excellent fishing but are very difficult to access.

During the first few weeks after opening, the park-bound Yellowstone is considered by many to offer simply the finest dry fly cutthroat fishing in the world. With the exception of a small salmon fly hatch occurring early in the season, the Yellowstone is a classic may- and caddisfly fishery. Adams, light cahills, house and lots, and elk hair caddis will all take fish. Attractors such as royal wulffs and humpies are also productive.

Madison River Drainage

The superlative Madison River starts in Madison Junction in the west side of Yellowstone at the confluence of the Gibbon and Firehole rivers. While the vast majority of the Madison is located outside the park in Montana, the fourteen miles inside Yellowstone Park receive more angling pressure than any other river fishery except the Yellowstone. This pressure is due partly to the location of two popular campgrounds lying adjacent to the river and partly to the fact than an east-west highway parallels its banks for most of this fourteen-mile stretch. The Madison is best fished early in the season or late in the fall because of warm water temperatures caused by thermal areas of the Gibbon and the Firehole. Serious anglers are cautioned to avoid fishing during the busy months of July and August when crowds are at their peak and when the fish are seldom on the bite because of tepid water conditions. Spring and fall fishing on this meandering meadow stream can be rewarding for skilled anglers.

The combination of a fly-fishing-only designation and the incredible number of fisherman has led to a wizened trout population. Early in the season, small flies and nymphs tied onto one- to three-pound test leaders are the rule. Muskrats,

gold-ribbed hare's ears, and pheasant tail nymphs will catch fish, as will dry fly patterns such as small elk hair caddis and light-colored variations of mayfly dun patterns.

September and October are accompanied by the change of color, an occasional early snowfall, and some prodigious brown trout that come up from Hebgen Lake to spawn in the Upper Madison. Eighteen- to twenty-inch fish are quite common at this time and it is not unusual to find many anglers here for whom this has become an annual trek. These big fish require a good amount of technique and casting ability and an even larger amount of patience; spawning fish unpredictably alternate between being aggressive and being unbelievably spooky. Some anglers swear by such flies as muddler minnows and hornbergs, whereas others prefer the more popular flies such as bitch creeks, girdle bugs, and woolly buggers.

Firehole River Drainage

Originating in the Madison Plateau and flowing right through some of the most spectacular thermal attractions in Yellowstone Park, the Firehole River is one of the most famous fly-fishing-only streams in the country. Although the fish in this picturesque river tend to be a little smaller, averaging ten to fourteen inches, the very idea of fishing a meadow stream with geysers and fumaroles for a backdrop is one that has intrigued anglers and sportswriters for years.

Even more so than the Madison, the Firehole suffers terribly from thermal shock during July and August. Accordingly, most anglers concentrate on the Firehole primarily in the fall and in early June. During the cooler weather, water temperatures are conducive to active feeding. The river's clarity and slow pace require delicate and controlled presentations of chosen flies. The Firehole, like the famous spring creeks of the Yellowstone, is often the domain of Latin speak and the three-weight line. Dry flies such as the elk hair caddis, adams, and various dun patterns (#16–20) will take fish. When there is no apparent rise on, anglers seem to have better luck with the larger attractor flies (#10–12) such as royal wulffs and house and lots. Dragon and damsel fly nymphs also work. The only consensus among Firehole anglers is that a light, *long* tippet is a must.

Slough Creek Drainage

Originating north of the park, in the southeastern edge of the Absaroka Range, Slough Creek flows south and forms one of the principal tributaries of the Lamar River. The sixteen-mile section that lies inside the park boundary is perhaps the most popular hike-in fishery found in Yellowstone. It was overfished in the late sixties and early seventies, but special catch-and-release regulations have brought about a fishing renaissance in this beautiful alpine stream. The average size of the cutthroats and cutthroat-rainbow hybrids (fifteen to eighteen inches), not the number, is what keeps anglers coming back. Some of the best fishing for these lunkers is located along a stretch within a forty-five minute hike of the campground. Farther upstream, in meadow areas, the number of fish increases, and size tends to diminish somewhat. Slough Creek has two principal advantages over other park fisheries. Due to its hike-in nature, the entire drainage is exceptionally pristine and, in spite of its popularity, offers the solitude necessary to enjoy the scenic beauty surrounding it. Additionally, Slough Creek does not suffer thermal stress in July and August and, consequently, the fishing can be excellent all season long. Hoppers are the premier dry fly especially in meadow sections. Large attractor patterns such as royal wulffs and house and lots are often effective when hoppers are not. Weighted dragon fly and hare's ear nymphs work well when bounced along the pebbled bottom. Like the Firehole, Slough Creek demands cautious wading and stalking techniques as these fish are easily spooked due to the incredible clarity of the water.

Ancillary Yellowstone Fisheries

In addition to the fisheries located within the park, many blue-ribbon streams are within an easy commute. The Jackson area to the south, within an hour-and-a-half drive, contains some outstanding river fisheries such as the Snake, Gros Ventre and Hoback rivers (see the section on the Jackson Area Fisheries for descriptions of these rivers). The Stillwater and Boulder rivers are to the north, and to the west the Bighole River draws a number of anglers, especially when a salmon fly hatch is on.

Three principal fisheries outside the park that attract Yellowstone anglers include the Lower Madison, Yellowstone, and Henry's Fork of the Snake. Whereas the Lower Madison and Yellowstone rivers originate in the park and continue to have excellent fishing outside park boundaries, Henry's Fork lies entirely outside the park runing just to the southwest of West Yellowstone.

Lower Yellowstone River Drainage

The lower Yellowstone, which flows out of the park near Gardiner, Montana, and continues north through the Paradise Valley, is very unlike its park-bound cousin. This big, brawny western river demands respect at all times, and anglers intent on fishing it for the first time should do so in the company of a professional guide. To maximize the amount of fishing time, most guides prefer to float the river. Although many different floats are available, perhaps the most renowned stretch of the lower Yellowstone lies from Mallards Rest to just below Livingston. This section requires more than a day to float and contains hundreds of riffles, islands, and bends, many of which offer superb angling. Locals have christened some of the more productive riffles with such colorful names as Weeping Wall, Whorehouse, and Warm Springs. Large rainbows up to five-pounds-plus predominate in this stretch, whereas browns and cutthroats form the majority of the population from Gardiner down to Mallards Rest.

Standard, high-floating dry flies include royal wulffs, goofus bugs (humpies), and hopper imitations in midsummer. Nymph patterns like gold-ribbed hare's ears and dark stoneflies produce big fish on dead drifts. Streamers such as the muddler minnow or dark spruce fly also work well when fished deep. A long, medium stiff, *minimum* 7 weight rod is recommended as lightweight gear is no match for the size of the lower Yellowstone nor for the strong winds that whip up along its length.

Nelson and Armstrong creeks are two small spring-fed creeks flowing into the Yellowstone River a few miles south of Livingston. These two world-class fisheries are quite different from the lower Yellowstone in that they require ultralight gear combined with perfect presentation. Four weight rods with 6–8X tippets are the rule here, as is a good knowledge of how to match the hatch. Local tackle shops in Livingston can outfit anglers with the proper flies to attract the two- to five-pound rainbows that inhabit these creeks. They can also make the necessary reservation as there is, unfortunately, a hefty rod fee for the privilege of fishing these beautiful Yellowstone tributaries.

Lower Madison River Drainage

The lower Madison River flows out of Quake Lake just outside of West Yellowstone. It is, perhaps, the most written-about trout stream in the world; the fifty-mile stretch between Quake Lake and Ennis, Montana, is the most heavily fished section of any river in Montana. A prodigious number of fish in the one- to three-pound class and sometimes incredible catch rates account for the river's popularity among anglers. A good day can produce up to fifty fish per rod. Special regulations put into effect in 1977 have made the lower Madison the quality fishery it is today: a thirty mile catch-and-release section was designated from Quake Lake to McAtee Bridge, special creel restrictions were applied along the river's entire length, and hatchery stocking was terminated. So successful were these regulations in helping to restore the Madison fishery that they have been copied on many other river systems nationwide. The end result is that the Madison, in spite of intense fishing pressure, is once again a world-class wild trout fishery.

The upper section of the river is one long series of riffles with some excellent boulder pocket water. The current is swift and, as a result, much of the best water is accesssed by float fishing. During the salmon fly hatch (usually around June 1 to 15), it's not unusual for more than fifty to seventy-five boats to be working this stretch per day. Eleven- to fourteen-inch rainbows predominate in the upper reaches with a good number of fish in the fifteen- to eighteen-inch class.

The section below the catch-and-release waters changes character when the river divides around a series of islands called the Channels. Most easily fished by wading, this water contains some classic dry fly water. It is advisable to hire a guide for the first couple of times through this area as, in its constant forking and dividing, the river becomes mazelike. Interestingly enough, brown trout outnumber rainbows almost two to one in the lower stretch.

Standard dry fly patterns (#10–16) such as royal wulffs, house and lots, and brown elk hair caddis will all take fish. Large salmon fly patterns (#2–6) such as sofa pillows and large grasshoppers (#4–10) will also work when a natural hatch is occurring. Stonefly nymphs (#2–4) will produce when cast on a dead drift. Streamer patterns such as woolly buggers, bitch creeks, and sculpins work well especially in the lower section when there are no apparent rises.

The Madison's large size and dependable afternoon winds require a good 6–8 weight rod. A dry line will suffice as long as nymphs and streamers are weighted for all but the deepest runs.

Fly shops in West Yellowstone and Ennis stock everything necessary to fish the Madison and are staffed by extremely attentive and knowledgeable fishermen who welcome newcomers.

Henry's Fork of the Snake River Drainage

Forty miles southwest of West Yellowstone, Henry's Fork of the Snake drains out of its origin, Henry's Lake. Although Henry's Lake itself is a first-class rainbow fishery, it is to Henry's Fork that thousands of dedicated anglers flock each year. With the possible exception of the famed Bighorn and Beaverhead rivers, there is no other fishery in the lower forty-eight states that supports more large fish than the Henry's Fork.

This river has quite a few different sections that have their own unique beauty and character. The upper stretch from Henry's Lake to Mack's Inn is predominately a marshy meadow river that doesn't receive much angling pressure. Fish tend to be smaller—up to three pounds—than in other sections and they are easily spooked. Between Mack's Inn and the head of Island Park Reservoir, the river is pocket and riffle water higher up before flowing through a steep canyon in the middle. Above the reservoir is a six-mile meadow stretch set in one of the most beautiful intermountain valleys found anywhere. Wildlife, the occasional bugling of elk, and little fishing pres-

sure due to few points of access make this section of the Henry's Fork the destination of anglers who prefer solitude in the heart of nature.

The main attraction of the Henry's Fork lies in the twenty-mile stretch below Island Park Dam which includes the famed Railroad ranch. At the top, the dam empties into Box Canyon, which contains some of the best fast-water nymph fishing on the river. It's a steep hike in and wading can be treacherous, but stonefly nymphs fished on a dead drift can bring up rainbows that sometimes top twelve pounds. Below the canyon on down through and below the ranch, the river is a series of mostly wadeable riffles, channels, and slack water. This section supports an incredible number of aquatic insects and, not surprisingly, large fish. Rainbows in the two- to five-pound class are common and every few years fish in excess of fifteen pounds are caught!

There are, however, two drawbacks to this section of Henry's Fork. It is crowded, especially from mid-June to mid-July when the green drake hatch is on. During this time there are as many as five hundred anglers working the water each day. Also, the hatches of insects are so prolific—occurring in bunches—that it can drive even the most hardened angler to distraction trying to figure out what these monsters are rising to. There are literally dozens of mayfly, caddis, and stonefly hatches that occur daily throughout the summer along almost the entire length of the river.

Fly shops in West Yellowstone and Island Park are invaluable resources for helping anglers match the hatch and providing the right equipment and required Idaho fishing license. Perhaps the two most important things an angler can bring to the Henry's Fork are patience and a sense of wonder that accompanies the knowledge that the angler is fishing in one of the Valhallas of trout fishing.

FIREHOLE RANCH

/o Rivermeadows, Inc., P.O. Box 347, Wilson, WY
3014. Phone: (307) 733-3674/2841. Contact:
Richard Albrecht, Rivermeadows, Inc.; Firehole
Ranch manager, Barry Morstad. Total capacity: 26.
Open June 1–October 1. Peak season: August and
eptember. Reserve 6 months in advance.

Accommodations: Five duplex cabins with living
quarters, private bath, and fireplace. Daily maid
ervice; laundry facility.

Meals: Three family-style meals daily on Ameri-
an Plan; hot breakfast with champagne, hot lunch
r elegant sack lunch, four-course gourmet dinner
/ith wine. Meals can be arranged to accommmo-
late late anglers. Beer, wine, liquor, and after-
linner cordials complimentary.

Rates: Expensive; fly-fishing vacation includes
odging, guided fishing, meals, local transportation,
quor, and ranch activities. Cash, check, or travelers
hecks.

How to Get There: Located 16 miles northwest of
Vest Yellowstone off Highway 20. Commercial air-
nes service West Yellowstone. Free pick-up. Rental
ar recommended for off-ranch travel.

The Firehole Ranch is located in Hebgen Lake
thirty minutes from West Yellowstone. Owned
by the same company that runs the famed Crescent H Ranch near Jackson, Wyoming, the Firehole Ranch is one of the true five-star fly-fishing
operations in the western United States. It is expensive, but, considering the accommodations
and services included in the package deal, the
price is not out of line.

The 500-acre ranch, originally known as Wat-
kins Creek Ranch, was run as a family-operated
cattle and dude ranch for over forty years before
it was purchased by Rivermeadows, Inc. in the
early eighties. Extensive remodeling and
redecorating have transformed this rather rustic
guest ranch into one of the most aesthetically
pleasing fly-fishing lodges found in the West.

Cabins situated in a forested glen below Coffin
Peak, a short walk from the main ranch house,
offer a unique blend of western elegance and styl-
ish comfort. Polished log walls, knotty-pine
paneling, and plush carpeting complement the
stone fireplaces and decorator curtains, bedspreads, and furnishings. The original main lodge
houses a formal dining area, full-service bar, and
living room dominated by a large stone fireplace.
It too has been extensively remodeled and updated with smart, oversize furnishings, English
antiques, and southwestern Indian rugs. The airy
dining room has a spectacular view of Hebgen
Lake and the Gallatin Range to the north.

Things to Do

Guests not interested in one of Firehole's fishing
programs can sign up for day-long horseback
rides up to alpine lakes or for shorter rides
around the ranch proper. Canoeing and swimming in Hebgen Lake are also popular pursuits.
Miles of hiking trails are reached by an easy commute from the ranch as are all the main geologic
attractions of Yellowstone Park.

Fishing

The Firehole is a destination resort for serious fly
fishers. It certainly qualifies as one of the top five
fly-fishing operations left still open to the general
public in the lower forty-eight. There are five
full-time guides on staff with additional local
guides on call when the ranch is busy. There are

never more than two anglers per guide and, often, guests receive one-on-one attention. Guests are assigned a guide for the week to take advantage of the familiarity that continuity breeds, both in assessing abilities and in camaraderie. Guides who aren't willing to fish hard from sunup to sundown or who hesitate to drag a boat back upriver to give a client one more chance at that trophy trout are not employed at the Firehole Ranch.

Guests meet with the ranch manager to discuss their fishing preferences and experiences. Each morning, they are picked up by their guide and taken to one of hundreds of local fisheries. Guides pay close attention to each guest's competence and patience and select fisheries accordingly. Highly skilled fishermen can be introduced to fisheries that will challenge everything they've got.

Licenses must be purchased in nearby West Yellowstone, but the ranch's full-service Orvis Fly Shop can fill all other angling needs.

LONE MOUNTAIN RANCH

P.O. Box 145, Big Sky, MT 59716. Phone: (406) 995-4644. Contact: Bob and Viv Schaap, part-owners. Total capacity: 45. Open year round. Peak season: July 4–August. Reserve 6 months in advance. No pets.

Accommodations: Four duplex and 11 individual cabins sleep 8; all have private bath and electricity. Daily maid service; laundry facility.

Meals: Three family-style meals daily on American Plan; hot breakfast, box lunch, full gourmet dinner, weekly barbecue and children's cookout. Alcohol available in Horsefly Saloon.

Rates: Expensive; weekly rates include lodging, meals, horse, and ranch activities. Discounts available for off-season and extended stays; 15 percent extra for stays less than 1 week. Special rates for children 2–12. Special packages include all-day alpine horseback and fishing trip, van tour of Yellowstone Park, raft trips, walk and wade trip, and float fishing trips. Extra charges: airport pick-up service. Check, VISA, MasterCard, or American Express.

How to Get There: One-hour drive from Bozeman or West Yellowstone, MT. From Bozeman, take Highway 289 west; turn south on Highway 85 which turns into Highway 191; turn west at resort sign and follow road 4 miles; turn north into ranch. From West Yellowstone, follow Highway 191 north to ranch. Commercial airlines service Bozeman. Rental car not required for local travel as ranch vehicles and guides are available.

Lone Mountain Ranch is located four miles west of the Gallatin River, just off the road that leads to Big Sky Ski Resort. A family-oriented guest ranch offering a wide variety of activities for people of all ages, Lone Mountain also provides superior access to the blue-ribbon fisheries of Yellowstone Park. The ranch was originally homesteaded in 1915 and has been run as a private resort off and on since the early thirties. In 1967 Chet Huntley and a group of investors purchased the ranch and used it as their base of operations while developing Big Sky. The Schaap family acquired Lone Mountain in the late seventies and have since formed a partnership with the current owner of Big Sky, Mike Ankeny. Both partners share a love for unspoiled wilderness, ensuring that the thousands of acres to the north of the ranch will remain undeveloped.

Cabins are scattered over the small mountain valley where the ranch is located. Several front a small creek, while the rest sit on a hillside overlooking the ranch and its beautiful backdrop of the mountains bordering Yellowstone in the distance.

The main log lodge, which serves as a gathering place for guests and locals alike, lies adjacent to the stables near the entrance to the ranch. It houses the Horsefly Saloon, open to the public.

Things to Do

The number-one priority at Lone Mountain Ranch is combining relaxation with exhilarating, family-oriented outdoor recreation. Recognizing that each family is a little different, the ranch crew schedules a wide variety of activities. Na-

ture walks and interpretive hikes guided by Bob Schaap are a favorite. Those in good physical condition will find miles of hiking and riding trails through the Spanish Peak Mountains surrounding the ranch. River float trips and guided excursions by automobile to view the spectacular geologic attractions in Yellowstone are also popular. Optional programs for children include campouts, scavenger hunts, a rodeo, and ice cream rides. For the truly laid back, a sundeck with a hot tub perches on a small hillside overlooking the ranch.

Fishing

Lone Mountain takes pride in its Orvis-endorsed fly-fishing program supervised by a full-time program director and guide. Along with free casting clinics, the ranch offers a number of trips designed for all levels of angling abilities: walk and wade trips, raft trips, and walk-and-float trips for women. Numerous alpine stream and lake fisheries within an easy day's hike or ride are capable of fulfilling any angler's wildest dream. Pack trips into the back country for cutthroats "as long as your arm" can also be arranged.

In addition to the Yellowstone Park fisheries, the ranch is only a few miles away from the lower Gallatin River. Although the Gallatin originates inside the park, the majority of its fishery lies in the stretch between Yellowstone Park and Gallatin Gateway to the north.

The most popular section of the Gallatin runs from just below the canyon area to the south of the ranch down to Gallatin Gateway. This lower section of the river has both browns and rainbows averaging twelve inches. Several feeder creeks easily accessed from the ranch also offer good fishing for rainbows and cutthroats. Unlike most rivers in Montana, the Gallatin is not a classic mayfly fishery. Sculpins, caddisflies, and terrestrials are the main diet here with preferred flies being royal wulffs, elk hair caddis (#10–16), dave's hoppers (#6–10), and muddler minnows (#4–8).

Fishing during an excellent salmon fly hatch in early June is often spectacular as long as the weather cooperates. The Gallatin, unfortunately, is notorious for going off color when it rains, though its upper reaches quickly clear up. Midsummer often sees dry fly fishing peaking with a variety of late-afternoon and early-evening hatches of mayflies coming off at once. Like most Montana rivers, however, the Gallatin really begins to shine in the fall. The river is clear and uncrowded and the fish really begin to put on the feed bag in preparation for the long winter ahead. Large streamers coupled with minute trico and other mayfly imitations can test any angler's patience, especially when matched against that fish of a lifetime.

MOUNTAIN SKY GUEST RANCH

P.O. Box 1128, Bozeman, MT 59715. Phone: 1-(800) 548-3392 or (406) 587-1244. Total capacity: 60-80. Open June 1-mid-October. Peak season: July and August. Reserve 6 months in advance. No pets.

Accommodations: Twenty-five cabins sleep 1-8; all with private bath. Daily maid service.

Meals: Three family-style meals daily on American Plan; hot breakfast or continental breakfast available, buffet or trail lunch, children served separately at dinner, full gourmet dinner for adults, weekly dinner ride. Meals can be arranged to accommodate late anglers.

Rates: Moderate; weekly rates include lodging, meals, horseback riding, special children's programs, and use of ranch facilities. Special rates for children under 6. Extra charges: airport pickup in Bozeman and Billings. Check, VISA, or MasterCard.

How to Get There: Located midway between Livingston and Gardiner, MT. From Livingston, follow Highway 89 south through Emigrant; 7 miles south turn west on Big Creek Road; follow signs to ranch. Commercial airlines service airports in Bozeman and Billings, MT.

The Mountain Sky Guest Ranch is set in a small, picturesque valley a few miles west of the lower Yellowstone River near Emigrant, Montana. This charming resort is among the few select Montana guest ranches to have received the AAA Four Diamond Award. Amenities at Mountain Sky include traditional western-style horseback riding, tennis, swimming in a heated pool with an adjoining Jacuzzi and sauna, and fishing.

Locals refer to the area surrounding the ranch as Paradise Valley—it's not hard to figure out why. The breathtaking scenery of northern Yellowstone is at their back door. Mountain vistas coupled with fir- and aspen-covered slopes and an incredibly clear blue sky lure people back to Mountain Sky Guest Ranch every year. This is first-class resort, only minutes away from the Yellowstone River and its renowned spring creeks, Nelson's and Armstrong's.

Wood-paneled cabins are comfortably furnished with sofas, easy chairs, and coffee tables; a small refrigerator is stocked with fresh fruit daily The main lodge, with its intimate cocktail lounge and dining room, recreation hall, and a newly constructed dance hall and meeting room, puts Mountain Sky a notch or two above the majority of Montana guest ranches. Attention to detail is evident throughout facilities that exude a feeling of casual western elegance.

Things to Do

Mountain Sky Ranch offers a large number of activities for guests to choose from. All guests old enough to ride are assigned a trail horse for their level of saddle skill. Rides into some of the prettiest country in Paradise Valley and the Yellowstone drainage depart daily except Sunday. Guided nature walks are available to those who prefer a more leisurely pace on foot. For guests spending a day at the ranch, options include tennis, volleyball, softball, horseshoes, and a swimming pool with Jacuzzi and sauna. The spacious ranch also has plenty of quiet, secluded spots just right for curling up with a good book.

Children's activities are pleasantly structured and well-supervised by professional counselors. Morning, afternoon, and evening activities include such favorites as nature hikes, arts and crafts, swimming, field games, and fishing in a stocked trout pond. Children of all ages have a special wrangler assigned to them for horseback riding instruction.

Fishing

Refer to the Yellowstone Park Area Fisheries section, notably the lower Yellowstone River and its spring creeks, located near the ranch, for more fishing information.

Fishing licenses, gear, and tackle should be purchased in Gardiner or Livingston prior to arrival at the ranch. The staff is happy to assist guests in making arrangements with local guides for float fishing trips on the Yellowstone River. Anglers should request that guide services are booked when making their lodge reservations as the best guides are booked up early in the season.

NINE QUARTER CIRCLE RANCH

Gallatin Gateway, MT 59730. Phone: ranch, (406) 995-4276; home, (406) 995-4876. Contact: Kim and Kelly Kelsey, owner/managers. Total capacity: 80–85. Open June–late September. Peak season: July and August. Reserve 6 months in advance. No pets.

Accommodations: Twenty cabins sleep 2–10; all with private bath and wood-burning stove. Daily maid service; laundry facility.

Meals: Three family-style meals daily on American Plan; breakfast cooked to order, hot lunch or sack lunch, children eat dinner separately while adults are at BYOB cocktail hour, western-style dinner. Barbecue or fish fry 2–3 times a week.

Rates: Moderate; weekly rates include lodging, meals, horseback riding, 2-day pack trip, childcare, fishing guide, and all ranch activities. Discounts offered for larger groups or extended stays. Special rates for children 5–14. Extra charges: vehicles available for rent, airport pick-up from Bozeman or West Yellowstone (children under 4, free). Cash or check.

How to Get There: Located midway between Bozeman and West Yellowstone. Take Highway 191 to Taylors Fork Road; turn west for 5 miles to ranch. Commercial airlines service airports in Bozeman and West Yellowstone. Ranch has private turf airstrip for small aircraft. A few vehicles are available to rent.

The Nine Quarter Circle Ranch, located a few minutes south of Big Sky, Montana, is one of the last truly authentic dude ranches left in the West. The Kelsey family has specialized in offering family-oriented western style vacations in a setting of rustic comfort for over forty years. A close to a 100 percent repeat booking rate in July and August attests to the success of this great Montana guest ranch. To families, one appealing aspect of the Nine Quarter Circle is that separate programs are offered for adults and kids. Family groups comprise the majority of clientele during the peak of summer, while fly fishers start moving in when the leaves start to turn in autumn — this is when fishing in nearby Yellowstone Park, the main fishery accessed by the ranch, gets red hot.

Cabins scattered over a half-mile stretch of ranch property are built of logs and knotty pine and comfortably furnished with wooden beds and dressers. The main lodge, a grand old building authentically western both in ambiance and decor that sits atop a small bluff overlooking the rest of the ranch, houses the dining room and Trophy Room, an informal gathering-spot replete with impressive racks and wall hangings. The cheery dining room is furnished with long wooden tables; this group arrangement ensures that everyone gets a chance to meet before the week is out.

Things to Do

As a working horse ranch, the primary activity at Nine Quarter Circle is horseback riding. The ranch raises its own Appaloosas and, with a string of 125 horses, all guests can be mounted daily. Horses are assigned according to riding abilities and riders keep the same mount for the entire week. Daily rides leaving from the ranch differ in length and level of difficulty; free lessons are available whenever they're needed. Every Saturday, humor and laughter abound when guests compete in the weekly gymkhana or horseback games.

The staff sees to it that children — from toddlers to older teenagers — have a good time. Riding, swimming in a mountain stream–fed swimming hole, square dancing, movies, nature hikes, volleyball games, and a weekly gymkhana are planned to introduce kids to a full range of western experiences. Youngsters too small to join the regular ride are led around the ranch atop a gentle horse. Toddlers spend time on the ranch playground equipped with swing sets and a warren full of domestic rabbits with which they inevitably became friends. Babysitting and childcare are provided for infants too young to take part in activities. The highlight of the teenager's week is a two-day wilderness pack trip that takes them through some truly unforgettable terrain.

Fishing

In addition to fisheries in Yellowstone Park, many local streams and creeks are easily reached via a short hike or ride from the Nine Quarter Circle. Cutthroats, rainbows, and browns in nearby drainages tend to be smaller (eight to ten inches) than park fish, but spectacular scenery and solitude can make for a very rewarding day. A fishing guide on staff will provide information on where the fishing's hot and make sure that anglers are properly outfitted. The ranch guide also helps in booking the services of local independent guides for float trips down the Yellowstone, Gallatin, and Madison rivers.

For additional fishing information, refer to Yellowstone Park Area Fisheries.

Fishing licenses as well as a full line of gear and tackle are available at the Nine Quarter Circle.

PARADE REST GUEST RANCH

7979 Grayling Creek Road, West Yellowstone, MT 59758. Phone: (406) 646-7217. Contact: Walt and Shirley Butcher, managers. Total capacity: 53. Open June 1–September 30. Peak season: July and August. Reserve 6 months in advance. No pets.

Accommodations: Fifteen log cabins sleep 2–6; all have private bath and gas or electric heat, wood-burning stove, or fireplace. Daily maid service.

Meals: Three buffet-style meals daily on American Plan; light or hot breakfast, lunch salad bar or outdoor barbecue in warm weather, trail lunch available on request, full dinner. Meals can be arranged to accommodate late anglers.

Rates: Moderate; daily rates include lodging, meals, horseback riding, and round-trip transportation to West Yellowstone airport. Special rates for children under 10. Cash, check, or travelers checks.

How to Get There: Located 118 miles north of Idaho Falls, ID, and 82 miles south of Bozeman, MT. Ranch is few minutes' drive from West Yellowstone airport. Regional airlines service airport June 1–September 30, depending on weather. Rental cars available at airport or from agencies in West Yellowstone.

Located eight miles north of West Yellowstone is Parade Rest Ranch, a quaint and rustic guest resort that has been in operation since the 1920s. Nestled in a grove of aspen and cottonwood trees, the 160-acre ranch caters to families and anglers looking for a quiet, relaxing setting from which to branch out and enjoy the superlative fishing and scenic wonders of nearby Yellowstone Park.

Rustic log cabins — some fronting Greyling Creek, a beautiful little trout stream that runs through the middle of the ranch — are simply yet comfortably furnished with beds, reading lamps, lounge chairs, and woven rugs with Indian and western motifs. A few paces away stands the original main lodge, now made over into a guest house for a large family or several couples.

Things to Do

Activities are unstructured, except for daily morning, afternoon, and all-day horseback rides into the Gallatin Range, which rises up from the ranch's back door. Guests who want to lounge around the ranch have use of a small library with card tables and a television in the lodge. A huge swing set, horseshoe pit, and areas for badminton and volleyball are set up in the surrounding yard. Nearby, a new lodge provides room to socialize and an outdoor hot tub.

Ranch staff will assist guests with booking local commercial outfits offering guided whitewater and scenic raft trips and sightseeing tours of Yellowstone Park and old mining towns in the vicinity.

Fishing

Refer to Yellowstone Park Area Fisheries for fishing information. The staff at Parade Rest work closely with numerous guides affiliated with the local fly shops in West Yellowstone. Guide services should be contracted when reservations are made to guarantee their availability at the time of your stay.

RAINBOW RANCH

42950 Gallatin Road, Gallatin Gateway, MT 59730. Phone: (406) 995-4132. Contact: Russell Estes, owner. Total capacity: 32. Open year round. Peak season: July and August. Reserve 6 weeks in advance. No pets.

Accommodations: Lodge rooms have private bath, electric heat. Large deck for sunbathing and 8-person Jacuzzi. Daily maid service; laundry facility nearby.

Meals: Hearty breakfast and dinners; sack lunch available for small fee. Full-service bar.

Rates: Inexpensive; daily rates include lodging and 2 meals. Rate without meals also available. Check, cash, VISA, or MasterCard.

How to Get There: Located between Bozeman and West Yellowstone on Highway 191. Regional airlines service airports in Bozeman and West Yellowstone. Free airport pick-up. Rental car recommended for local travel.

Located on the banks of the Gallatin River twelve miles north of Yellowstone Park, Rainbow Ranch is open year round. In summer the ranch caters primarily to groups of fishermen who seek a comfortable place to hang their hat. Most guests are on the river or enjoying other activities during the day, using the ranch as a home base.

The original ranch was built in the early 1920s; new facilities were built in 1957 and completely remodeled in 1983. Immediately upon entering the main lodge, guests are struck by its homey feeling. The main lounge and living area is appointed with an inviting stone hearth and over-stuffed furnishings conducive to the kind of gatherings and stories told on fishing vacations.

In the main lodge, a two-story wood and stone building facing a meadow, a stone hearth separates the kitchen and dining room area from a full-service bar and lounge. The lounge is furnished with comfortable oak furniture, a well-stocked bookcase, and a bridge table. Vintage guest rooms with the patina of years of usage are situated downstairs from the main lounge and dining area. Large lockers, filled with the gear of annual returnees, line a hallway that leads to modern lodgings. Sliding glass doors open onto a deck—with ample room for sunbathing and an eight-person Jacuzzi—overlooking the meadow between the lodge and the Gallatin River. A rec hall equipped with a pool table, foosball, table tennis, and satellite television lies beyond the spa.

Things to Do

Most guests prefer to make their own plans; the ranch staff are happy to assist with bookings for local guides, horseback rides, and raft trips. Numerous hiking trails nearby lead to high alpine meadows filled with wildflowers and occasional wildlife. The golf course at Big Sky Resort is only ten minutes down the road and Yellowstone Park is a short drive to the south.

Fishing

Refer to Yellowstone Park Area Fisheries section and to Lone Mountain Ranch for a description of local fisheries.

OREGON

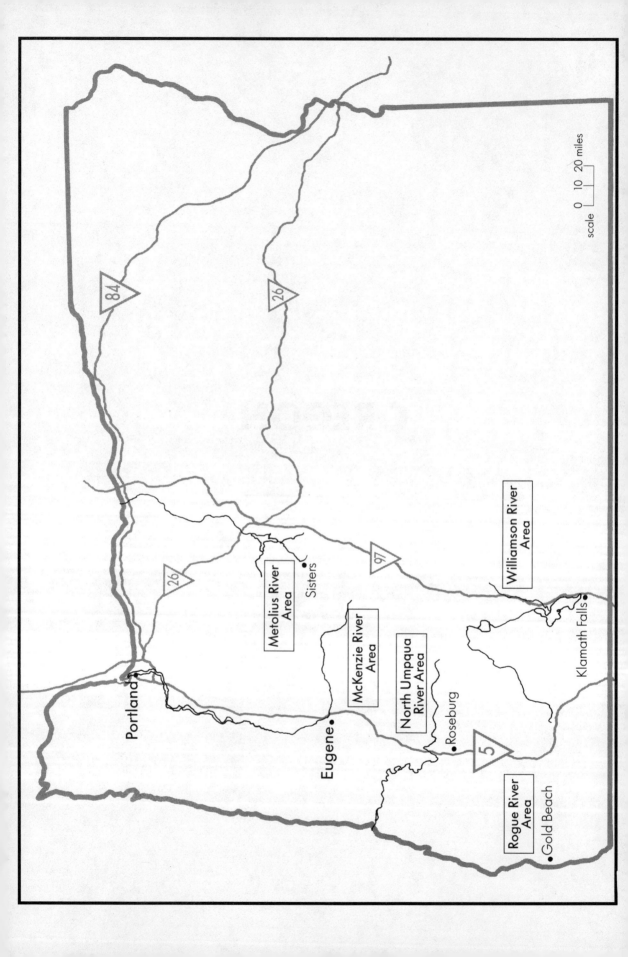

EUGENE

McKenzie River Area Fisheries

The McKenzie River Valley is one of Oregon's most pristine mountain playgrounds. The region has a natural, untampered quality that attracts outdoor recreationists who want to fish the McKenzie and explore the beauty of the Cascade Mountains surrounding it.

McKenzie River Drainage

The McKenzie River is recognized as one of the country's premier trout streams and one of the state's great natural playgrounds. Its swift, crystal-clear waters have long been a favorite of anglers who come to test their skills against the beautiful native red-side rainbows, cutthroats, and cutthroat-rainbow hybrids. The river is heavily stocked with hatchery rainbow fingerlings in the spring, but unfortunately many of them do not survive the rigors of the wild river. Although the McKenzie produces a good number of native rainbows in the twelve- to seventeen-inch range, the bulk run between seven and ten inches. A good angler is likely to take at least two larger fish and will easily fill the limit of five smaller fish per day. The McKenzie also yields spring-run chinook salmon that migrate upriver in May and June. Summer-run steelhead averaging seven pounds show up as early as the end of April in the lower river, increasing in number along the entire length of the river between July and October.

The McKenzie has its headwaters in the heart of Oregon's spectacular Cascade range just west of Clear Lake and flows eighty-nine miles west to where it joins with the broad Willamette River near the urban center of Eugene-Springfield. It is followed along most of its length by Highway 126, better known as the incredibly scenic McKenzie River Highway. In its upper stretches the river—and the highway—travels through old-growth forests of red cedar, mountain hemlock, and 100- to 300-year-old douglas firs. Streamside moss and lichen-covered boulders and trees create a magical effect as the swift riffles of the upper McKenzie mellow out below its confluence with

the Blue River. From Blue River down, the McKenzie runs mostly through private property, making drift fishing from McKenzie boats—extremely maneuverable flat-bottomed boats with a wide girth and tapered bow and stern—the most popular and preferred method of angling. Bank and walk-and-wade fishing on the upper reaches of the McKenzie is made easy by a number of campgrounds and state parks bordering the river. Chest waders with traction devices are highly recommended since swift currents and large, round boulders make footholds extremely difficult. Also, wet wading for any length of time is unlikely to be comfortable because of average water temperatures of 42 to 48 degrees. Contracting the services of one of the numerous, professional float guides is guaranteed to produce larger fish simply because both sides of long stretches of river can be covered. Guides also have a better handle on where fish lie, an unpredictable enterprise on the McKenzie. Anglers claim to hook fish "where you'd least expect them"—in deep, fast slicks—as well as in their usual holding spots in pocket water and on the edge of riffles.

Effective all-season patterns for trout include nymph and adult imitations of golden stones (#8), mckenzie river specials (#10–14) with a green chenille body and deer-hair wings, and yellow and orange elk hair caddis (#8–14). Patterns that match seasonal hatches include small yellow stoneflies (#14) in June and big caddis (#8) that mimic a prolific natural hatch in October. Hare's ears (#8) and zug bugs (#8–10) are productive nymph patterns to use. Popular old standbys for summer steelhead fishing are the green butted skunk (#6), silver hilton (#8), and purple peril (#6–8). Steelhead will also go for the same orange caddis (#8) the trout go after in October. Green or blue comets (#4–6)and egg flies (#6–10) are the most popular flies used for spring-run chinook. An 8½- to 9-foot, 6–7 weight rod with floating (preferred) or sink-tip line will handle any situation on the river nicely.

McKenzie River Tributaries

Horse, Lost, and Deer creeks are all tributaries of the McKenzie with populations of native and stocked rainbows. Additionally, Horse Creek holds a few salmon and Deer Creek yields a good number of cutthroats. Several reservoirs easily accessed by roads and a myriad of hike-in alpine lakes can also be fished within a day's journey from any of the lodges located on the upper river near McKenzie Bridge. The two-hundred-thousand-acre Three Sisters Wilderness Area has over three hundred lakes offering some of the best stillwater fishing in North America. Besides abundant numbers of rainbow, brook, and brown trout, high lakes yield cutthroat and lake trout, Atlantic and kokanee salmon, and a smattering of landlocked coho and chinook salmon.

Popular lake patterns include brown, black, and olive leech patterns (#4–10), carey specials (#6–12), zug bugs (#8–14), and hare's ear nymphs (#16–18). Multiple hatches of dry flies emerging simultaneously make it extremely difficult to decipher what trout are feeding on. However, any of the hair-wing caddis variations such as the bucktail, elk hair, or tied-down caddis will take surface rising fish all season long. Damsel and dragon fly imitations are extremely productive from midsummer through September. The trick is to carry a variety of patterns in different sizes.

The Caddis Fly in Eugene is the largest supplier of fly-angling gear and tackle in the area. A multitude of roadside stores that dot the McKenzie River Highway also sell licenses and stock a limited selection of tackle. Professional guide services can be contracted through the Caddis Fly or by writing to the McKenzie River Guides Association in Vida, Oregon.

McKenzie River Area Attractions

The beautiful McKenzie River canyon offers an unequaled variety of recreational choices for a canyon of its relatively small size. The McKenzie River Highway travels the length of the river and is thickly covered with old-growth forests laced with sparkling streams. Lower down, where the canyon widens out to the Willamette Valley, fruit and nut orchards, tree farms, lush meadows, and acres of cultivated flowers awaken the eye. Sahalie Falls, where the swift McKenzie gushes over a

rocky ledge and boils down into a pristine mountain pool surrounded by moss-covered boulders, is one of the most popular stops along the scenic east-west route. Surprisingly enough, one of Oregon's top five eighteen-hole public golf courses, Tokatee, is tucked in a setting of snow-capped mountains and towering firs.

Six land tracts contained within the Olallie Ridge Special Interest Area are preserved for geologic exploration, hiking, and sightseeing. The entire area lies between the South Fork of the McKenzie and the western boundary of the Three Sisters Wilderness in the magnificent Oregon Cascade range. The Olallie Trail, along with the McKenzie River National Recreation Trail and a plethora of smaller trails around Cougar and Blue River reservoirs, gives hikers and backpackers convenient access to a variety of backcountry terrains. The Delta Old Growth Grove located near Cougar Reservoir is one of the few old-growth areas set aside for public enjoyment. An interpretive loop leads visitors through majestic 200- to 500-year-old douglas fir and red cedar.

The McKenzie River presents a real challenge to drift boats, whitewater canoes, kayaks, and rubber rafts. Numerous licensed companies offer exhilarating rides through whitewater rapids. Some include gourmet streamside buffets, fish fries, or barbecues. After partaking in the thrilling—and strenuous—adventures of the canyon, indulge in a soak in hot mineral water swimming pool at Belknap Springs. An unusual sidelight is the House of Horses Museum east of Vida, with displays of pioneer history that demonstrate what horse power has accomplished through the years.

CEDARWOOD LODGE

McKenzie Bridge, OR 97413. Phone: (503) 822-3282. Contact: Tony and Jean Puddefoot, owners and hosts. Total capacity: 28. Open March–December. Peak season: July–September. Reserve 6 months in advance. Pets per prior arrangement.

Accommodations: Seven housekeeping cabins with private bath, fireplace, deck, kitchen, and barbecue sleep 2–6. Daily maid service (extra charge); laundry facility.

Meals: N/A; meals can be obtained at the Log Cabin Inn down the road. Groceries available in town.

Rates: Inexpensive; rates vary according to length of stay. Prefer 3-night minimum stay. Cash or check.

How to Get There: Located 50 miles east of Eugene on Highway 26. Commercial airlines service airports in Eugene and Redmond; light planes can land on strip in McKenzie Bridge. Rental car recommended for local travel.

The Cedarwood Lodge, in operation as a guest lodge for sixty years, is a place of peace and tranquility arranged throughout a dense forest of cedars fronting on the McKenzie River. The absence of phone and television makes it the perfect place for adults and anglers who find their own creative enterprises entertainment enough for a relaxing vacation.

Fully furnished cabins with cozy interiors have cafe curtains, braided throw rugs, and a unique blend of country furniture.

Things to Do

Guests pursue individual interests at their own leisure. The Puddefoots highly recommend — and are available to help — anglers contract the services of local guides to get the most out of their time on the McKenzie. A small assortment of rods and reels is kept on hand for novices and youngsters. The Puddefoots are also active hikers and enjoy sharing their knowledge of the various trails throughout the valley.

Refer to McKenzie River Area Attractions for a complete listing of activities the McKenzie Valley has to offer.

Fishing

Refer to McKenzie River Area Fisheries for further information on fishing.

THE COUNTRY PLACE

56245 McKenzie Delta Road, McKenzie Bridge, OR 97401. Phone: (503) 822-6008. Contact: Wally and Myke Burnark. Total capacity: 20–22. Open year round. Peak season: June–September. Reserve 1 year in advance. Pets allowed.

Accommodations: Three rustic cabins sleep 2–4; with private bath, fireplace, kitchenette or full kitchen (full kitchen has washer and dryer), and wood. Lodge sleeps 6–24; with several baths, fireplaces, full kitchen. No daily maid service; laundry facility in nearby trailer park.

Meals: Fixed-price western-style cook-out every Saturday night; sack lunches available daily with advance notice. Meals catered for large groups and seminars by prior arrangement.

Rates: Inexpensive; daily and weekly rates available for units with full kitchens or kitchenettes, and for lodge. Required 3-day minimum stay. Cash, check, travelers checks, MasterCard, or VISA.

How to Get There: Turn south off Highway 126 onto Horse Creek Road, east of McKenzie Bridge; turn right onto McKenzie Delta Road and follow it to ranch. Commercial airlines service airports in Eugene and Redmond. Rental car recommended for local travel.

The Country Place is an inviting retreat tucked away in a peaceful forest of douglas firs. A tumultuous whitewater stretch of the beautiful McKenzie River is the only thing that moves along at a frantic pace here.

Rustic cabins nestled amidst a towering stand of trees along the McKenzie River have outdoor decks and porches and simply decorated contemporary interiors. A separate facility, the Lodge, is a Dutch Colonial mansion perfect for smaller family groups vacationing together. The spacious, wood-paneled living room has two stone fireplaces and exposed-beam ceilings. Large picture windows offer serene views of a manicured lawn bordered by lush flower gardens and thick forest.

Things to Do

Besides taking advantage of all the recreational activities the valley has to offer, guests at the Country Place can settle back and enjoy the quiet surroundings of the resort. A common rec hall contains pool and Ping-Pong tables as well as a small library. A central lawn area has a swimming pool with a slide and sundeck; equipment is provided for badminton.

Fishing

Refer to McKenzie River Area fisheries for more information on fishing. Assistance is gladly given to anglers wishing to make arrangements with local guides.

LOG CABIN INN

McKenzie Bridge, OR 97413. Phone: (503) 822-3432. Contact: Tony and Jean Puddefoot, owners and hosts. Total capacity: 30. Open March–December. Peak season: June–September. Reserve 3 months in advance; 2-night minimum for advance reservations. Pets allowed by prior arrangement.

Accommodations: Six duplex cabins with private bath, fireplace, and covered deck; two additional cabins have fully equipped kitchen. Four rooms in bed-and-breakfast lodge.

Meals: Log Cabin Inn serves three full meals daily; complimentary continental breakfast in bed-and-breakfast lodge. Full bar service.

Rates: Inexpensive; daily rates for cabins and bed-and-breakfast accommodations. Cash, check, MasterCard, or VISA.

How to Get There: Located 50 miles east of Eugene on Highway 126. Commercial airlines service airports in Eugene and Redmond; airstrip for small planes located in McKenzie Bridge. Rental car recommended for local travel.

The Log Cabin Inn is one of the oldest buildings in western Oregon and dates back to 1906; in fact, it is the oldest three-story building west of the Rockies and was originally a stagecoach stop. Located on six-and-one-half acres of prime McKenzie riverfront property reserved for the exclusive use of guests, the inn has excellent catch-and-release fishing.

Cabins are located on a perch overlooking the river a short walk away from the restaurant, the Log Cabin Inn, which serves the finest food on the river. All have lava rock fireplaces with free split wood and a covered deck and are decorated in an eclectic blend of early American and country comfortable.

Things to Do

Guests are left on their own to come and go as they please at the Log Cabin Inn. Tony and Jean Puddefoot, hosts, are very knowledgeable about the river canyon and can provide information on hiking, places of interest, and guide services. Refer to McKenzie River Area Attractions for a complete listing of activities.

Fishing

A stretch of the McKenzie running through the Log Cabin Inn property is reserved for the exclusive use of guests with fishing limited to catch and release only. This policy has increased both the quantity and quality of fishing found on the river in this section in the recent years.

Refer to McKenzie River Area Fisheries for more information on fishing.

THE WAYFARER RESORT

Star Route, Vida, OR 97488. Phone: (503) 896-3613. Contact: Mike and Karen Rodgers. Total capacity: 20. Open year round. Peak season: April 30–October 1. Reserve 1 month in advance. Pets allowed and childcare available with advance notice.

Accommodations: Thirteen cabins sleep 1–8; with private bath, pot-bellied stove, free firewood, and fully equipped kitchen and barbecue. One cabin serves large groups or seminars; with wet bar and semiprivate grounds. Daily maid service; laundry facility.

Meals: N/A

Rates: Inexpensive; daily and weekly rates. Three-day minimum stay April 20–September 15. Extra charges: baby and pet care services, maid service. Cash, check, or travelers checks, MasterCard, or VISA.

How to Get There: Located 25½ miles up Highway 126 from I-5 in Eugene. Cross river on covered bridge and follow Goodpasture Road 4 miles to lodge. Commercial airlines service airport in Eugene. Rental car recommended for local travel.

The ten-acre Wayfarer Resort blends luxury with rustic charm, and a secluded location with easy access to shopping, dining, and the arts in Eugene, making it a destination to which regulars have been returning for more than twenty-five years.

Cabins outfitted with comfortable, contemporary furnishings, and pot-bellied stoves overlook the McKenzie River and glacier-fed Maarten Creek.

Things to Do

A large lawn area is maintained for guests to enjoy volleyball, badminton, and croquet; a top-quality tennis court is only a short walk away from the cabins. Children under eleven can have fun fishing in the Wayfarer's stocked pond. The lodge provides a cozy home base from which to explore the variety of recreational activities the McKenzie River Valley has to offer. The host family will gladly help to arrange guide services and provide hiking maps for those who are interested.

For additional activities refer to McKenzie River Area Attractions.

Fishing

See McKenzie River Area Fisheries for more information on fishing.

SISTERS

Metolius River Area Fisheries

East of the McKenzie Valley, in the steep foothills of central Oregon's Cascade mountains, lies the beautiful Metolius River Recreation Area. Geographically, the region is nestled between the high desert, sagebrush plateau of the central and eastern part of the state and the lush, alpine country that shoulders the snow-capped peaks of the Cascades. Old-growth ponderosas, white firs, and lodgepole and tamarack pine reach above a forest floor overgrown with manzanita, wild huckleberries, and mountain laurel. The sheltered eastern side of the Cascades receives less than twelve inches of precipitation annually, ensuring bright, sunny days and cool evenings most of the summer. Besides perfect weather, the Metolius region enjoys another advantage making it an ideal vacation spot for the entire family: It is conveniently located within an hour or two of several resort areas, including Black Butte Ranch, Bend, and Sun River, all of which offer a variety of cultural and recreational opportunities.

Metolius River Drainage

The beautiful spring-fed Metolius is the main fishery that draws anglers to the Camp Sherman area. Alpine lakes and streams throughout the Deschutes National Forest and the Sisters and Mount Washington wilderness areas also offer excellent fishing opportunities for small- to fair-sized rainbows, brooks, and browns.

The Metolius River percolates up to the surface from natural springs running beneath Black Butte. From its headwaters, the river travels thirty-one miles north, then east, eventually emptying into Lake Billy Chinook—a high-use recreational spot for waterskiing, board sailing, and lake trolling. The Metolius averages thirty to forty feet in width with a year-round water temperature of 49 to 52 degrees. Eight- to fourteen-inch rainbows are the predominate trout species, with a goodly number of browns. A few dolly vardens reaching the five- to ten-pound range, with a seventeen-pounder being one of the largest recorded, are also present.

Although experienced anglers consistently take up to six good-size fish of twelve to fourteen inches per day, the Metolius is not an easy river to fish. The water's clarity and relatively slow pace make fly presentation critical. The absence of boulders and logjams that would ordinarily provide good cover and create holes for fish to hold up in also inhibit a higher catch rate. As guide John Harken of the Patient Angler Fly Shop in Bend puts it, "It takes a lot of finesse to do well knowing that fish can be anywhere in the river."

Prolific caddis (#14–18) and mayfly (#14–20) hatches occur on the Metolius all year round with ant patterns (#14–16) producing well all summer long. Green drakes (#9) perform from the end of May into June until dry golden stones (#8–10) take over the end of June. Golden stones stay on the river well into August and up to September, when the local hatch comes full circle, returning to caddis and mayfly patterns. A large, orange caddis (#8–10) hatch finishes out the season in October. The best time of day to fish is from midday to evening as tree cover along the banks slows the morning hatch rate.

The Metolius is closed to fishing from a floating device and all native fish must be returned to the river unharmed. A limited number of hatchery fish, identified by a clipped fin, can be kept. Waders are not necessary as much of the fishing is done from the bank, requiring average casts of twenty-five feet and under. The river is restricted to fly fishing only from Lake Creek down to Bridge 99.

Secondary Metolius River Drainages

Secondary fisheries that can be reached within a day's drive from the Metolius area include the Deschutes and Crooked rivers, both of which carve deep canyons through the high-desert country of central Oregon. Fly anglers wishing to fish either the Deschutes or Crooked rivers can contact the Patient Angler or the Fly Box in Bend for guide information. On the western slopes of the Cascades, the McKenzie River is also fairly accessible. For more information on the McKenzie refer to McKenzie River Area Fisheries.

The Camp Sherman Store and Fly Shop in Camp Sherman is the most centrally located outlet for purchasing licenses. It carries a wide selection of hand-tied flies and custom-made rods and also sponsors a number of fly-fishing classes and seminars conducted by experts in the field. Topics range from specialty fly tying, casting and streamside entomology, to photography for fishermen. Classes are limited; advanced registration is necessary to assure a space. Contact the Camp Sherman Store for an itinerary of their summer workshops. The store also works closely with local Metolius River guides and can arrange their services for interested anglers. The Patient Angler and the Fly Box in Bend are additional sources for licenses, tackle, gear, and guide information.

Metolius River Area Attractions

The Metolius River Recreation Area offers fishing, horseback riding, hiking, boating, sailing, and waterskiing. The Sisters Ranger District of the Deschutes National Forest publishes a directory of day hikes within the forest and its two wildernesses, the Sisters and Mount Washington areas, located in close proximity to the Metolius region. Several local packers offer full accommodation and spot drop trips into the back country as well as rent saddle horses for guided scenic trail rides. Most of the trails access streams and alpine lakes with fair to good fishing for small rainbows, brooks, and browns. West of Camp Sherman, Blue Lake Resort has a marina for boat rentals, a restaurant, a swimming pond, and stables that offer guided rides, pack trips, and hayrides. Located a little farther west of Blue Lake, the beautiful McKenzie River Highway's upper reaches are well worth a day's ride.

East of Camp Sherman, Black Butte Ranch has two eighteen-hole golf courses with additional public courses located in Redmond and Bend. The restored, western town of Sisters hosts the "biggest little rodeo in the world" each June and is a short drive away. Northeast of Sisters, off Highway 97—the main north-south route through central Oregon—the towering pinnacles of Smith Rocks offer challenging rock climbing.

Between Redmond and Smith Rocks, the highway crosses over the 403-feet-deep Crooked River Gorge—breathtakingly sheer lava walls created by the river's carving action.

South of Redmond, the bustling, four-season resort town of Bend is an oasis in the high desert offering the widest variety of cultural and recreational opportunities east of the Oregon Cascades. The restored downtown sector is situated along the scenic banks of the Deschutes River against the stunning backdrop of the mountains. First-class restaurants, art galleries, and chic boutiques dot the main streets along with classic eateries, antique shops and book and gift stores. The town hosts a variety of summertime events including performances by a reputable community theater, the Cascade Festival of Music, and a spectacular Fourth of July celebration. A short drive south of Bend, Lava Lands Visitor Center and the Oregon High Desert Museum entice those interested in the region's natural history.

Summer events visitors should also include in their travels are Redmond's Deschutes County Fair and Camp Sherman's Camp Sherman Days. The Days are an excellent opportunity for everyone to experience what early community life was like. Events include a square dance, fishing derby, an old-fashioned picnic, and tours of the Community Hall and Schoolhouse.

HOUSE ON THE METOLIUS

P.O. Box 601, Camp Sherman, OR 97730. Phone: (503) 595-6620 and (415) 964-8585. Contact: Kendra Van Patten, manager. Total capacity: 20–23. Open mid-May–early October. Peak season: June and September. Reserve 4–6 months in advance. Pets by permission only.

Accommodations: Two cabins, one duplex, and four studio units sleep 2–6; with private bath, fireplace, free wood, kitchen or kitchenette, and deck or courtyard. Daily maid service for stays longer than 1 week.

Meals: N/A. Restaurants and grocery stores in Camp Sherman area, and in Sisters, Redmond, and Bend.

Rates: Inexpensive; daily rates include lodging and private fishing on the Metolius. Cash, check, travelers checks, or VISA.

How to Get There: Located 2 miles downstream from Camp Sherman. Follow Highway 20 for 10 miles west of Sisters and follow signs to Camp Sherman. Commercial airlines service airport in Redmond; airstrip for small planes in Sisters, Bend, and Redmond. Buses stop in Sisters daily. Rental car recommended for local travel.

House on the Metolius embraces two-hundred acres of scenic ponderosa pine forests and lush meadowlands on the eastern slopes of central Oregon's Cascade Mountains. Quaint housekeeping cabins with deck or stone courtyard and a charming splash of flowers displayed in window boxes, hanging planters, and miniature gardens either front a gorge section of the Metolius or overlook a meandering meadow stretch that disappears in the distance against a majestic backdrop of snow-capped Mount Jefferson and Three-Fingered Jack. The House on the Metolius is particularly appealing to anglers who want to fish on the resort's private, one-half-mile section of river, thereby avoiding the more crowded stretches open to the public.

The units are widely spaced along a beautifully manicured lawn, dotted with mammoth ponderosas and douglas firs, with a playground complete with swings and slides. Guests also have use of the Tamarack Room, which houses a small library, board games, and a VCR.

Things to Do

Fly fishing on the Metolius and exploring the natural wonders of the surrounding Deschutes National Forest are the primary recreational pursuits of guests staying at House on the Metolius. Refer to Metolius River Area Attractions for a variety of local activities in the area.

Fishing

Within the resort's boundary, the Metolius moves through a narrow, barely accessible gorge section into a meandering meadow stretch averaging forty feet to seventy feet across. Grassy banks provide ample casting room; wading is not required as the river is fairly free of obstructions that require tricky mending. Angling on the property is restricted to fly fishing, barbless hook only. General restrictions for the river that require catch-and-release of all native fish apply here as well. A limited number of hatchery fish, identified by a notched fin, can be kept. The resort's staff are happy to assist anglers in setting up professional guide services for float trips on the McKenzie or Deschutes rivers. Anglers must provide their own transportation.

LAKE CREEK LODGE

Star Route, Sisters, OR 97759. Phone: (503) 595-6331. Contact: Diana Peperling, manager. Total capacity: 35–60; 25-guest minimum to reserve entire facility. Open year round. Peak season: July and August. Reserve 1 year in advance. No pets in summer.

Accommodations: Four cottages with private bath, refrigerator, and porch sleep up to 4; 12 homes with fully equipped kitchen, screened-in porch, and private bath sleep 2–8. Daily maid service in cottages; laundry facility in Camp Sherman.

Meals: A la carte breakfast; buffet-style dinner; lunch available in cafe in Camp Sherman. All alcohol is BYOB.

Rates: Moderate; weekly and daily rates for homes and cottages include lodging and dinner July–October. Cash, check, or travelers checks.

How to Get There: Located west of Sisters off Highway 20. Commercial airlines service airport in Redmond; airstrip for small planes in Sisters, Bend, and Redmond. Free airport pick-up by prior arrangement. Buses stop in Sisters daily. Rental car recommended for local travel.

Located in the midst of the Deschutes National Forest in Metolius River country, Lake Creek Lodge exudes the serene ambiance of a country inn where comfort and hospitality are trademarks. Cottages, "homes," and a main lodge, nestled beneath a canopy of old-growth ponderosa pine and douglas fir around scenic Lake Creek Pond, feature knotty pine walls and electric heat. The centrally located main lodge houses a dining room, a rec hall, and a lounge area that serves as a gathering place for guests.

Things to Do

Guests are free to do as they like: fish the clear, spring-fed waters of the Metolius, golf ten minutes away, bicycle, hike, and horseback ride. A local outfitter, High Cascades Adventures, offers hayrides every Wednesday night as well as daily guided trail rides throughout the Deschutes National Forest. Outdoor activities offered at Lake Creek include volleyball, shuffleboard, horseshoes, swimming in a heated pool, paddle tennis, and tennis. Guests also have use of pool and Ping-Pong tables in the main lodge.

Fishing

The lodge staff works with the Camp Sherman Store to set guests up with professional guides on the Metolius, McKenzie, and Deschutes rivers. The store is also the most convenient place to purchase fishing licenses and a wide variety of gear and tackle.

Refer to the Metolius River Area Fisheries section for additional information on fishing.

ROSEBURG

North Umpqua River Area Fisheries

The legendary summer steelhead and spring chinook fishery of the North Umpqua is touted as being the "finishing school for fly angling steelheaders." The upper stretch above Winchester Dam is also home to rainbow, brook, and brown trout. Originating high in the Oregon Cascades at Diamond Lake, this treasured stream carves its way through miles of old-growth timber on its way to the southern part of the state. The river's rich heritage is attributed in part to such legendary figures as Zane Grey, Jack Hemingway, and Ernie Schwiebert, who have spent many summers challenging the tenacious seagoing rainbows that inhabit this pristine mountain fishery.

North Umpqua River Drainage

Strong currents, tricky wading on slick, lichen-covered boulders, and sixty- to eighty-foot casts make the North Umpqua extremely difficult to fish. In addition, steelhead are notorious fighters and very unpredictable. Anglers have gone away year after year without a hook-up only to return again for the hoped-for thrill of nailing one of these powerful silver-bodied torpedoes. The North Umpqua's gin-clear, emerald-tinged water is another distinguishing feature of the river. Its clarity allows steelheaders to "spot" their quarry as they drive along Highway 138, which runs along most of the thirty-six-mile section designated for fly fishing, catch-and-release only. Steelhead inhabiting the North Umpqua average six to ten pounds with fish up to fifteen to twenty pounds recorded. Although it's possible to hook fish on a fly anytime of year, the pace is usually slow until the middle of July, with the best fishing occurring between August and October. Wet fly fishing for steelhead requires precise and continual mending of line so that the swing of the fly is as slow as possible.

A good selection of productive, dark-patterned wet flies (#8-10) includes skunks, green butt skunks, silver hiltons, muddler minnows, and black gordons. In October large, bushy dry patterns that float well such as caddis, steelhead bees, and royal wulffs work the best. Smaller rainbows, cutts, and browns will go after old-favorite standbys such as spruce flies, bucktail coachmans, and tied-down caddis. Nine-foot to ten-and-a-half-foot, 7-10 weight rods are required for steelhead fishing, while lighter rods will handle smaller trout. Line selection includes floating, sink tip, and shooting heads for special situations where long casts are required. Recommended tippets run from 6-10 pounds, and, as the water clears in late summer, 12-15 foot leaders are the norm. Wading shoes (or traction devices of any type) are a must; a wading staff is advised. Numerous local guides offer half- and full-day walk-and-wade trips on the upper river and float trips on the stretch below the fly-angling-only water.

Steelheaders can contact the Umpqua Fisherman's Association, P.O. Box 2083, Roseburg, OR 97470, to obtain a list of active guides. A number of small convenience markets up and down the river sell licenses and a limited selection of tackle.

North Umpqua River Area Attractions

Fly angling for steelhead is the major recreational pursuit of visitors to the upper North Umpqua area. Bait-and-lure angling from drift boats is popular on the lower river. Whitewater raft trips offered by local companies challenge Class 3 rapids on the river. Swimming and kayaking are also popular sports on the main river as well as on numerous feeder creeks.

Hikers and backpackers have easy access to countless trails throughout the North Umpqua National Forest, which borders the river along most of its length. Diamond Lake and famous Crater Lake are two scenic attractions located in the middle of the nearby Cascade Range. Diamond Lake has horseback riding, fishing, marina facilities with boats to rent, and a lodge and restaurant. Crater Lake, surrounded by Crater Lake National Park, is renowned for its beauty and unique location in the center of an ancient volcanic crater. Wildlife Safari and several Oregon wineries are also within an easy day's drive.

STEAMBOAT INN

Tokette Route, Box 36, Idleyld Park, OR 97447. Phone: (503) 496-3495/498-2411. Contact: Jim and Sharon Van Loan. Total capacity: 32–40. Open year round. Peak season: July–October. Reserve 3 months in advance for weekends. No pets.

Accommodations: Eight riverside cabins with bath and porch; 4 cabins with bath, fireplace, and kitchenette. Daily maid service; laundry facility.

Meals: A la carte breakfast and lunch open to the public; gourmet dinners by reservation only. Wine served with dinner.

Rates: Inexpensive; daily rates include lodging only. Children under 16, free. Extra charges: Fisherman's dinner, pick-up from Roseburg airport. Cash, check, travelers checks, MasterCard, or VISA.

How to Get There: Located 38 miles east of Roseburg, OR, on scenic Highway 138. Commercial airlines service airports in Eugene and Medford, 2½ hours away; airstrip for small planes in Roseburg.

The Steamboat Inn sits halfway along a thirty-six-mile stretch of the North Umpqua River reserved for fly angling only. From its gravel turnout along Highway 138, the Inn looks like a typical quick-stop roadhouse. However, inside Steamboat's public restaurant the ambience is that of a quiet, country wayside retreat. Featured in *Country Inns and Back Roads* and a member of Unique Northwest Country Inns, Steamboat attracts two types of visitors: anglers who come to fish the North Umpqua and gourmets in search of exquisite dining.

Pine-paneled cabins tucked serenely along the high bank of the North Umpqua in a majestic setting of ancient Douglas firs share a covered veranda overlooking the roiling river below while guest cottages approximately one-half mile away, nestle into the trees along Steamboat Creek. The main lodge houses an intimate dining room open to the public, a well-stocked fly shop, and an area with snack items and beverages.

Steamboat Inn is renowned for its exceptional food. A half-hour after sundown, a closed sign is posted in the window and only those with reservations can partake of one of the most delightful dining experiences to be found on the Pacific Coast. The event is so spectacular that people drive the long distances from Seattle, Portland, Ashland, and Eugene to indulge. Aperitifs and hot hors d'oeuvres are served before guests sit down to a twenty-foot long table sawed from a single slab of sugar pine and set with linens and candles, while a fire crackles in a stone hearth in the corner.

Fishing

Steamboat's Fly Shop sells licenses and stocks a good selection of rods, reels, and tackle. Local guide services can also be arranged through the shop. See North Umpqua River Area Fisheries for more fishing information.

TIMBER RIVER

22113 North Umpqua Highway, Idleyd Park, OR 97447. Phone: (503) 496-0114. Contact: Ray or Patty Lillard, managers. Total capacity: 12. Open year round. Peak season: March–November. Reserve 3 months in advance. Pets are allowed outdoors only.

Accommodations: Modern riverside cabins with full kitchen, bath, sleeping lofts, and fireplace sleep 2–6; towels and linens provided. Daily maid service; laundry facility.

Meals: N/A. Meals available at Red Barn, Muchies, and Steamboat Inn.

Rates: Inexpensive; daily rates. Cash, check, or travelers checks.

How to Get There: Located in Idleyd Park, one-half hour drive east of Roseburg, OR, on Highway 138. Commercial airlines service airports in Eugene and Medford. Rental car recommended for local travel.

Timber River, located a few miles west of the thirty-six mile stretch of the North Umpqua's fly-angling-only water, has guest facilities that are ideal for those looking for the low-budget alternative that only housekeeping accommodations can offer.

Things to Do

Refer to North Umpqua River Area Attractions.

Fishing

Refer to North Umpqua River Area Fisheries for more fishing information.

GOLD BEACH

Rogue River Area Fisheries

Staying at one of a handful of remote, riverside hideaways accessible only by boat or foot travel is vital to discovering what the Rogue River canyon in southern Oregon is all about. Although steep banks covered with dense vegetation and boulders interspersed with sheer basalt bluffs make travel extremely difficult, hearty Sierra Club types return annually to enjoy the beauty, peace, and serenity of this wild canyon.

Rogue River Drainage

The Rogue River is a top-producing fishery for spring and fall chinook, summer and winter steelhead, and trout in its upper reaches. Although busy jetboat traffic and intense angling pressure have had adverse effects on the quality of the river's once world-class fishery, local efforts and the creation of a salmon-trout enhancement program promise to renew — indeed, have already immensely improved — the Rogue's legendary status. It is also one of the few federally designated wild and scenic rivers.

The Rogue originates near Crater Lake in the Oregon Cascades and flows 215 miles to the Pacific Coast at Gold Beach. Although the river is accessible by road in its lower part, most of the river is reached only by whitewater boat and hiking trail. Rafting permits are required on the wild and scenic section and only a limited number of permits are issued by a lottery to preserve the river's natural environs. Numerous jetboat companies run tours and shuttles up the river, and close to fifty guides offer float trips between the mouth and the upper limits of salmon and steelhead angling.

The lower river from the mouth thirty miles upstream has good fishing through summer and fall. Spring-run chinook enter the river in May and continue into July when summer steelhead begin to make their run. Feisty half-pounders — steelies that move into the ocean in March and return upriver in midsummer — averaging twelve to eighteen inches and from one and three-quarter

pounds to three pounds also move into the Rogue in July, migrating upriver through October. Larger winter steelhead averaging eight to ten pounds are abundant November through March. Fall chinook salmon and a smaller number of coho show up in the lower river in July and October and progress upstream through December. Rogue chinook average twenty pounds with fish up to thirty to forty pounds taken occasionally. The best time to fish is during fall and winter when the armada of recreational jetboaters, canoers, kayakers, and rafters diminishes, allowing the contemplative angler relative peace.

Stonefly hatches start near the mouth in mid-May moving upriver until the end of July. Coachman-type streamers (#6–8) and split-wing

flies pulsed through the water two to four inches below the surface like a nymph are popular and effective. The recommended gear is a 8½-foot, 7–9 weight rod with 10-foot sink-tip or dry line.

Tackle shops in Gold Beach sell the required licenses and steelhead and salmon permits. They also carry all the gear and tackle for the Rogue and can provide information on local guides. A limited selection of angling items are available at the Cougar Lane Store across the river from Agness and at Illahe Lodge.

Rogue River Area Attractions

The Rogue Wilderness encompasses the Wild and Scenic Rogue River canyon and is included in the one-million-acre Siskiyou National Forest. The Siskiyou Mountains, which bridge the Cascade and Coast ranges extending between Oregon and California, are referred to as the "botanist's paradise." A diverse variety of plants within this area are indigenous to different east-west and north-south climes and protected under federal law.

The most popular route of travel through the wilderness, the Rogue River Trail has numerous, well-marked side paths for hikers and backpackers to explore. The forest is inhabited by an abundance of black-tailed deer, elk, and raccoon with rare sightings of black bear and mink. An array of birds commonly seen include the blue heron, merganser, kingfisher, cliff swallow, osprey, and bald eagle.

Rafting, tubing, and jetboating are a popular way for summer visitors to tour the scenic Rogue River canyon. Several commercial raft and jetboat companies in Gold Beach and Grants Pass offer half- and full-day adventure trips with lunch stopovers at a wilderness lodge.

HALF MOON BAR LODGE

Agness-Illahe Road, Agness, OR 97406. Phone: (503) 476-4002. Contact: Willis Crouse, manager. Total capacity: 20. Open April 15–November 15. Peak steelhead season: August–November 1. Reserve 6 months in advance. No pets.

Accommodations: Eight guest rooms share baths; electricity available though kerosene lamps are encouraged. Clean linens daily; laundry facility.

Meals: Three family-style meals daily on American Plan; hot breakfast, lunch, gourmet dinners. Wine served with dinner; all other alcohol is BYOB.

Rates: Moderate; daily rates include lodging, meals, jetboat "spotting service" for anglers, and lodge activities. Cash or check only.

How to Get There: Reach by jetboat service daily from Gold Beach or Agness, OR. Pick-up by lodge boat if necessary. Backpackers can hike in on the Rogue River Trail, 11 miles upriver from Foster Bar boat landing near Agness. Charter flights available from Mike Wilson, Pacific Flight Service, Medford-Jackson County Airport, (503) 779-5445.

Half Moon Bar Lodge, tucked deep within the Rogue River Wilderness surrounded by mountains rising several thousand feet above its perch on a horseshoe bend of the river, is set amidst majestic 200- to 300-year-old fir trees, bay laurel, oak, wild azalea, and iris. Half Moon's gracious, highly personal, and informal hospitality gives it a unique quality that places the lodge in a class of its own.

Guest rooms are modestly and comfortably furnished with warmth provided by propane heaters and country patchwork quilts. Although electricity is provided by a portable generator, the use of kerosene lamps is encouraged to preserve the peace of the surrounding wilderness. A spacious building with dining area, library, and pool table, the main lodge's pot-bellied stove, open-beam ceiling, thick, vertically stacked log walls, and lounge chairs attract guests dedicated to comfort.

Things to Do

Life at Half Moon is simple and guests pursue their own diversions. The lodge offers a jetboat spotting service that taxis steelhead and salmon anglers to choice wading water, where they're dropped off for a predetermined span of time. If notified beforehand, Half Moon will book the services of an independent guide for interested guests.

Besides fishing, the brisk, clear-running waters of the Rogue also offer opportunities for gold panning, tubing, and swimming. Wilderness hiking trails and self-guided nature and photography walks radiate in all directions from the lodge. Those who wish to hike the Rogue River Trail are ferried across the river to where the trail parallels the river and picked up later on. Between leisurely jaunts in the wilderness, guests can grab a good book off the shelf in the lodge, play pool, or relax in a sauna nearby. Lawn games such as volleyball and horseshoes can be set up for guests who want to play.

Fishing

See Rogue River Area Fisheries for more information on fishing.

ILLAHE LODGE

37709 Agness-Illahe Road, Agness, OR 97406. Phone: (503) 247-6111. Contact: Ernest, Violet, or Carolyn Rutledge, owners. Total capacity: 26. Open year round. Peak season: mid-August–November 1. Reserve 1 year in advance. No pets.

Accommodations: Twelve bedrooms in lodge sleep 2–3. Daily maid service; laundry facility.

Meals: Three family-style meals daily on American Plan; breakfast, hot lunch, dinner. All alcohol is BYOB.

Rates: Moderate; daily rates include lodging and meals. Extra charges: guide services and boat. Cash, check, or travelers checks.

How to Get There: Located 37 miles upriver from Gold Beach and 7 miles upriver from Agness on Agness-Illahe Road. Illahe accessible by road from Roseburg via Highway 42 in Powers. Commercial airlines service airport in Medford. Jetboat service daily from Gold Beach or Agness, OR. Rental car recommended for local travel.

Illahe Lodge/Guide Service was started in 1943 by Ernest Rutledge's grandfather and is presently into its third generation of owner/operators. The Wild and Scenic Rivers Act now prohibits vehicular travel in the wilderness starting just upstream from the lodge, so Illahe Lodge is the last road access on the Rogue. The Rutledges specialize in fall fly fishing for half-pounders from mid-August through October. They also guide fly-fishing trips for winter steelhead and spring salmon, although artificial lures and trolling have become the most popular angling method.

Simply furnished guest facilities consist of the main lodge and an out building; a downstairs bedroom with a private bath is reserved for guests unable to climb the stairs. The main lodge, a two-story wood structure with cedar shingles, has a serene view of the Rogue River from its hillside perch; it houses the dining room and a spacious knotty pine–paneled living room used for socializing. Roomy lounge chairs take advantage of a crackling fire in the rock fireplace, and guests have use of a piano, organ, and accordion stored here for evening entertainment.

Things to Do

Illahe Lodge accommodates sightseeing excursions on the river. The Rogue River Trail passes between the lodge and the river, providing hikers with easy access to the Rogue Wilderness upstream.

Fishing

Guided fishing trips outfitted by the Rutledges have kept the lodge in business by word-of-mouth since 1943. Guides fish two customers per motor-powered alumiweld boat (designed by Ernest Rutledge). Most groups average six customers to three guides, with smaller and larger groups accommodated by special arrangement. Anglers are taken to choice spots on the river to fish while guides row. Illahe is about the only guide service working this stretch of river that encourages fly casting rather than trolling. Although experienced anglers prefer to bring their own gear, equipment is available at no extra charge.

Licenses are available at the Cougar Lane store located approximately seven miles downstream. Locally tied flies are sold at the lodge.

PARADISE LODGE

Box 456, Gold Beach, OR 97444. Radio phone: (503) 247-6022. Contact: Allen and Meryl Boice, owners. Total capacity: 40. Open year round. Peak season: July–October. Reserve in advance for July and August. Pets allowed.

Accommodations: Seven motel rooms with private bath sleep 2; cabins with private bath and pot-bellied stove sleep up to 8. Daily maid service; laundry facility.

Meals: Three family-style meals daily; fixed-price all-you-can-eat buffet breakfast and lunch, sack lunches available, full dinner. Full-service bar.

Rates: Moderate; overnight rates include meals and lodging. Family and group rates negotiable. Special rates for children; children under 4, free. Extra charges: guide services. Cash, check, travelers checks, MasterCard or VISA.

How to Get There: Reach by jetboat service daily from Gold Beach or Agness, OR. Pick-up by lodge boat if necessary. Backpackers can hike in 11 miles on the Rogue River Trail from Gold Beach or Agness. Paradise's private air charter, Rogue Air Service, has room for 3–5 passengers from Gold Beach or Medford; arrange through lodge.

Paradise Lodge sits eighty feet above the Rogue River at the lower stretch of the designated "wild and scenic" section fifty-two miles east of Gold Beach, Oregon. It is at the top end of the longest trip—104 miles round-trip—offered by commercial jetboat services out of Gold Beach. Paradise is the designated luncheon stopover for these tours, and the lodge accommodates many overnight passengers who want to split their river trip into two days. Paradise is much more public than Illahe or Half Moon Bar, and many guests enjoy the congenial hosts and the choice of cabin accommodations it has to offer.

Modern, motel-type rooms offer contemporary furnishings and a river view. Outlying cabins situated in a grassy meadow overlook four acres of fruit trees and vegetable gardens uphill from the lodge. Interiors are a homey blend of country-western featuring braided rugs, cafe curtains, pot-bellied stoves, refurbished stage trunks, carved oak rockers, and a combination of cedar shingle and wood-paneled walls.

The main lodge, built in 1953, is an impressive wooden structure that serves as a restaurant to resident guests and jetboat passengers alike. Drop-beam ceilings, pine paneling, a pot-bellied stove, and a huge collection of historic and humorous photographs welcome travelers. Long picnic tables decked with cheerful white and brown checked cloths have been set up in rows to seat large crowds. A half-wall partition allows diners to observe cooks preparing all-you-can-eat meals on antique, wood-burning stoves.

Things to Do

The Rogue River Trail passes right through the lodge property, giving hikers and backpackers easy access to the surrounding wilderness. Horseshoes and volleyball are set up for visitors who just want to relax around the lodge and enjoy the scenic beauty. Paradise Lodge will also set guests up for professionally guided raft trips in summer and steelhead fishing trips in fall.

Fishing

Refer to Rogue River Area Fisheries for more fishing information. Guests must come equipped with fishing gear; tackle and licenses can be purchased at tackle shops in Gold Beach.

KLAMATH FALLS

TAKE IT EASY FLY FISHING RESORT

P.O. Box 408, Fort Klamath, OR 97626. Phone: (503) 381-2328. Contact: Randy and Cynthia Sparacino, owners. Total capacity: 22–30. Open last weekend of April–October 31. No pets.

Accommodations: Five duplex cabins with private bath and electric heat sleep up to 4.

Meals: Hot breakfast and gourmet dinner daily on modified American Plan; nominal fee for sack lunch; cocktails and barbecue on Friday night. Wine served with dinner.

Rates: Moderate; daily rates include lodging, 2 meals a day, fishing in ranch streams, ranch activities, and use of ranch facilities. Two-night minimum stay. Extra charges: wade trip on headwaters of the Williamson, float trip on the main Williamson, Rogue River jet trip, guided trips on the Wood and Sprague rivers, pick-up from Chiloquin airport. Cash, check, travelers checks, MasterCard, or VISA.

How to Get There: Located on Highway 62 at junction of Highway 232, one-half hour from Klamath Falls, OR. Commercial airlines service airport in Klamath Falls; airstrip for small planes at Chiloquin airport, 15 minutes from ranch. Rental car recommended for local travel.

Located in the beautiful Wood River Valley of south-central Oregon, Take It Easy is one of a handful of western lodges catering specifically to fly anglers. Superb fishing opportunities on guided trips on the Williamson—a large spring-fed river with sections yielding native rainbows in the three- to twelve-pound class—and on the Rogue River, renowned for the largest number of summer-run steelhead on the West Coast, lure anglers back year after year. Trophy-size rainbow, brown, and brook trout are also found in abundance in a number of lakes and other secondary streams nearby, such as the Sprague and Wood rivers and Spring Creek.

Superb meals, guided float and wade trips, and personalized instruction in fly tying and casting make Take It Easy the premier location for anglers who want to experience the quality and variety of fishing that southern Oregon has to offer.

Modern duplex cabins nestled in a secluded, forested setting along Fort Creek are decorated with attractive contemporary furnishings accented by arched cathedral ceilings and large picture windows overlooking cozy front porches and the creek beyond.

The single-story, ranch house lodge complex is located a short walk from the cabins across a footbridge. The main lodge dining room is an intimate, natural log building with an immense stone fireplace and a long wall of windows overlooking a streamside lawn. A complete fly shop stocked with all the gear and tackle anglers will need along with rods and waders to rent adjoins the dining room by way of a sheltered veranda. Next to the fly shop, a fly-tying and activity room is equipped with tying tables, vises, tools, and a wide selection of fly-tying materials. This room also has an impressive library of fishing magazines and books, and a comfortable arrangement of couches and lounge chairs for relaxing, slide presentations, and other regularly scheduled programs. Next door, the Ruckus Room has a pool table, Ping-Pong table, piano, and card tables.

Things to Do

Although most guests here indulge in fly fishing to their heart's content, a number of nearby points of interest are worth a visit. Scenic Crater

Lake National Park in the middle of the high Cascades is easily reached by good paved road and the views are breathtaking. Collier State Park has a unique logging museum covering acres of land, and Lava Lands National Monument is a short drive away. South of Fort Klamath, Agency Lake and Upper Klamath Lake abut wilderness areas and a wildlife refuge. The area is also known for a population of white pelicans that summers there. Across the road from Take It Easy, the Fort Klamath Museum offers a small tribute to pioneer days in the Wood River Valley. Hikers and backpackers have easy access to unlimited trails throughout the Winema National Forest adjoining the ranch.

Fishing

Two spring-fed creeks flowing through the ranch harbor rainbows up to four pounds and are designated fly-fishing-only, catch-and-release with barbless hooks.

The major fisheries covered by Take It Easy's professional guide service include the Williamson and the Rogue. The fishing season starts off with walk-and-wade trips on the headwaters of the Williamson the last weekend of May through June 30. Rainbows in this large, meadow-spring creek made famous by its black drake hatch run up to twenty-two inches. Native brooks run up to fourteen inches.

From June 15 through October 15, a seven-mile float beginning at the junction of the Sprague River and the main Williamson becomes the main angling attraction. From this confluence—known as Blue Hole—on down, the warmer waters of the Sprague combine with the cooler spring-fed waters of the upper Williamson to create ideal water temperatures for native rainbows, which can run well over ten pounds as a result. Eighteen inchers are a common occurrence. These large rainbows grow rapidly—up to twenty inches in a three-year cycle—in Klamath Lake and move into the river from late June through October to escape the lake's summer warming trend. Good-size browns also inhabit the river below Spring Creek. Private landholdings on both sides of the lower river plus tricky floating and tackle regulations almost necessitate the use of a knowledgeable guide.

Prolific caddis and mayfly hatches predominate in June and July, with a large October caddis hatch taking over in the fall. Black and white patterns such as the marabou leech and muddler or bucktail coachman will carry the peak of the season from August through September.

From August 20 through October 31, float trips down the famous "wild" Rogue River for summer steelhead are offered. Refer to Rogue River Area Fisheries for more fishing information.

Take It Easy also arranges trips on the Sprague and Wood rivers in the Fort Klamath area. The Wood River is a perfect, crystal-clear, spring-fed fly-water stream requiring light, long leaders. Generally less than fifteen feet in width, the river is characterized by undercut banks, logjams, and deep pools as it meanders through meadowlands. Native rainbows and a fair number of browns run up to four to five pounds. Fair-size brooks are also present in the stream. Permission is needed to fish lower sections which run through privately owned grazing lands.

The Sprague River has its headwaters in the mountains southeast of Bly, Oregon. Managed for wild trout, the river offers good fishing for rainbows, with a fewer number of browns, up to three pounds and better. The Sprague is an early-season producer with its peak fishing period occurring in late spring and early summer. Large streamers and bucktails are the preferred patterns. Angling is restricted to artificial flies and lures only below the Chiloquin Dam.

The Take It Easy Fly Shop is well equipped to handle the angling needs for any of the fisheries in the Fort Klamath area. Fly-casting and fly-tying lessons are provided at an hourly rate and fly-fishing schools are arranged for larger groups.

WASHINGTON

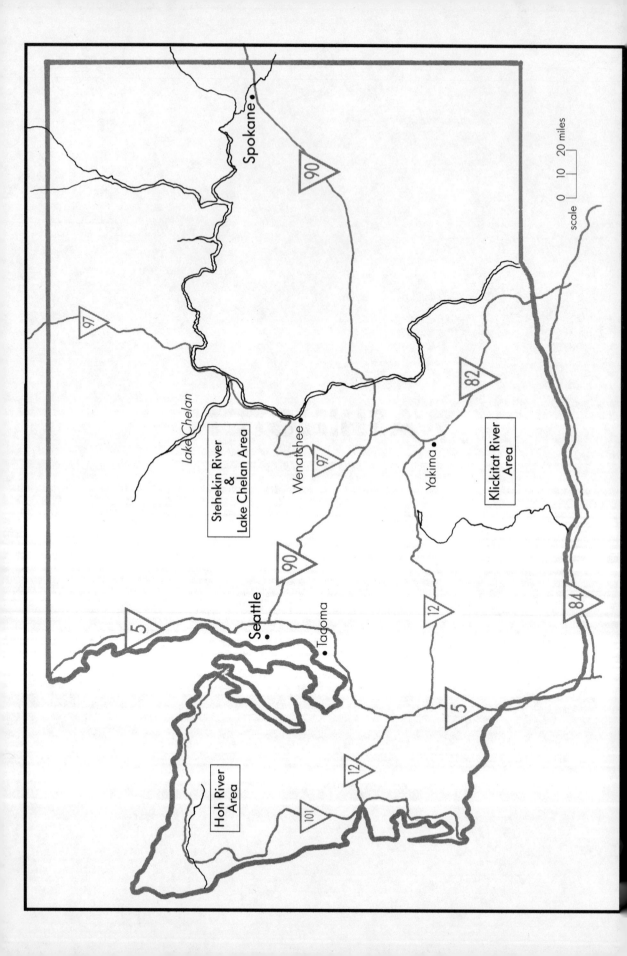

OLYMPIC PENINSULA

LAKE QUINAULT LODGE

P.O. Box 7, Quinault, WA 98575. Phone: 1 (800) 562-6672 (toll-free in Washington State) or (206) 288-2571. Total capacity: 150–200. Open year round. Off season: October 1–May 30. Peak season: June 1–September 30. Pets allowed only in Lakeside Inn.

Accommodations: Bedrooms with private bath in main lodge; motel rooms with private bath, gas fireplace, and balcony adjoin main lodge. Separate facility houses additional rooms. Daily maid service; laundry facility.

Meals: A la carte meals available in lodge dining room. Full-service bar.

Rates: Moderate; daily rates include lodging only. Convention rates available September 16–April 30; honeymoon rates available May 1–October 31. Cash, check, travelers checks, MasterCard, or VISA.

How to Get There: Located 4 hours from Portland, OR, and 3½ hours from Seattle, WA. Take Highway 101 north 40 miles from Aberdeen-Hoquiam; take Lake Quinault South Shore Recreation Area exit; follow South Shore Road 2 miles to lodge. Commercial airlines service airport in Seattle; commuter airlines connect with Aberdeen's Bowerman Field. Float plane service to Lake Quinault Lodge can be arranged through Chrysler Air out of Lake Union in Seattle. Rental car recommended for local travel.

Lake Quinault Lodge, a quietly elegant yet informal retreat, is located in the heart of northwest Washington's Olympic Peninsula. Surrounded by the Olympic National Forest, Olympic National Park, and the Quinault Indian Reservation, the lodge and its guest facilities are graciously ensconced in a lush rain forest unique to the Pacific Northwest. The dramatic difference between austere coastal beaches and rugged snow-capped mountains in the Olympic Peninsula's interior can be viewed in a leisurely day's drive. Premier fishing for summer- and winter-run steelhead and fall- and spring-run chinook on the Soleduck, Calawah, Bogachiel, and Hoh rivers can be found nearby.

The main lodge, built circa 1926, embodies a rare blend of antique charm coupled with modern convenience. Lavish banquet and convention facilities and a spa with a heated indoor pool, Jacuzzi, and saunas all harmonize within a structure that is a stunning piece of period architecture. Intricate designs stenciled on wood-beamed ceilings in the lobby and an immense fireplace in the lounge exhibit the talents of many artisans and craftsmen who worked together to complete the lodge (it took a mere ten weeks and $90,000 to build). Antique wicker chairs, settees, desks, and tables inspire a feeling of nostalgia for an elegant period gone by. Everywhere, the beauty of natural, polished wood permeates the interior's quiet ambience.

The lodge houses several dining and multipurpose rooms, a cocktail bar, and a lounge bedecked with trophy mounts and artifacts from the area's logging period. The main dining room overlooks Lake Quinault set against a stunning backdrop of distant snow-capped mountains.

Rooms in the main lodge are charmingly furnished and include iron bedsteads, wicker bureaus, and desks from the lodge's original collection. A few rooms have trundle beds. Motel-type rooms adjoin the main lodge by way of a breezeway and have balconies overlooking Lake Quinault. A separate guest facility, Lakeside Inn, built circa 1923, served as the original lodge. Remodeled twenty years ago, it now has guest rooms with knotty pine paneling and antique wicker furnishings.

Things to Do

Guests staying at Lake Quinault Lodge have use of a spa with an indoor heated swimming pool, Jacuzzi, and sauna, and a rec room equipped with pool and Ping-Pong tables and video games. Yard games include horseshoes and volleyball, and, down by the dock, rowboats, canoes, and paddleboats are for rent. In the evenings, live entertainment is provided by bands playing contemporary hits. A piano bar in the lounge offers a more intimate scene.

Surrounding the lodge, Olympic Park and the Olympic National Forest occupy the peninsula's mountainous interior. Hikers and backpackers can explore the beautiful environs of lush rain forests dissected by hundreds of trails. Ancient two-hundred-foot spruce trees drip with tendrils of moss, and a thick undergrowth of ferns bathed in dew creates a tropical effect.

Grays Harbor, a forty-five minute drive south of Quinault, with its principle twin cities of Aberdeen and Hoquiam, is the commercial-tourist hub of the western side of the peninsula. The harbor is one of Washington's leading industrial and sportfishing ports. Clam digging, whale watching, surf and deep-sea fishing for salmon, tuna, and rockfish, and combing wild ocean beaches for driftwood and Japanese glass floats are activities that require little money and only a sense of adventure to enjoy.

Many interesting attractions lure visitors to the tiny towns along the coast and surrounding harbor. Grand, historic mansions built by lumber barons line the bluff. Hoquiam hosts the Polsom Park Museum filled with antiques and logging memorabilia and Hoquiam Castle, a twenty-room mansion built by a lumber tycoon. Nautical buffs will find the Maritime Museum in Westport educational. From Westport, a tour of charming seaside communities along the Pacific Coast can be enjoyed on a leisurely day's drive.

Colorful, summertime events begin with Grayland's Cranberry Blossom Festival in June. During July and August, small towns play host to various celebrations such as Aberdeen's Americanism Days, Elma's Harbor Park horse racing, and the Slug and Saltwater festivals in Westport. In September Loggers Play Day in Hoquiam attracts contestants and spectators from throughout the Northwest.

Fishing

Most of the quality fishing near Lake Quinault is located in the Forks area an hour's drive north of the lodge. The spring-fed Soleduck, Calawah, and Bogachiel rivers all offer fantastic fishing for summer- and winter-run steelhead and fall- and spring-run chinook in the ten- to twelve-pound, thirty-inch to thirty-one-inch class. Big rocks create plenty of holding pocket water in both the Soleduck and the Calawah; however, long white-water sections with big rapids make these rivers extremely challenging for even the most experienced boaters. On the other hand, the Bogachiel — or Boggie as it is referred to by locals — is characterized by wide gravel bars that require less skill to maneuver. Lush cedar and fir rain forests choked by dense underbrush prohibit easy bank access on all three rivers, making drift fishing the preferred method of angling.

A fourth major fishery, the Hoh River, is the largest and most powerful of all the rivers in the Forks area. Being a glacier-fed stream, it is also the most temperamental river and remains discolored by snow runoff all summer long. The huge gravel bars characterizing the Hoh are in a constant state of flux. When the river mellows out in June, it produces excellent fishing for summer-run eight- and nine-pound steelhead averaging twenty-eight inches to thirty inches. The best fishing occurs in September through October, when high-mountain temperatures drop, thereby stalling further snowmelt. In effect, this is the first time the river clears all season, expanding its normal window of visibility of eight to ten inches to fifteen to eighteen inches. When the Washington monsoon season begins in mid- to late-October, the Hoh becomes virtually unfishable through January.

The Hoh probably receives the most fishing of all the rivers around Forks. Bank access is extremely easy; 60 percent of the river is reachable by back-country roads and Highway 101. In addition, private landowners along the river cooperate with conscientious anglers who respect their property rights. Much of the river runs through public land belonging to the National Forest and Park services and the Department of Natural Resources.

Closer to the lodge, the Quinault River runs from Lake Quinault to the Pacific Ocean and offers spectacular seasonal fishing for rainbows, sea-run cutthroats, and steelhead. Permission to fish is needed on the lower river, which runs through the Quinault Indian Reservation.

Heavily dressed marabou attractor patterns (#4–6, 3–4XL) in black, purple, and orange are the most common flies used for steelhead on these rivers. A piece of hot pink tied into attractors also works occasionally. A 9-foot, 6–7 weight rod with either a floating line or sink tip will handle average forty- to fifty-foot casts. Rain gear and warm gloves with the fingers cut out are essential.

The Tackle Box in Forks sells licenses, gear, and a wide assortment of tackle. Twenty-six guides are listed with the Olympic Peninsula Guides Association, which can be contacted through their president, George Wing, P.O. Box 932, Forks, WA 98331. He's also a good resource for up-to-the-minute information on water and weather conditions. Quinault Lodge also keeps a list of guides on hand for guests making their own arrangements.

WHITE SALMON

FLYING L RANCH

Mailing address, Glenwood, WA 98619. Phone: (509) 364-3488. Contact: Darvel, Judith, or Ilse Lloyd. Total capacity: 20. Open year round. Peak season: June–September. Reserve 2 weeks in advance.

Accommodations: Seven bedrooms in lodge; 1 light housekeeping cabin with kitchen and private bath sleeps up to 4. Shared kitchen facilities available. Daily maid service; laundry facility located in Glenwood.

Meals: Home-style breakfast in ranch cookhouse; lunch available for groups, otherwise restaurants located nearby; dinners available at ranch by prior arrangement.

Rates: Inexpensive; weekly and daily rates include lodging and breakfast. Cash, check, Master-Card, or VISA.

How to Get There: Located on I-84 east to Hood River, OR; cross to Washington State and take Highway 141 north 12 miles; at BZ Corner, turn east and continue 18 miles to Glenwood; follow signs to ranch 1 mile northeast of town. From Wakima, WA, take Highway 97 south to Goldendale; then go northwest 35 miles to Glenwood. Free pick-up for guests arriving by bus or train in Bingen or Hood River. Commercial airlines service airport in Hood River; airstrip for smaller planes in Trout Lake and Goldendale.

The 160-acre Flying L Ranch is nestled on the eastern slopes of the Cascade Mountains in south-central Washington's Glenwood Valley. Majestic Mount Adams rises above the floor of a valley comprised of farms, ranches, and a small logging town. Here, the community carries on its quiet commerce amidst dense pine forests and lush meadowlands. The Flying L has been owned and operated by the Lloyd family for over forty years. Best described as a bed-and-breakfast country inn, the ranch is an ideal setting for weekend seminars, short-term getaways, and small group retreats. It is especially well known for its annual art and photography workshops.

A two-story guesthouse, built by the Lloyds in the sixties, and a light housekeeping cabin are decorated with simple, comfortable furnishings and original artwork. The main lodge, built circa 1946, has a spacious living room with a fireplace and library. Guests are welcome to use the piano and stereo. An eclectic collection of artifacts from around the world—Taiwan, Peru, Costa Rica, Yugoslavia, and the American Southwest—are attractively displayed throughout.

Things to Do

The ranch is an ideal place for guests to simply relax and recharge their batteries in a pastoral setting. A shallow lake in the meadow is used for rafting and swimming and a gentle horse stands ready for short guided rides. Lawn games include volleyball and horseshoes. In the evenings, Darvel Lloyd may entertain guests with informative slide shows of Mount Adams or his international travels.

The ranch also serves as a home base for a number of off-ranch recreational activities. Horse-drawn wagon rides and guided trail rides are offered by the Mount Adams Adventures Guide Service. Hikers and backpackers have direct access to miles of trails in the Upper Klickitat Canyon in the vast Mount Adams recreational area—including the Indian Heaven Wilderness—

and in the Columbia River Gorge National Scenic Area. Certain areas in lower elevation forests are havens for seasonal harvesting of mushrooms and huckleberries. Snow and ice climbing on Mounts Hood and Adams, bicycling in the Mount Adams foothills, whitewater rafting, kayaking on the Klickitat and White Salmon rivers, and sailboarding on the Columbia River are challenging activities awaiting those in good physical condition.

Visitors who prefer a more leisurely pace have a wide variety of choices to select from. State parks with developed recreational facilities within an easy day's commute include Brooks Memorial, Horsethief Lake, and Maryhill and Goldendale Observatory state parks.

The Maryhill Fine Arts Museum houses an impressive collection of Rodin sculptures and nineteenth and twentieth century art. Close by, a replica of England's Stonehenge commemorates soldiers lost in World War I. A trip to Goldendale should include a visit to the Observatory's Interpretive Center, which houses the nation's largest public telescope, and a stop at Presby Mansion, built circa 1902, containing the Klickitat County Historical Museum. Another museum worth a visit is the Gorge Heritage Museum in White Salmon.

Following Route 141 north from the Columbia River Gorge, visitors can sample wines from the Mount Elise Vineyard and the Charles Hooper Family Winery in Bingen and Huseum respectively. Huseum also has a nine-hole public golf course. White Salmon is a charming village with spectacular views of Mount Hood. North of White Salmon, scenic Trout Lake Valley offers horseback riding, self-guided treks through ice caves and lava fields, and good road access to Mount Adams. The Conboy Lake National Wildlife Refuge, located east of Glenwood, is a mountain oasis for bald eagles and migratory waterfowl.

While touring the area's attractions, visitors can also enjoy summertime festivities including Community Days, county fairs, and rodeos. Bingen's Huckleberry Festival and Timber Carnival in August is one of the biggest summer events and draws tourists from all over the Northwest.

Fishing

The Klickitat and White Salmon rivers are the two primary fisheries within an easy day's drive from the Flying L. Both are presently under consideration for protection by the National Wild and Scenic River Act.

The Klickitat River offers excellent fishing from June through November for naturally producing steelhead averaging ten to twelve pounds. Salmon are caught near the river's confluence with the Columbia River. The Klickitat is characterized by long sweeping gravel bars along its entire length, with a steady gradient of eighty-five feet per mile in the upper section. Lower down, the gradient eases off to a consistent fifteen to twenty feet. The streambed averages between fifty and hundred feet across and is generally unbroken, with the exception of a few deltalike sections where it divides into several channels. Float fishing from dories is the preferred method of angling on the Klickitat as bank access is somewhat prohibited because of private landholdings. Designated access points can be as many as eleven miles apart.

The Klickitat is a quality stream rather than a numbers stream. Experienced anglers work hard at getting one to two hook-ups a day. Steelhead weighing up to twenty-four pounds—with the bulk being between nine and fifteen pounds—hold up in slots and pools up to five feet deep, which makes fighting with them a matter of skill. The fish enter the Klickitat in June and August and remain in prime health through September because of the river's relatively cold temperatures, caused in part by glacier meltwater and snow-fed springs. Angling reaches its peak in August.

The combination of the river's speed, its lack of pools, and the fact that it is a glacial stream that never completely clears creates a situation where submerged patterns work the best. Productive nymph patterns (#2–4) include green butt skunks, reverse green butt skunks, purple perils, and woolly worms. Traditional skunk and muddler patterns also work well. Two patterns popular with local guides are rick's favorite and a version of the shrimp fly tied with a dark pink body, green back, and ginger-colored hackle. Fishermen who want to challenge surface feeders will find that steelhead and October caddis (#4–6) perform well. Guides suggest a 9- to 9½-foot rod with 7–8 weight sink-tip line to handle the typical twenty- to fifty-foot casts.

The White Salmon River, traditionally known as a whitewater rafting river, can produce fair fishing for rainbows and cutthroats averaging twelve inches, with fish in the four-pound class recorded. It is a difficult river to access—it is embedded in a fault line with 135-foot sheer rock walls from Trout Lake Valley all the way down to the Columbia River Gorge—and a difficult river to float. The frequency of concurrent Class 2½ and Class 3 rapids requires the skill of a professional guide. The White Salmon yields rainbows, cutthroats, and eastern brooks running between nine and fifteen inches with catches up to three to four pounds. The Conduit Dam, built near the White Salmon's confluence with the Columbia River, prevents steelhead from entering the river. The dam forms Northwestern Lake, which yields ten- to fourteen-inch rainbows and a few brook trout.

The broad Columbia River is a spectacular fall, bright chinook and coho salmon fishery. Estimates predict that out of four hundred and fifty thousand fish returning up the Columbia, one out of a thousand will be six-year salts averaging between eighty and a hundred pounds. The numbers of big fish are increasing each year. The Columbia also contains thriving populations of rainbows, cutthroats, and walleyes. Prehistoric sturgeon up to fifteen feet long also inhabit the river. Troll fishing on the Columbia is a unique experience shared by the multitudes, for the river is also host to commercial fishing, sightseeing cruises, boardsailing, and a variety of water sports.

Lake fishing opportunities also abound throughout the area. Smaller lakes in the Mount Adams Wilderness produce native rainbows and brooks averaging eight to ten inches, while larger lakes stocked by the Yakima Indians yield fish in the ten- to twelve-inch class. Many small lakes in the Indian Heaven Wilderness west of Trout Lake offer outstanding trout fishing. A special permit is required to fish the southeastern side of the wilderness owned by the Indians. Several outfitters in Trout Valley service fishing and hunting trips into more remote mountain regions of the Cascade Range within the Gifford Pinchot National Forest. A few of the packers, such as the Mount Adams Adventures Guide Service, have aligned themselves with local fishing guides offering a unique combination float-and-pack trip. The Lloyds are happy to assist guests in booking the services of local guides.

A limited selection of tackle is available from two general stores located in Glenwood and from the Klickitat Fly and Rod Shop just outside Glenwood. Goldendale has several sporting goods stores that carry a larger variety of fishing tackle and gear. The best bet is to stop in Hood River or the Dalles on the Oregon side of the Columbia River.

CHELAN

NORTH CASCADES LODGE

P.O. Box 275, Stehekin, WA 98852. Phone: (509) 682-4711; connects with Lake Chelan Recreation, Inc, in Chelan; no phone at lodge. Contact: Steve Gibson, manager. Total capacity: 90. Open May 1–October 15. Peak season: June–September. Reserve 1 month in advance.

Accommodations: Bedrooms and housekeeping suites in main lodge, 2-bedroom apartment, triples, chalet, and A-frame sleep from 2–8; all have electric heat and private bath. Outdoor hot tub available. Daily maid service; laundry facility.

Meals: A la carte meals available; grocery stores in Chelan and in lodge cater to guests in housekeeping units. Beer and wine available.

Rates: Inexpensive; daily rates. Higher rates for holidays, weekends, and peak season. Cash or check only.

How to Get There: Accessible by cruise ships leaving from Chelan daily or by chartered seaplanes operated by Lake Chelan Recreation, Inc. Contact Jim Courtney at Chelan Airways. Backpackers can reach lodge by back-country trails connecting with the Cascade Pass Trail or Pacific Crest Trail. Write to District Ranger, North Cascades National Park, Stehekin District, Stehekin, WA 98852, for possible routes.

North Cascades Lodge claims to be one of the most isolated mountain resorts in the contiguous forty-eight states. There are no phones, mail is delivered by boat, communications are via radio, and the only way to get to the lodge is by boat, float plane, or hiking trail. Situated in the small wilderness community—year-round population is eighty—of Stehekin on the north shore of Lake Chelan in northwestern Washington, the lodge serves as a popular starting point for back-country hikes and pack trips into one of the largest complexes of national parks and recreational areas in the United States. The immense five-hundred-and-five-thousand-acre North Cascades National Park Service Complex—a tract of federally protected lands—extends all the way to the Canadian border and includes North Cascades National Park, Ross Lake, and Lake Chelan National Recreation Areas, along with the Paysaten and Glacier Peak wildernesses. Mount Baker, Okanogan, and Wenatchee national forests all abut the periphery of the park and encompass some of the most impenetrable, northernmost reaches of the Cascade Range. Snow-covered peaks ring hundreds of glacier-carved valleys and subalpine hillsides carpeted with wildflowers during summer. Tall western red cedar and douglas fir shade the deltalike maze of small streams on the eastern slopes forming the Stehekin River and Lake Chelan watershed, the area's major fishery.

North Cascades Lodge sits at a strategic location in the Strehekin Valley along one of the few routes of access into the heart of the rugged North Cascades. Visitors should note, however, that the lodge is situated right at the boat landing in Stehekin where some of nearly forty thousand annual travelers disembark every midday for half an hour.

Despite the brief crowds and the fact that angling can be strenuous and fish not up to trophy size, the voyage to and stay at Stehekin may very well be one of the most unforgettable experiences of a lifetime.

A variety of guest lodgings set among towering firs and pines are furnished in comfortable, contemporary decor. The main lodge's rustic dining room and outdoor picnic deck receive the brunt of cruise-ship traffic. Bicycle and boat rentals are all handled by the lodge. A gift shop and park service visitors center, which houses natural history displays and exhibits of Stehekin Valley memorabilia, are situated uphill from the lodge away from guest lodgings.

Things to Do

Day hikes, backpacking, mountaineering, boating, fishing, horseback riding, and river rafting are available to the hardy adventurers that the Stehekin Valley and Upper Lake Chelan attract. Approximately three hundred miles of well-groomed trails provide hikers and riders with spectacular views of timbered ridges and snow-capped mountains. Trailheads at Prince Creek and Moore Point, reached via a hitch aboard the cruise ship, provide access into the Lake Chelan–Sawtooth Wilderness. A ride farther south aboard ship deposits hikers in the community of Lucerne, from which the fishing resort of Domke Lake can be reached with a two-mile hike. It's a steep, rugged one-mile hike from Cottonwood Camp to Trapper Lake but well worth the rewards, with some of the best cutthroat fishing in the region. Miles of primitive dirt roads within the Wenatchee National Forest provide access to bird watching, mushroom hunting, and berry picking. The park service also runs a shuttle bus up the valley where visitors take a short hike in to marvel at scenic Rainbow Falls.

Dense underbrush can make lower elevation off-trail routes formidable or impassable, limiting access to experienced hikers in good physical shape. A better alternative to those unfamiliar with the terrain is to enlist the guide services of the Courtney family at Stehekin's Cascade Corrals. They offer a variety of back-country day and extended-stay hiking and horseback trips into the North Cascades.

Short excursions from the lodge, either by foot or rented bicycle, lead to the historic Buckner Orchard Farmstead and the Old Schoolhouse, in use since its construction in 1921.

Fishing

Lake Chelan, the Stehekin River, and the many streams and mountain lakes in the Stehekin watershed are the principal fisheries located near North Cascades Lodge. Lake Chelan produces rainbows and cutthroats up to nineteen inches with larger fish up to twenty inches not uncommon. Landlocked (kokanee) salmon average twelve to sixteen inches, while chinook can run up to thirty pounds. Lake Chelan, at fifty-five miles long by a mile-and-a-half wide, is one of Washington's largest inland freshwater lakes. It is also probably the most scenic body of water in the entire Northwest. The snow-capped peaks engulfing the lake's north shore travel southward and are interrupted by yawning canyons and precipitous rocky cliffs inhabited by wildlife—among which are mountain goats rarely seen elsewhere.

Fishing for kokanee starts at the south end of Lake Chelan in early spring and moves up the lake throughout the summer. Trolling in fifteen- to twenty-foot depths with small wobblers such as dick nites, red martins, and canadian wonders is the most common method of angling on the lake. In September, the kokanee move into the Stehekin River to spawn, laying their eggs in the shallow feeding troughs of cutthroats and rainbows. This overabundance of natural caviar cripples autumn fly fishing because fish inhabiting the river become sated.

Fishing for cutthroat and rainbow in the lake gets hot when spring runoff begins in late April and early May. Trout fishing is most productive near the mouths of small feeder creeks where food sources are plentiful. As the runoff slows, bigger fish move up against the steep shoreline and eventually enter larger feeder streams in late summer. Prince and Fish creeks and the Stehekin River are major Lake Chelan tributaries stocked with rainbows and cutthroats that remain fishable into fall.

The Stehekin River is a large, powerful, flood-prone glacial river that produces some large rainbows and cutthroats up to sixteen to eighteen inches with average fish being in the ten- to fourteen-inch range. The best and most accessible section to fish is at the river's mouth on Upper Lake Chelan, where a submerged meadow provides a lush feeding shelf for silvers and rainbows. The lower five miles of the river, from its mouth to Harlequin Bridge, is broad and slow-

STEHEKIN RIVER & LAKE CHELAN AREA

moving with long riffle sections and abundant back eddies and holding pockets. A preponderance of snags and a boulder-strewn bottom can unravel many a good angler's confidence and cause the demise of flies too heavily weighted to stay within the premium trough six to eight inches above the bottom. Private landholdings and dense undergrowth make bank access difficult; angling from drift boats and large rubber rafts is the preferred method of fishing this section. The Stehekin River Trail on the west side of the river and several short trails on the east bank afford limited access to a number of holes. When in doubt of trespassing, seek the advice of park rangers.

As the fishing season progresses and water levels drop, angling on the Stehekin's middle section, between Harlequin Bridge and Bridge Creek, becomes productive. This usually coincides with the invasion of spawning silvers into the river's lower section. A steep gradient, strong currents, and spots that require sixty- to seventy-foot casts keep the midsection challenging even for experienced fishermen.

Higher up, between Bridge Creek and High Bridge, the Stehekin River becomes quieter and shallower. Pools and irregular stair steps are interrupted by an impenetrable eighty- to one-hundred-foot gorge section. This rugged, unpredictable stretch should be addressed only by surefooted anglers who don't mind the relatively meager rewards of rainbows and cutts averaging eight to ten inches.

Above High Bridge, logjams, beaver dams, and pools created by clogged glacier debris typify the river and its tributary streams. Intermittent canyons, steep slopes, and thick underbrush inhibit access to these higher fisheries but rewards can be surprising. Places exist where it is possible to take several fish, one after another, in pools no bigger than six by ten feet. One-pound fish up to sixteen inches have been caught, although they are the rare exception to fish averaging eight to ten inches.

Boulder, Bridge, Company, Devore, Flat, Park, and Rainbow creeks all offer fair to excellent fishing for rainbow, dolly varden, brook, and golden trout. Access to productive alpine lakes in the Stehekin drainage is limited by rough, ungroomed terrain. The best fishing in these emerald-colored, glacier-fed lakes is in early July,

right after the ice goes off. Brightly colored rainbows and cutthroats average nine to twelve inches while monsters up to twenty-one inches have been caught in a few of the lakes. Float tubes are recommended to ensure unobstructed backcasts on these pristine lakes with depths varying from marshy to shallow to deep. Trapper, Rainbow, Dagger, McAlester, and Doubtful lakes are all reachable via road or hiking trail. Backcountry anglers should be aware that distances on a map can be deceiving in rough terrain. What looks like an easy day in and out may very well require an overnight. A good source of information on the Stehekin drainage is *Fishing Stehekin Waters*, by Lloyd Bell, a local who has fished this neck of the woods since 1948. Flyers published by the North Cascades National Park Service available at the Stehekin visitors center and ranger station are another excellent source of information about fisheries in this region.

Productive flies on the Stehekin include (#12–14) mcginty mosquitos, mayflies, renegades, black ants, and black gnats. Blue duns are good all-season patterns. Gray or white streamers and gray or brown hackles have appeal early in the season, while terrestrials such as the yellow jacket (#10) produce the best results later on. When fish don't seem to be on the bite, a switch to a provoker pattern such as a colorado, indiana, or french spinner will spur them into action. The best time of day to fish is from late afternoon until sundown, when natural hatches pepper the air. A 5½-foot rod with medium action is required to fish small bushy creeks while a 7½- to 8-foot rod will handle the Stehekin River and Upper Lake Chelan. Fishing licenses, regulation booklets, and a very limited selection of tackle are available at North Cascades Lodge. Anglers will find a wider selection of fishing gear and tackle in a variety of sporting goods stores in Chelan at the south end of the lake.

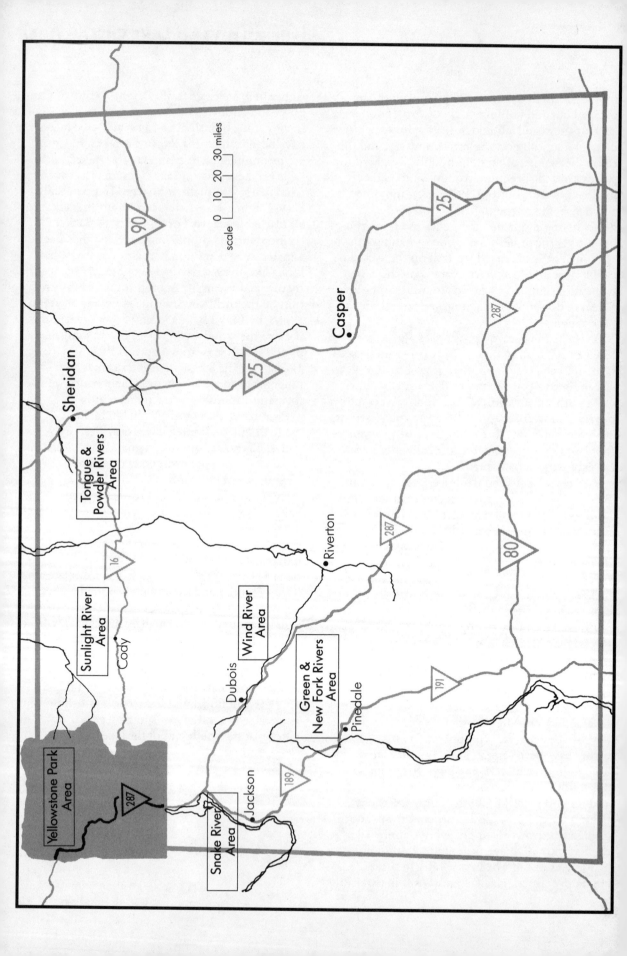

WYOMING

PINEDALE

Pinedale Area Fisheries

The principal access point for these two world-class fisheries is Pinedale, Wyoming. Pinedale is a small western town—population 1,200—located in the foothills of the Wind River Mountains an hour's drive south of Jackson. At an elevation of 7,000 feet, it is surrounded by big sky, high-desert sagebrush country that ends abruptly to the east where the snow-capped peaks of the Wind Rivers travel north to south as far as the eye can see. Float trips down the spectacular rainbow fishery, the Green River, and the top-notch brown trout stream, the New Fork, are the premier fishing attractions in the area. Alpine lake fishing within the 385,000-acre Bridger Wilderness is also reputed to be some of the best in the western states. Although the Bridger Wilderness encompasses some of the most rugged terrain in the entire Rocky Mountains, it is one of the most accessible back-country tracts in the continental United States.

Pinedale is not the place for a luxury, catered vacation. It is, however, the ideal spot for independent outdoor types looking for a no-frills vacation with an abundance of angling and wilderness experiences at their doorstep or tentflap. Accommodations tend to be very rustic and are, for the most part, affiliated with outfitter and pack operations. Lodging facilities are basically used as a convenient base camp from which wilderness treks depart and return.

Green River Drainage

The Green River is a world-class rainbow fishery that flows through the outskirts of Pinedale. Known to a select few anglers until as recently as ten years ago, the river is quickly losing its anonymity. Reports of average fifty-fish days have increased the number of anglers on the river at least fourfold. However, in spite of the influx of anglers, the Green still produces a high catch ratio—only the size of the average fish caught has decreased.

Local politics makes the river a particularly tricky river to fish. Public access is protected by law in the river's upper reaches within the Bridger National Forest. The problem arises in the blue-ribbon waters of its lower stretch below the forest boundary. Here the river meanders through miles of privately owned range lands that are strictly guarded by ranchers. Access to these sections is limited to float guides who know where put-ins and take-outs are located. Float fishermen unacquainted with the area are discouraged from trying to go it alone, as ranchers do not hesitate to prosecute trespassers. Contracting the services of local guides will guarantee a hassle-free trip.

The Green River originates in a plethora of high mountain lakes, streams, and glaciers in the Wind River Range. Its tributaries drain the western slope of the mountains emptying into lakes with populations of golden, cutthroat, and rainbow trout up to sixteen inches. Smaller brooks average eight to twelve inches. Mackinaw as large as four pounds and an increasing number of montana graylings are also found in the upper reaches of the Green. In the most heavily fished section below Pinedale, twelve- to fourteen-inch rainbows predominate, with fewer numbers of browns—some of which are in the two- to five-pound class.

The Green ranges from thirty to sixty-five feet in width with deep-water pockets connected by long riffle sections. Clearing from spring runoff by mid-July, the river remains extremely sensitive to changing weather conditions until early October. August and September are peak fly-fishing months for most of the Green, with the exception of its upper reaches, which experience a fast and furious season from late June to mid-July. A prolific mayfly hatch in late June is a difficult one to match; royal wulffs, elk hair caddis, humpies, house and lots, and adams (#12–14) will provoke action out of surface-feeding fish anywhere on the river. Large browns in lower sections below Pinedale are easily coaxed by heavily weighted (#4) yuk bugs, girdle bugs, and woolly buggers. An 8- to 9-foot, 6 weight rod is adequate for most angling situations. Since guides can usually put fly fishers within easy casting distance of a rise, long casts are not required. Chest waders may come in handy for occasional midriver wading.

Secondary streams feeding into the Green southeast of Pinedale near Big Piney include North, Middle, and South Piney creeks. North and Middle Piney offer good fishing for cutthroats and brooks up to ten to twelve inches. Select lakes in the Middle Piney drainage have some rainbows with larger browns and mackinaw up to five pounds. Rainbows, brooks, and cutthroats averaging ten inches are found in South Piney Creek. Some creek sections are restricted to the use of artificial flies and lures only and special catch limits apply.

New Fork River Drainage

The New Fork River, a major tributary of the Green, originates in alpine lakes and streams draining the western slopes of the Wind River Range. Primary creeks in the upper New Fork watershed such as Willow, Pine, Fremont, Pole, Fall, and Boulder creeks sustain populations of fair-sized rainbows, goldens, brooks, rainbow-cutthroat hybrids, and a few browns. Grayling and mackinaw are also present. The New Fork leaves Bridger National Forest just below the two lakes forming the New Fork Lake group, which harbor mackinaw up to twenty inches and ten- to fifteen-inch rainbows. The river flows southward from there, eventually merging with the East Fork River. Farther south, the New Fork joins the Green River just east of Big Piney.

The New Fork usually clears before the larger Green—around the first week in July—with the peak season lasting through August and September. Like the Green, the New Fork is a popular floating river in its lower reaches where browns in the two- to three-pound range are consistently taken. Occasional lunkers up to six and eight pounds are also caught, giving the New Fork the reputation it has as one of the finest brown trout fisheries in the West. Twelve- to fourteen-inch rainbows and smaller brooks also inhabit the river.

Again, floaters are advised to hire the services of a professional guide, as some hostility towards anglers by private landowners exists here, as it does on the Green. Guides are also a good idea

because they are familiar with the numerous obstacles to be avoided while floating the river. Narrow, sinuous stretches overhung by willows, stick jams, and barbed wire fencing crossing the river require skillful navigation. These hazards can also present problems for unhindered casting, which makes this river one to be challenged by anglers with some experience behind them. Another potential source of frustration for novices is the size (#2–6, heavily weighted) of the average fly the huge browns in the New Fork seem to prefer.

Tackle boxes should include a variety of attractor patterns (#4) such as yuk bugs, girdle bugs, bitch creeks, flutter mice, and muddler minnows. Elk hair caddis and royal wulffs (#12–14) cast next to the bank are used when arms tire of casting the larger patterns. Eight- to nine-foot, 6-7 weight rods are sufficient on the New Fork in most instances. Heavier rods can come in handy when afternoon winds kick up.

Secondary Fisheries

Secondary fisheries in the Pinedale area that receive far less pressure than either the Green or the New Fork are the East Fork and Big Sandy rivers. Together they drain a sizable portion of the southern Wind River Range before converging with the New Fork and the Green. Both offer fair to good fishing for cutthroats and rainbows in their upper reaches. The main branch of the East Fork has browns and cutthroats in the eight- to fifteen-inch class while the Big Sandy has rainbows, cutthroats, small browns, and unfortunately, a large number of suckers.

The Wind River Range contains nearly one thousand three hundred named — and at least that many unnamed — alpine lakes between seven thousand five hundred and eleven thousand five hundred feet. Varying from three to over two hundred acres (with ten acres being the average size), many of these crystalline lakes are rarely ever fished during an entire season. This is due to the fact that the Wind River Range is so rugged. Sheer escarpments, upthrusted cirques, treacherous boulder fields, and rock slides make the going rough on over five hundred miles of horseback and hiking trails. Elusive golden trout ranging from ten to twenty-five inches are the most prized species of fish inhabiting the higher climes. Eastern brook and rainbows between eight and sixteen inches, native cutthroats to twenty inches, rainbow-cutthroat hybrids, german browns, montana graylings, and mackinaw are also present but unevenly distributed in lakes where late ice-offs mean feast or famine. In planning a trip into the Bridger Wilderness, anglers should write ahead to the USDA Forest Service, Intermountain Region, Ogden, Utah 84401, or to the Wyoming Game and Fish Department, Cheyenne, WY, 82002, for a copy of *A Guide to Bridger Wilderness Lakes*.

Popular lake fisheries easily accessed by roads in lower elevations include Fremont, Soda, Half Moon, Meadow, Burnt, and Boulder lakes. Five-thousand-acre Fremont Lake is a bustling summer resort area with a boat launch, restaurant, and several public campgrounds. Sailing, sailboarding, and lake trolling for trophy-size mackinaw — an occasional twenty pounder is pulled from depths up to six hundred feet — are

Fremont's biggest attractions. Fly fishing for brooks, cutthroats, and rainbows inhabiting Fremont's shallower waters receive far less attention. Soda Lake, lying just south of Fremont Lake, offers good fishing for ten- to fifteen-inch brooks and two- to three-pound browns. Half Moon is primarily a mackinaw fishery with fish averaging fifteen inches. The lake also produces an occasional wily brown in the six- to eight-pound category. Meadow Lake has excellent fishing for grayling while Burnt and Boulder lakes yield small brooks, twelve-inch rainbows, and mackinaw up to three pounds.

Wind River Sporting Goods in Pinedale sells licenses and carries a wide variety of angling gear and tackle.

Pinedale Area Attractions

Pinedale serves as the gateway to the Bridger-Teton National Forest and the Jim Bridger Wilderness Area. Scenic drives meander through high-desert rangelands and along rivers and streams eventually ending in the alpine terrain on the western slopes of the Wind River Mountains. The Green River and New Fork lake groups, Fremont Lake, and Half Moon Lake are popular turn-around points for short day excursions. Trails encircling the lakes head off into spectacular back-country hiking and wilderness fly fishing. Kendall Warm Springs, located north of Pinedale, is another popular day venture for road travelers. The springs have the distinction of being the only place in the world where the tiny Kendall dace is found. This small fish grows to a maximum of two inches and spends its entire life in the 84 degree spring water.

Visitors to the Pinedale area can also take a drive up to Jackson, an hour and a half each way, to shop in western stores and art galleries and sample a variety of cuisines in the town's many fine restaurants.

Western theme festivities scheduled throughout summer include a county fair, Mustang Days, the Round-up Days Rodeo, the Fourth of July Chuckwagon Days, and an Annual Chili Cookoff. Art exhibits, civic club barbecues, softball tournaments, and the Little America Cup Sailing Regatta on Fremont Lake are other events that attract an impressive number of tourists to Pinedale.

BIG SANDY LODGE

Box 223, Boulder, WY 82923. No phone. Contact: Bernie and Connie Kelly, owner/managers. Total capacity: 35. Open June–mid-September. Peak season: mid-July–Labor Day. Reserve by May. Pets allowed.

Accommodations: Five housekeeping cabins with antique cookstove and 5 sleeping cabins sleep up to 6; all share bathhouse. Daily maid service.

Meals: Fixed-price family-style breakfast and dinner served in lodge; trail lunches available on request. All alcohol is BYOB.

Rates: Moderate; daily rates include lodging only; weekly rates include 6 nights lodging, all meals, and 4 days guided trail rides. Extra charges: all-accommodation pack trips, spot pack and gear drops, guide/packer, and pack horses. Cash, check, or travelers checks.

How to Get There: Located 44 miles east of Boulder, WY, south of Pinedale on Route 191. From Boulder, take paved road east for 18 miles until road turns to gravel; follow Forest Service signs. Commercial airlines service airports in Jackson or Rock Springs; airstrip for small planes in Pinedale. Rental car recommended for local travel.

Big Sandy Lodge, located close to the Jim Bridger Wilderness boundary, is the most remote resort destination in the Pinedale area. It is literally at the end of the road. Established as a fishing camp in 1929, Big Sandy presently specializes in providing outfitter services near the Continental Divide region of the Wind River Mountains. Its main lodge and ten rustic cabins—without phones, electricity, or indoor plumbing—afford basic yet comfortable accommodations to families and adventure-bound wilderness trekkers who want to vacation in quiet seclusion.

Cabins with lodgepole pine walls and wide plank floors are attractively, albeit simply, furnished. The rustic log lodge, built in the 1940s, stands like a sentinel at the edge of Big Sandy Opening at the base of the Continental Divide. An alpine lake out front mirrors the reflection of magnificent snow-capped peaks in the background. The lodge consists of two enormous cathedral-ceilinged rooms on either side of an immense main foyer. Massive twin stone fireplaces dominate each room, one of which serves as the dining room and the other as a lounge and social room.

Things to Do

Hiking and horseback riding on hundreds of miles of trails in the Jim Bridger Wilderness are the highlight of a vacation at Big Sandy. The lodge has saddlehorses for rent by the day or half-day, with guides provided at no additional cost. The lodge also offers all-accommodation back-country pack trips completely outfitted with a guide, cook, camping equipment, supplies, and horses. Other excursions include spot drop trips, which leave guests at a wilderness camp with wranglers returning for them at a predetermined time, and gear drop trips, designed for campers who want to hike in without the added burden of heavy packs.

Fishing

Nearly one-hundred alpine lakes and numerous streams lie within a day's hike or horseback ride from the lodge, and at least that many more can be reached by extended back-country pack trips. Mud Lake in front of the lodge offers excellent fishing for browns and small brooks. Nearby

Johnson Lake has produced grayling up to one-and-a-half pounds and a plethora of tiny lakes are inhabited by ten- to eighteen-inch rainbows, cut-throats up to twenty inches, and brooks that average twelve inches. The upper reaches of the East Fork and Big Sandy rivers are within hiking distance from the lodge. Streams in the surround-ing watershed range from delicate ribbons cascading down heavily timbered slopes to mean-dering meadow creeks averaging five to ten feet in width.

Anglers should be sure to purchase a license and stock up on tackle before leaving Pinedale, a long hour-and-a-half drive each way.

BOX R RANCH AND OUTFITTERS

Box 23, Cora, WY 82925. Phone (307) 367-2291. Contact: Irv and Laura Lozier. Total capacity: 25. Open June–November. Peak season: July and August. Reserve 4 months in advance. No pets.

Accommodations: Fifteen log cabins with kerosene lamps share bathhouse; modern cabins have private bath, kerosene lamps, and wood-burning stove. No electricity. Daily maid service; laundry facility.

Meals: Three family-style meals daily on American Plan; hearty breakfasts, hot lunch or sack lunch, full dinner. Outdoor barbecue once a week. Beer and wine available; all other alcohol is BYOB.

Rates: Moderate; a variety of package rates include travel from Jackson Hole, meals, lodging, cowboy guides, horses, and ranch activities. Special packages include the Ranch River Wrangler, Ranch River Round-Up, Ranch Wagonmaster, Wind River Ranger, High Country Wrangler, and Alpine Explorer. Cash, check, money order, bank draft, or travelers checks.

How to Get There: Located 20 miles north of Pinedale outside of Cora, WY. Ranch sign posted on Wyoming Highway 352; ranch is located 8 miles from highway on a narrow dirt road. Call ahead to find out road conditions. Commercial airlines service airport in Jackson Hole, WY; airstrip for small planes in Pinedale. Free ranch pick-up from airfield in Pinedale.

The Box R Ranch operates primarily as a year-round working western cattle ranch. Surrounded on three sides by the Bridger-Teton National Forest, the ranch consists of 1,590 acres of high-desert rangeland. The Box R was originally homesteaded by the Loziers in 1900 and still remains in the family three generations later. Rustic cabin quarters for twenty-five guests and full-service guided pack trips into the Bridger Wilderness are summertime pursuits that keep life busy for Box R's wranglers and ranch hands.

One-room log cabins are located across an open hillside from the main lodge. Cabins without indoor plumbing share a common bathhouse. Lighting is provided by kerosene lamps, and wood-burning stoves are used for heat since none of the cabins have electricity. Interiors feature woven scatter rugs and exposed-beam ceilings; the walls combine wood paneling and log-and-mortar. The main log lodge, originally built in the early 1900s, has recently been remodeled. It houses a dining room and separate living room and library. Trophy mounts, animal pelts, and western art are displayed throughout. Guests can browse through family photo albums in the lodge or gather informally in the centrally located rec hall with bar and sitting area furnished with comfortable lounge chairs and card table.

Things to Do

Those who want to experience all the adventures of the West can elect the Box R's most comprehensive vacation package, the Ranch River Wrangler. The Wrangler combines three days of ranch life—which includes wrangling in the "cavy," sorting and moving cattle, packing stock salt, branding calves, and roundup camp-outs—and fishing with a one-day float on the Green River and a three-day wilderness pack trip. A variety of other ranch and river combinations is also available. Each year the Loziers offer three ultraspecial extended pack trips for a limited period during the summer. Past treks have penetrated deep into the Gros Ventre Wilderness, the Popie Agie Wilderness, and high into regions of the Continental Divide and Yellowstone's Thoroughfare. The majority of roving camps along these routes are situated at nine thousand feet, with sites changing every two to three days.

Fishing

Tremendous alpine lake and stream fishing accessed by extended wilderness trips highlights an angling vacation at the Box R. Outfitters have earmarked lakes with brook trout averaging one pound and lunker cutthroats in the two- to three-pound class. Opportunities for excellent rainbow and California golden trout fishing also abound in back-country lakes.

Guests staying on the ranch have access to over five miles of private trout streams and two stocked ponds with seven-pound trophy rainbows up to thirty inches in length. Willow Creek offers super brook and brown trout while the lake it empties into south of the ranch, seven-mile-long Willow Lake, yields ten- to twenty-inch mackinaw, rainbows, and a few browns.

Anglers must provide their own equipment, tackle, and fishing license, all of which can be purchased a half-hour drive down the road at Wind River Sporting Goods in Pinedale.

DARWIN RANCH

Box 511, Jackson, WY 83001. Phone: (307) 733-5588. Contact: Loring Woodman, owner/manager. Total capacity: 20. Open June 20–September 9. Peak season: July 18–August 24. No pets.

Accommodations: Four rustic log cabins with porch, electricity, and wood-burning Franklin stove sleep 2–8; several cabins have private bath.

Meals: Three family-style meals daily on American Plan; breakfast cooked to order, hot lunch cooked by chefs recruited from noted San Francisco restaurants, sack lunch, full-course gourmet dinner. All alcohol is BYOB.

Rates: Moderate; daily rates include lodging, meals, guide service, and horse. Special rates for children over 5. Extra charges: pack trips, airport pick-up from Jackson. Personal checks accepted.

How to Get There: Located 2–3 hours from Pinedale or Dubois, WY. Driving instructions available when reservations are confirmed. Airport pick-up from Jackson. Rental car recommended for local travel.

The Darwin Ranch, a small, informal operation with lodging for twenty guests, is the highest and most isolated guest ranch in the Wyoming Rockies. The 160-acre homestead lies in the middle of Teton National Forest at the head of the Gros Ventre River. The nearest town, Pinedale, is three-and-a-half hours and fifty miles away over extremely rough dirt roads. Darwin's owner of nearly twenty-five years, Loring Woodman, is a steadfast conservationist who is dedicated to preserving the wilderness surrounding the ranch.

Rustic log cabins with original exteriors dating back to the turn of the century have been renovated with new foundations, front porches, and picture windows. All cabins have log-beam ceilings and hardwood floors, lodgepole pine furnishings, homespun curtains, and country print bedspreads, all of which combine to create a cozy ambience. The main lodge looks much as it did fifty years ago. It houses the main dining room and a living room with an enormous stone fireplace. Western furnishings are embellished with colonial and American antiques and new knotty pine walls. Guests also have access to a corral, stables, and homemade sauna on the banks of the chilly Gros Ventre River flowing only feet away.

Things to Do

Darwin's recreational agenda is pretty much play-it-by-ear. Rubber rafting on the Gros Ventre is enjoyed during late June and early July when the river is too high from spring runoff to fish. Even though the ranch has a few rubber rafts on hand, guests are encouraged to bring their own. The riverside sauna is extremely rustic but effective in steaming the chill off after an exhilarating raft run. Well-trained, gentle horses are available for guided rides in the surrounding wilderness. Competent riders are free to ride on their own. The Gros Ventre peaks are within an easy day's range for backpackers and hikers wanting to explore endless high-country terrain. Ranch guides can also direct climbers to a few easy ascents up nearby peaks. Naturalists and photographers will enjoy the variety of wildlife and flowers that thrive undisturbed in this pristine alpine environment. Darwin Ranch is also a licensed outfitter for pack trips into wilderness areas of the Teton National Forest.

Evenings are relaxing times for guests to gather in front of a roaring fire in the main lodge, stargaze on the front porch, or curl up with a good book in the solitude of their cabins.

Fishing

Spectacular purist fly fishing is found on the upper reaches of the Gros Ventre as it meanders through ranch lands. Cutthroats averaging twelve inches compete with a fair number of lunkers in the eighteen- to twenty-inch class, with fish up to twenty-six inches having been recorded. Above the ranch, vigorous ten- to twelve-inch brookies inhabit the river's headwaters. Tremendous fly fishing occurs after spring runoff in late July and continues through mid-October, with the peak of the season occurring in early August. When the Gros Ventre clears, it remains gin clear—and slow, averaging fifteen to twenty feet in width—through the end of August. The river's clarity can be frustrating to novice fly fishers because good presentation and casting accuracy are essential. Experienced anglers claim there are days when every cast produces a strike. Average days are more likely to produce five to six good fish—twelve- to fifteen-inch cutthroats—per hour for those who work hard at it. Clear Creek, a nearby tributary of the Gros Ventre, is a secondary fishery that offers fairly good cutthroat fishing earlier in the season when the main river is still high.

Fishing on the ranch is restricted to the use of flies only; catch-and-release is strongly encouraged. Enforcement of these strict measures over the last twenty years accounts for the quality of fishing found on the Darwin Ranch. Lorin Nauman and several ranch hands are more than willing to help novices with casting instruction and to act as guides occasionally. A 8½- to 9-foot, 4–7 weight rod, felt soles, and hip boots will handle any angling situation found nearby. A good selection of flies (#14–16) to bring include humpies, wulffs, adams, and elk hair caddis. Hare's ear nymphs, muddler minnows, woolly worms, and matukas (#4–6) are surefire bets when fish are feeding below the surface. Be sure to stock up on fishing provisions and purchase a license before leaving Pinedale or Jackson as the ranch does not supply any tackle or equipment.

PONDEROSA LODGE

P.O. Box 832, Pinedale, WY 82941. Phone: (307) 367-2516. Contact: Sue and Larry Weiss. Total capacity: 26. Open year round. Peak season: July–September. Reserve 2 months in advance. No pets.

Accommodations: Cabins with private bath, wood or propane heat, electricity; one housekeeping cabin with fully equipped kitchen. Daily maid service; laundry facility in Pinedale.

Meals: Three family-style meals daily on American Plan; western breakfast, hot lunch, and full dinner. Guests can also order a la carte from regular menu. Full-service bar.

Rates: Moderate; weekly and daily rates available. Extra charges: boat and horse rental, guided pack trips, spot and gear drops, airport pick-up. Groups rates negotiable for special packages. Cash, check, MasterCard, or VISA.

How to Get There: Located 10 miles east of Pinedale on Skyline Drive. Commercial airlines service airports in Jackson or Rock Springs; airstrip for small planes located in Pinedale. Airport pick-up available.

Ponderosa Lodge is comprised of a public restaurant and marina and five rustic cabins nestled into aspen and pine groves on the north shoreline of beautiful Half Moon Lake. The ranch's 200 acres of privately leased land lie within the Bridger-Teton National Forest at the base of the Wind River Mountains north of Pinedale. In addition to having lodge and cabin facilities, the Ponderosa serves as the base of operations for guided pack trips into the spectacularly rugged and scenic Jim Bridger Wilderness Area.

The Ponderosa's rustic log-and-mortar walled cabins overlook the waterfront lodge. The fifty-five-year-old lodge, jutting out over Half Moon Lake from its shoreline perch, serves primarily as a public restaurant with an adjoining enclosed porch. Large picture windows dominating two walls give diners a serene view of the lake. A public marina and horseback riding stables are located a short walk from the lodge.

Things to Do

Ponderosa guests use the lodge as a base of operations for independently planned activities. The lodge has horses and six horsepower fishing boats for hire; a special waterskiing boat is also available. Hikers and backpackers have easy access to miles of trails in Bridger-Teton National Forest which surrounds the ranch. Trails are also used for guided horseback rides designed for fishing, sightseeing, or photographing wildlife.

The Ponderosa is well equipped to provide wranglers, guides, and pack animals for longer back-country trips. Spot drops are available to clients who want to be dropped off at a wilderness camp and left until wranglers return for them at a prearranged time. On privately guided trips, wranglers, cooks, and guides remain in camp throughout the duration of guests' wilderness stay.

Fishing

Nine-hundred-acre Half Moon Lake is primarily a mackinaw habitat with fish averaging twelve to fifteen inches in depths up to 280 feet. Three- to six-pound browns are also produced occasionally. Lake trolling with small powerboats is the most popular method of angling in Half Moon. On its southern tip, the lake is drained by Pole

Creek, which connects with numerous wilderness lakes offering good fishing for cutthroats, rainbows, and brooks. Many of these lakes are reached within a day's round-trip from the lodge. Spectacular high-mountain lake fishing in more remote areas requires more than a day in the saddle—or on foot—under the guidance of a packer. Anglers are expected to provide their own fishing tackle, equipment, and personal gear on extended wilderness treks. Wind River Sporting Goods in Pinedale is an invaluable resource for all angling supplies, licenses, and numerous publications and maps on Wind River fisheries.

WHITE PINE LODGE

P.O. Box 1449, Pinedale, WY 82941. Phone: (307) 875-7067. Contact: Rick and Carla Miller, managers. Total capacity: 60. Open year round. Peak season: July and August. Reserve pack trips 3 months in advance. No pets.

Accommodations: Eleven bedrooms with private shower adjoin main lodge; 2 rustic cabins without indoor plumbing share group shower. Groups of 6 or more can stay in dormitories with communal showers and bunks. Daily maid service; laundry facility.

Meals: A la carte meals offered in lodge's public restaurant; optional American Plan also available. Beer and wine; liquor is BYOB.

Rates: Moderate; daily rates. Special packages also available include all-accommodation pack trips, spot pack drop, horseback day fishing trip, day float trip, Wind River ride, elk photo ride, bighorn sheep photo ride. Extra charges: airport pickup in Jackson or Rock Springs. Cash, check, or travelers checks.

How to Get There: From downtown Pinedale, follow Skyline Drive 11 miles north to lodge. Commercial airlines service airports in Jackson or Rock Springs; airstrip for small planes in Pinedale. Airport pick-up can be arranged.

Located near the Elkhart Park entrance to the Bridger Wilderness, White Pine Lodge was originally homesteaded in 1910 and has been a hunting and fishing camp for over sixty years. At one point it was owned by the Faler family, legendary names in pioneering the development of hunting and fishing lodges in the West. In winter the lodge caters to alpine and nordic skiiers and snowmobilers using the White Pine Ski Area; in summer its motel-style units serve primarily as a base camp for the lodge's wilderness outfitting and pack operations.

Lodge bedrooms feature knotty pine walls and conventional, comfortable furnishings. Groups of six or more can elect to stay in one of two separate dormitories with communal showers and bunk beds arranged youth hostel fashion. Rustic cabins without indoor plumbing are also available. The lodge's main dining room, with cathedral ceiling, is decorated with an array of trophy mounts, pelts, and stuffed specimens of western wildlife. At one end, a wall that combines modern wood paneling and cedar shingles abuts a massive rock fireplace. Large picture windows frame a gorgeous view of a meadow surrounded by pine forests.

Things to Do

A majority of guests staying at White Pine contract the services of the lodge's affiliated outfitter and pack operations. Horses can be rented by the hour for leisurely guided scenic and wildlife observation rides. All-day rides to alpine lakes and streams are geared to anglers intent on fishing in the back country.

Pack trips range from a fourteen-day Wind River ride to seven-day rides for photographing elk and bighorn sheep. Customized combined fishing-photography trips into the Bridger wilderness are designed for small parties of six to eight people. Spot drops portage clients and gear into a wilderness camp until wranglers return for them at a prearranged time.

Fishing

Access to superb golden trout waters within White Pine's concessioned area and experienced guides who are accomplished anglers distinguish the lodge's outfitter services from other local pack operations. Goldens in some of the alpine lakes range from eight to twenty-five inches with eight to twelve inches being the average catch. A monstrous eleven-pound, four-ounce golden holds the record to date. Guides claim that anglers with ordinary skill have enjoyed one-hundred-catch days, with experienced fishermen likely to take at least five or six fifteen- to twenty-five-inch fish in a day, depending on weather. Populations of rainbows, brooks, cut-throats, rainbow–cutthroat hybrids, browns, grayling, and mackinaw also inhabit the lakes.

Day-long rides and longer back-country treks are tailored to the needs of individual anglers. Guides carry backup tackle but, as on all back-country treks, clients are expected to provide their own tackle, equipment, and fishing license, all of which can be purchased at Wind River Sporting Goods in Pinedale.

JACKSON

Jackson Area Fisheries

The Snake River runs through the heart of the historic Jackson valley on the western slope of the Continental Divide in northwestern Wyoming. Rimmed by the Teton Range to the west, the Absarokas to the east and north, and the Gros Ventre, Hoback, and Snake River ranges to the south and east, the valley measures fifty miles long and fifteen miles wide. Grand Teton National Park, Teton National Forest, and Bridger-Teton National Forest surround this region, which contains nearly ten million acres of uninhabited land. Combined with Yellowstone Park, contiguous with Teton County, the area has one of the largest wilderness systems in the lower forty-eight states. The Snake, along with the Gros Ventre River, is the home of the legendary Snake River cutthroat. These two fisheries alone absorb most of Jackson's fishing pressure. Other local drainages such as the Hoback, Greys, and Teton rivers also offer excellent blue-ribbon fishing in sections.

The cosmopolitan, western town of Jackson is the commercial hub of the valley, catering to the thousands of visitors that tour Grand Teton and Yellowstone national parks each year. Jackson also serves as one of the main attractions to hundreds of guests staying at one of the numerous dude ranches in the vicinity.

Angling opportunities range from challenging float fishing on large — and populated — waterways such as the Snake and Gros Ventre rivers to hip boot wading on more obscure, underrated fisheries such as the Hoback, Greys, and Salt rivers. The fabulous fly-fishing waters of Yellowstone Park are also easily within a day's reach. (Refer also to Yellowstone Park Area Fisheries.) The Green River, touted as having one of the highest catch ratios of browns and cutthroats of any river in the lower forty-eight, and the New Fork River are secondary drainages within easy commuting distance from Jackson. (Refer to Pinedale Area Fisheries section.) Ancillary fisheries on the Idaho border include the Fall and Teton rivers and Bitch Creek. These border watersheds are mentioned only in passing, as most anglers who visit the area rarely exhaust the fishing possibilities found closer to Jackson.

With national parks, forests and wildlife refuges making up over 90 percent of Teton County, ample opportunities for alpine lake and stream fishing exist to appease anglers of all persuasions. Hundreds of walk-in lakes and creeks sustain hearty populations of small- to fair-sized (nine- to fourteen-inch) rainbows, native cutthroats, eastern brooks, and a few german browns. Travel in federally protected areas is generally limited to foot and horseback, hence many of these fisheries are rarely fished at all.

Snake River Drainage

The Snake River, one of the most popular float rivers in the country, flows along the base of the Tetons. The snow-covered peaks jut up a breathtaking thirteen thousand feet above the valley floor, creating a spectacular backdrop. Abundant wildlife include deer, bison, moose, and the lesser creatures that inhabit aspen and conifer forests along the river's edge, while ospreys and the protected American bald eagle nest overhead. Good fishing for spotted cutthroat, native to only seventy miles of the Snake between Yellowstone Park and the Idaho border, has improved due to special restrictions implemented by the Wyoming Game and Fish Department. A permit system within the park and cooperation among commercial guides minimize the chances of overcrowding and assure relative solitude for parties floating the Snake.

As is true for most western mountain streams, the river remains unfishable through May and June because of heavy spring runoff. When the water clears in early July, the dry fly fishing gets better through October, with the peak season occurring in August and September. The river sustains bountiful numbers of twelve-inch cutthroats in riffles, back eddies, and undercut banks, while bigger cutthroats up to twenty inches cruise the tricky depths of omnipresent logjams.

The Snake River tributaries of Pacific and Buffalo Fork creeks offer good fishing for cutthroats up to twelve inches, small six-inch to ten-inch brooks, and a few browns. Flat Creek, which enters the Snake eight miles south of Jackson, is a haven for fly-fishing purists. This gin-clear, meandering meadow stream averages ten to fifteen feet in width, with sections designated fly fishing only. The open marshlands of the elk refuge surrounding Flat Creek make stealthy approaches essential. Wary cutthroats averaging twelve inches and frequently larger holding in deep-water pockets in oxbow turns spook easily. Smaller eight-inch to ten-inch brooks are found in shallow riffle waters and along edges of sandy bars. Unhindered backcasts and short forward casts make Flat Creek ideal for novices.

Alpine lakes in the higher reaches of the Snake River watershed have populations of rainbows averaging ten inches, cutthroats up to twelve inches, and some mackinaw. It is worth noting that many of the high-country lakes in Grand Teton National Park are sterile due to late ice-offs and frigid water temperatures that inhibit the growth of natural vegetation. Enquiring of local anglers and fly shops in Jackson will help anglers decide which lakes to avoid. Popular lakes with good fishing include Jackson, Jenny, String, and Leigh lakes. Jackson Lake, a resort area with marina facilities, is home to lunker mackinaw (yielding a record-setting forty-four pounder in 1967) best fished for by trolling the lake's depths. Jenny Lake, south of Jackson Lake, has lodging and marina facilities catering to a large number of campers and tourists. Jenny Lake yields monstrous mackinaw and twelve- to fourteen-inch cutthroats with marginal populations of rainbows and brooks. Anglers in search of more solitude can canoe from Jenny Lake to String Lake and portage a mile by trail up to Leigh Lake. These smaller lakes have fish populations similar to Jenny Lake but do not suffer from the amount of angling pressure the larger lake endures.

The Snake River drainage is primarily a caddis and mayfly habitat with large hatches occurring throughout summer and fall. Subsequently, caddis and mayfly imitations (#10–16) in a variety of colors are absolute winners when fish are surface feeding. Productive all-season attractor patterns include royal wulffs, royal trudes, and yellow humpies. Muddler minnows, black woolly buggers, yellow woolly worms, and gray matuka streamers are effective wet fly patterns. Hare's ears — or any dark-colored nymphs — also work well. During August, hoppers and other terrestrial patterns (#6–12) will inevitably tease a strike.

Gros Ventre River Drainage

The Gros Ventre River enters the Snake north of Jackson. Access along its canyon section is via paved road that quickly turns to gravel; ease of travel along it is dependent on the weather. The Gros Ventre was formerly reputed to be one of the best cutthroat fisheries in the Jackson Valley. Its popularity declined in recent years because of heavy irrigation and the devastating effects of overfishing. Even though irrigation still remains an issue, the river's loss of popularity has resulted in a big comeback of its trout population. In fact, some locals claim it's better than ever.

Reliable fishing in this volatile river cannot be counted on before the end of July as the end of spring runoff varies as much as three weeks from year to year. Prime fly fishing occurs right after spring runoff and continues through early October with the season peaking in August. This low, fast river, ranging from twenty to fifty feet in width, is characterized by long, gravelly riffles interrupted by languid, deep pools. Cutthroats averaging twelve inches to fourteen inches inhabit the river's entire length while populations of mackinaw and brooks up to twelve inches inhabit its lower and upper reaches. A few sections with grassy overhangs frequently yield one- to two-pound cutthroats. Eighteen-inch to twenty-inch cutthroats are not uncommon in remote stretches that rarely see any angling action. Primary tributaries of the Gros Ventre such as Crystal, Cottonwood, and Fish creeks harbor ten-inch to twelve-inch cutthroats and brooks.

Adams, elk hare caddis, and gray hackle yellow-bodied humpies (#14–16) will produce fish on the Gros Ventre and its tributary streams as will woolly worms and matukas. In August, muddler minnows (#4–12) fished dry to imitate hoppers are likely to incite action.

Hoback River Drainage

The Hoback River is a highly underrated, hence underfished, cutthroat fishery that joins the

Snake below Jackson. The Hoback weaves a sinuous path back and forth under Highway 187 for a good thirty miles, making it a perfect fishery for drive-and-fish anglers in need of easy bank access. Riffles and pools along its entire length produce cutthroats averaging ten inches. Smaller cutthroats are found in numerous feeder streams draining into the Hoback from the western side of the Teton Range. Productive tackle includes small humpies, royal wulffs, and muddler minnows.

Greys River Drainage

The Greys River is another offbeat fishery in the Jackson area that receives very little attention. The river splits the Wyoming Range from the Salt River Range west of Jackson, eventually emptying into the Palisades Reservoir on the Idaho border. It offers especially good fly fishing for ten-inch to sixteen-inch cutthroats. A policy of catch-and-release is strongly encouraged to preserve the Greys' delicate environs.

Salt River Drainage

The Salt River enters the Palisades Reservoir from the south after winding its way through the Star Valley, known as the little Switzerland of Wyoming. Although siltation prevents the Salt from being the fly-fishing stream it once was, it does have some excellent fishing for cutthroats, browns, and a few brook and rainbows after spring runoff. Locals insist that "anything approximating the size of an insect" will spur these unselective feeders into action.

A number of independent guide services and float companies operate out of Jackson. The town offers several well-stocked sporting goods and fly angling shops with guide services and special float trip packages. Fishing licenses can be purchased in sporting goods stores in town or at a number of convenience markets in smaller outlying towns; Jackson, however, has the largest selection of tackle and equipment.

Jackson Area Attractions

The Jackson area offers an abundance of cultural and recreational opportunities. In town, visitors can browse through several fine art galleries with one of the biggest overall selections of quality western and American Indian art found anywhere on the continent. The McCallum Winchester Collection, located off the town square, features historic and educational western life displays and is one of the best-traveled private collections of Winchester Arms.

Jackson also has fine gift, clothing, and souvenir shops, fitness centers, and restaurants offering a variety of cuisines. Spending an hour in the Teton Hot Pots (hot tubs) after exploring the town is a fun and soothing way to relax. The Jackson Hole Golf and Tennis Club has an eighteen-hole championship course, six tennis courts, a clubhouse, and a swimming pool in a spectacular setting at the base of the Tetons.

Visitors can ascend the lofty Tetons via an aerial tram operating out of Teton Village or scale them under the professional guidance of instructors at the Exum Mountain Guide Service. River-runners zip along the valley floor in rafts operated by one of the twelve concessionaires in Grand Teton National Park or by a number of commercial outfitters in Jackson who offer whitewater and scenic float trips. Breakfast and dinner cruises on Jackson Lake are also popular with tourists.

The National Elk Refuge, located just outside of Jackson, serves as a winter feeding ground for elk and is a great location to view the protected trumpeter swans during summer. The spectacular sights in Grand Teton and Yellowstone national parks are well worth the easy round-trip from town.

Performing arts include the world-class Grand Teton Music Festival of Symphonic and Chamber Music and several theatrical companies presenting old-fashioned melodramas. The Jackson Hole Rodeo is one of the top wild West shows in existence, with a special kids arena for goat tail tying and calf scramble events. Equestrians will also enjoy regularly scheduled quarter horse shows and polo matches.

CRESCENT H RANCH

c/o Rivermeadows, Inc., P.O. Box 347, Wilson, WY 83014. Phone: (307) 733-3674/2841. Contact: Richard Albrecht. Total capacity: 32. Open June 2–October 13. Peak season: mid-July to end of September. Reserve 6 months in advance. No pets.

Accommodations: Single and duplex cabins with private bath and electric heat sleep 2–4, a few with fireplace; fresh fruit and embossed stationery complimentary. Daily maid and laundry service.

Meals: Three family-style meals daily on American Plan; breakfast cooked to order, breakfast ride once a week, hot lunch or sack lunch, full gourmet dinner, outdoor barbecue several nights a week. Meals can be arranged to accommodate late anglers. Wine served with meal; complimentary full service bar.

Rates: Expensive; daily rates. Special rates for children under 12. Six-night minimum in peak season. Special packages (including lodging, meals, guide, and local transportation): girls adventurer program, five-day fly-fishing school, five-day fly-fishing vacation. Cash, check, or travelers checks.

How to Get There: Take Route 22 for 8 miles from Jackson to Wilson; turn up Fall Creek Road and follow it 2½ miles to ranch. Regional airlines service airport in Jackson. Free pick-up from Jackson Airport. Rental car recommended for local travel.

The 1,500-acre Crescent H Ranch is one of the West's premiere fly-fishing guest ranches. In addition to its access to the variety of public fisheries around Jackson, the Crescent H is well endowed with private waters reserved exclusively for guests. Cutthroats up to twenty-two inches are not uncommon in Fish Creek, the ranch's primary fishery, and in three other spring-fed creeks on the property. Three well-stocked ponds and five miles of private bank access along the Snake River contribute to making the Crescent H the most desirable destination resort for serious fly fishers. While the family angler pursues his or her passion, the rest of the family is well taken care of by a professional staff that caters to personal needs in ways that only world-class resorts can afford.

Cabins are well appointed, with brass bedsteads, lodgepole pine tables and lounge chairs, electric hurricane lamps, and matching print bedspreads, throw pillows, and curtains. Fresh fruit and embossed ranch stationary are complimentary and place these accommodations in the realm of the luxurious.

The main lodge sits in the middle of a grassy meadow hemmed by a semicircle of guest cabins. In the lodge, fresh bouquets of flowers grace massive coffee and end tables. Giant couches and regal, high-backed chairs upholstered in suede and leather, and a unique and exquisite blend of English antiques, western artifacts, and American Indian weavings create a luxurious impression. Dining tables set with silver, pewter, and crystal and an ornate armoir stocked with respectable brands of complimentary liquor for the cocktail hour round out that special feeling.

Things to Do

Miles of trails for all levels of experience throughout the Grand Teton National Forest await horseback riders and hikers. Individual riding skills are assessed before guests are assigned a horse and saddle for the week. After that, everyone rides as much or whenever they please. On the Teton tour, a special weekly event, picnic lunches are packed and guests are transported via ranch vehicle to Grand Teton National Park for an exciting day of picnicking, boating, and wildlife photography.

Kids will have the time of their lives on the ranch down at one of the stocked ponds where canoes and tepees await daytime use or overnight camp-outs. Guests also have access to a skeet range, swimming pool, and tennis courts on property adjoining the ranch.

A special twenty-four-day residency program is designed to teach twelve- to fourteen-year-old girls the techniques of fly fishing as well as general outdoor recreational skills. Camping, horseback riding, canoeing, float trips on the Snake, and fishing a variety of waters in the Jackson area and Yellowstone Park keep the girls busy during their tutelage under well-qualified women counselors.

Fishing

While there are a number of activities offered, fly fishing is undoubtedly the main attraction at the Crescent H. Several fly-fishing vacation packages are designed to meet the needs of both novice and experienced anglers. Anglers not enrolled in a fishing package can enlist the services of a ranch guide at a daily rate for expeditions on any of the fisheries in the Jackson area.

Implementation of an extensive stream habitat improvement program by the Crescent H on the five miles of private spring creeks flowing through ranch property has created a situation where five- and six-pound cutthroats are not un-

heard of. The spring creeks provide excellent early-season fishing with both wet and dry flies. Numerous hatches can occur at any one time with caddis, pale morning duns, and blue duns being the most popular — and successful — patterns. The streams vary in width from twelve to twenty-five yards, offering a variety of slow and fast clear-water fishing.

Three ponds stocked with cutthroats averaging fourteen inches, with lunkers up to five pounds recorded, are reserved for casting practice and for occasional keepers prepared by the chef. Fishing on the ranch is restricted to catch-and-release fly fishing only. Anglers may purchase equipment, gear, tackle, and licenses at the Orvis Shop conveniently located on the ranch.

LOST CREEK GUEST RANCH

P.O. Box 95, Moose, WY 83012. Phone: (307) 733-3435. Contact: Wanda Smith, manager. Total capacity: 50. Open early June to end of September. Peak season: mid-June–mid-September. Reserve 1 year in advance. No pets.

Accommodations: Deluxe single and duplex cabins with private bath; several with fireplace.

Meals: Three family-style meals daily on American Plan; breakfast cooked to order, sack lunch available, lunch ride features cookout once a week, full traditional dinner as well as gourmet dinner, barbecue twice a week. Optional separate dinner hour for children. All alcohol is BYOB.

Rates: Expensive; weekly rates include lodging, meals, and horse. One-week minimum stay. Prices vary according to size of party; discounts for longer stays. Special rates for children under 5; infants free. Cash, check, or travelers checks.

How to Get There: Located 2 miles off Route 25/187 about 20 miles north of Jackson. Regional airlines service airport in Jackson. Free pick-up from airport in Jackson. Rental car recommended for local travel.

Lost Creek Guest Ranch is a small, exclusive resort with a sweeping view of the Tetons. With luxury furnishings and a four-star rating by Mobil Travel Guide, the ranch is showplace quality. Special amenities include courtesy airport pick-up, and fresh coffee or hot chocolate delivered to your cabin every morning and a bucket of ice each afternoon.

Log cabins have recently been redecorated; polished log walls, exposed-beam ceilings, and roomy front porches tie together in the classic western tradition.

In the main lodge, furnishings feature a large collection of western art, and oversized couches, chairs, and coffee tables arranged in several lounging areas enclosed by large picture windows. A welcoming fire is kept burning in a brick fireplace that extends from the floor up to vaulted cathedral ceilings. The attractive dining room opens onto an enormous wood sundeck with an inlaid stone firepit in the center. A children's playroom and a card room with a BYOB stocked bar for adults are also housed in the main lodge.

A heated swimming pool, tennis courts, riding corral, skeet shooting range, and garage equipped with a river raft for scenic floats complete the amenities the lodge offers.

Things to Do

Instructional and recreational horseback riding are the main features at Lost Creek Guest Ranch. Two- to three-hour morning and afternoon rides are scheduled daily, with special all-day rides planned on request. The Grand Teton National Park and the Teton National Forest are contiguous with ranch property, providing a variety of terrains. Competitive horse games are scheduled weekly in the arena for guests who want to show off their newly acquired riding skills. Lost Creek is also experienced in guiding longer pack trips into the Gros Ventre Wilderness where relaxation means fishing in alpine streams and lakes, hiking, and photography. Rafting on the Snake is another popular pastime with ranch guests, who are free to use the ranch's rubber raft anytime.

Those wishing to spend a leisurely day on the ranch can loaf by a heated swimming pool, play tennis, or practice their marksmanship on the skeet range. While tennis rackets are provided, guests must bring their own shotguns from home. High-altitude tennis balls and shells can be purchased at the ranch office.

Special evening activities include musical entertainment, slide shows, and a weekly trip to the Jackson rodeo. Card players can usually find a lively game in session in the adult's social room, while youngsters are kept busy with board games or Ping-Pong in the children's playroom.

Fishing

Lost Creek Guest Ranch is centrally located to a variety of river, stream, and lake fisheries in the Jackson vicinity. Less experienced anglers or those who are unfamiliar with the area can have ranch staff contract the services of an independent guide. Fishing tackle and licenses must be purchased in Jackson as the ranch does not stock these items. Refer to Jackson Area Fisheries section for further fishing information.

RED ROCK RANCH

P.O. Box 38, Kelly, WY 83011. Phone: (307) 733-6288. Contact: Ken Neal, manager. Total capacity: 30. Open mid-June–September. Peak season: July and August. Reserve 6 months in advance. No pets.

Accommodations: Rustic cabins with private bath, porch, and Franklin stove sleep 4–6. Daily maid service; laundry facility.

Meals: Three family-style meals daily on American Plan; breakfast cooked to order, lunch and trail lunch, full dinner, steak barbecue each Sunday. Special dietary needs can be accommodated with advance notice. Children eat before adults. All alcohol is BYOB.

Rates: Moderate; weekly rate includes lodging, meals, horse, and ranch activities. Recommended 7-night minimum stay; no overnights. Discounts before July 1 and after September 1. Extra charges: pack trips, round-trip airport pick-up. Cash, check, or travelers checks.

How to Get There: Six miles north of Jackson, turn off Highway 26 heading east towards Kelly; 1 mile past Kelly, turn up Gros Ventre Road; follow it 16 miles to ranch. A dirt/gravel road to ranch is well maintained.

Red Rock Ranch lies in the heart of the Gros Ventre mountains surrounded by the Bridger-Teton National Forest. One of Wyoming's remaining authentic cattle ranches, Red Rock operates as an informal family-oriented guest ranch during the summer months. Nestled in spectacular red rock country from which its name is derived, the ranch is a perfect retreat for a relaxed vacation in a secluded canyon setting.

Rustic log cabins lining the edge of a grassy canyon draw are comfortably furnished. The main lodge is a short distance across the meadow from the cabins. It houses the dining room, living room, and two separate recreation rooms for adults and children. Unique lamps crafted from western farm implements, dropped-beam ceilings, woven Indian rugs, high-back leather lounge chairs, and a collection of trophy mounts create a friendly atmosphere. A massive stone fireplace occupies an entire wall.

Things to Do

Horseback riding on trails throughout Teton National Forest is the primary activity at Red Rock. Guests are matched with suitable mounts upon arrival and are guided on daily morning and afternoon rides by experienced wranglers. All-day rides into spectacular alpine meadows in the upper Gros Ventre Range are scheduled every weekday except Sunday.

Longer pack trips into more remote, higher regions of the Bridger-Teton National Forest can be arranged prior to arrival. These are quite popular and require special scheduling. Exhilarating float trips on the Snake with independent guides from Jackson usually require only a day's notice as there are many outfitters offering these trips.

On-ranch activities include sunbathing at poolside, swimming, hiking, volleyball, and pickleball (played on a dwarf tennis court with a paddle and wiffle ball). Between children's activities supervised by a full-time counselor-wrangler, kids can enjoy foos-ball, bumper pool, and board games in their own rec hall. Adults have use of a separate rec hall equipped with Ping-Pong, pool, and card tables. To wind down in the evenings, guests relax in front of a fire in the main lodge or take a sauna before settling in for the night. Square dances make for a festive evening several times during the summer.

Fishing

Two-and-a-half miles of Crystal Creek wind through ranch meadowlands en route to the Gros Ventre and Snake rivers. Crystal Creek is a fast-running hip boot stream; native cutthroats average thirteen inches here, with occasional fish up to eighteen to twenty inches recorded. Spring runoff usually lasts until July; superb dry fly fishing occurs from August through mid-September. Nymph patterns work best before the water drops in July, with (#14) renegades, adams, humpies, and royal wulffs working well all season long. Joe's hoppers (#10–12) and muddlers (#14) fished dry are the most productive patterns during August. Fishing on ranch property is restricted to fly fishing, catch-and-release only. Guests who want to sample local trout can keep fish from a stocked pond used primarily for casting lessons.

Sections of the Gros Ventre and Snake rivers are reached by an easy day's ride from the ranch. Ranch vehicles are available for guests without cars. Serious anglers in good physical condition usually opt for a pack trip into the Bridger-Teton National Forest or Upper Gros Ventre Range, where dozens of mountain lakes and miles of undisturbed streams are reachable by foot or on horseback only. A long day in the saddle can bring satisfaction in the form of genuine solitude and deep-bellied twelve-inch cutthroats.

The ranch keeps a few flies and leaders on hand as a backup; however, fishermen are expected to have their own equipment and tackle as well as a license, all of which can be purchased in Jackson.

R LAZY S RANCH

Summer: P.O. Box 308, Teton Village, WY 83025. Phone: (307) 733-2655/7655. Winter: 2479 Holiday Ranch Loop Road, Park City, Utah 84060. Phone: (801) 649-8086. Contact: Bob and Clair McConaughy, managers. Total capacity: 45. Open mid-June–September 30. Peak season: July and August. Reserve 6 months–1 year in advance. No pets.

Accommodations: Log cabins with electricity, private bath, and front porch sleep 4–6; dormitories also available. Daily maid service; laundry facility.

Meals: Three family-style meals daily on American Plan; breakfast cooked to order, hot buffet lunch or sack lunch, dinner buffet and once-a-week seafood buffet, regular cook-outs.

Rates: Moderate; weekly rates include lodging, meals, horse, guide service, and ranch activities. One-week minimum stay unless by special arrangement. No children under 6. Extra charges: pack trips and fishing guide service. Check or travelers checks.

How to Get There: Located off Route 390 on western side of Snake River. From Jackson, follow Route 22 to Route 390; follow 390 1 mile north of Teton Village to ranch. Regional airlines service airport in Jackson. Free airport pick-up to and from Jackson. Rental car recommended for local travel.

The 350-acre R Lazy S Ranch lies adjacent to the south boundary of Grand Teton National Park. Guest quarters and the main lodge are scattered in tall stands of aspens throughout grassy meadows, against the majestic backdrop of the Tetons. The ranch's eastern boundary is formed by the cutthroat haven, the beautiful Snake River. Children's counselors, a wide range of daily activities, and attractive log cabins make the R Lazy S perfect for families with children of all ages.

Cabins are fully carpeted and feature a combination of original log and wood-paneled walls and exposed-beam ceilings. Matching curtains and bedspreads, handsome lodgepole pine furniture, Indian rugs, and western art place these lodgings a notch above rustic. A cozy log lodge contains separate dining rooms for children and adults, a library, and a living room with a massive stone hearth. Western ranch furnishings are nicely complemented by polished log walls, drop-beam ceilings, and chandeliers fashioned from old wagon wheels. Across the meadow, a children's rec room equipped with a Ping-Pong table and foosball machine adjoins the corrals.

Things to Do

Although a full and varied program is scheduled, guests are encouraged to do exactly what they want. Guided horseback rides throughout the Teton National Forest and Grand Teton National Park are the featured activities at the R Lazy S. Riders are assigned a mount at the beginning of their stay and all guests receive instruction to ensure their comfort and safety on the trail. Rides cover a variety of terrains depending on abilities and interests. A fully supervised activities program for children 6–12 years old highlights horseback riding instruction and trail rides to a nearby lake or warm springs pool for swimming. Water sports include scenic and whitewater float trips on the Snake (arranged through independent outfitters) and swimming in the ranch swimming hole.

Guests who want to spend a leisurely day on the ranch can participate in games of softball, tetherball, volleyball, and horseshoes. In the evenings, the main lodge livens with weekly square dances, western swing dance lessons, slide shows, and singalongs. A drive into Jackson to visit the

rodeo, sightsee, and indulge in the nightlife is a special treat whenever people are interested.

Fishing

R Lazy S guests have private access to several miles of the Snake River, which forms the ranch's eastern boundary. Most guests who return annually know the river well enough to fish it on their own. Day trips down the Green and New Fork rivers outside Pinedale and the Teton River are also available. A fishing guide will help novices with casting on a stocked, private fishing pond. Catch-and-release fly fishing is encouraged on all ranch waters, with the exception of the stocked pond where guests are allowed to keep an occasional catch to be prepared by the chef. Serious anglers can take advantage of two- or three-day pack trips into high-mountain lakes and streams with an abundance of eight-inch to ten-inch brooks and cutthroats. Favorite spots include the upper reaches of Snake River tributaries and Pacific and Buffalo creeks. Knowing where and what to fish is never a matter of concern because R Lazy S guides are all accomplished anglers.

Equipment, tackle, and licenses can be purchased in Jackson or in Moose or at a tackle shop, Westbank Anglers, ten minutes down the road.

Refer to Pinedale Area Fisheries for more fishing information.

TRIANGLE X RANCH

Moose Post Office, Jackson Hole, WY 83012. Phone: (307) 733-2183. Contact: the Turners, owners/operators. Total capacity: 75–80. Open mid-May–mid-October. Peak season: June–August. Reserve 6 months in advance.

Accommodations: Twenty-two fully heated log cabins with private bath sleep 2–6. Daily maid service; coin-op laundry facility.

Meals: Three family-style meals daily on American Plan; optional sunrise breakfast floats, horseback picnic rides, evening dinner floats, and cookouts. All alcohol is BYOB.

Rates: Moderate; weekly rates include lodging, meals, horse, and ranch activities. Seven-day minimum stay. Special rates available before June 10 and after September 20. Discount for children too young to ride. Extra charges: fishing guide service, pack trips, float trips, deli lunch float, sunrise wildlife float, evening wildlife float, evening supper float, overnight float, airport pick-up from Jackson Hole airport. Cash, check, or travelers check.

How to Get There: Located 25 miles north of Jackson on Route 26/187. Regional airlines service airport in Jackson Hole. Rental car recommended for local travel.

The Triangle X Ranch is an authentic working dude ranch owned and operated by the Turner family for four generations. With lodging for eighty guests, a special children's program, and well-planned daily activities, the Triangle X is truly the granddaddy of all the dude operations in the Jackson Hole Valley. Surrounded by Grand Teton National Park, the Triangle X has the distinction of being the only guest ranch in the United States that is a leased concessionaire of the federal park system. Wilderness pack trips and river float trips offered to the public as well as to guests combine to make the Triangle X a massive 24-hour operation. For families who want a choice of activities that only a large outfit can offer, the Triangle X manages to do so in a relatively relaxed atmosphere.

Log cabins situated in a rolling meadow with an incomparable view of the Teton range are attractively and simply furnished in traditional western ranch style—braided throw rugs, homespun curtains, ribbed bedspreads, comfortable lounge chairs, writing desks, and dressers.

Several dining rooms—preteens and adults dine separately—and cozy living and sitting areas are housed in the ranch's spacious main lodge. Western-style furnishings take advantage of the magnificent views afforded by large floor-to-ceiling picture windows. A gift shop stocked with convenience store items is located near the lodge, along with the corrals and tack barns for Triangle X's pack horse and float operations.

Things to Do

Daily activities are structured around guided horseback rides. Guests are assigned a horse at the beginning of the week and receive free instruction before heading out on rides designed for beginning to advanced riders. By the end of the week, most guests are in good enough shape to go on a twenty- to twenty-five-mile ride. On Saturday, the real diehards compete in the weekly gymkhana or games on horseback while "wranglers" twelve years and under are kept busy in their own well-supervised program. Kids' activities include horseback rides and lessons, arts and crafts, and swimming trips to a side channel of the Snake River.

Shopping excursions into Jackson and guided

fishing trips can be arranged on request. Guests can also combine their ranch stay with an unforgettable pack trip into the Teton Wilderness. Scenery, solitude, and some spectacular cutthroat fishing await back-country travelers. A float trip down the Snake River with Triangle X's professional guides could very well be the highlight of this vacation. The scenic float trips include a hearty western meal and a chance to see a variety of wildlife at close range.

Activities don't slack off at sunset. The ranch offers moonlight horseback rides, wildlife float trips, square dancing, slide shows, and card games to those with any zest left at the end of a busy day. A ranch vehicle will also take guests into Jackson for a night on the town.

Fishing

Approximately two miles of the prime cutthroat fishery, the Snake River, flows through the ranch. Even though rafts and guide services are available, some experienced fishermen return annually with their own boats. A powerboat kept on Yellowstone Lake is also available to ranch guests. Catch-and-release fly fishing is encouraged. Ranch guides are fully qualified to guide on any river or stream fishery in the Jackson vicinity, but they're quick to point out that the best fishing is found in wilderness areas reached only by horse-

back or on foot. Parties of five to seven fishermen led up to the headwaters of the Snake, Yellowstone, and Buffalo rivers can experience twenty- to thirty-five-catch days for cutthroats averaging twelve inches to fourteen inches. Alpine lakes with populations of cutthroats, brooks, and rainbows rarely see any angling action all season.

Fishing licenses, tackle, and equipment can be purchased at sporting goods stores in Jackson a half-hour down the road from the ranch. A limited number of locally tied flies are available to guests through ranch guides as well, but this resource serves primarily as a backup to the shops in town.

SUNLIGHT BASIN

7 D RANCH

Sunlight Valley, P.O. Box 100, Cody, WY 82414. Summer phone: (307) 587-3997; winter phone: (307) 587-9885. Contact: Marshall and Jane Dominick, managing partners. Total capacity: 30. Open June 14–September. Peak season: July 12–August. Reserve 6 months–1 year in advance.

Accommodations: Eleven log cabins with pot-bellied stove and private bath sleep up to 8; a few with front porch and open stone fireplace. Daily maid service.

Meals: Three hearty family-style meals daily on American Plan; breakfast, weekly breakfast ride, lunch, full dinner with cook-outs each week. All alcohol is BYOB.

Rates: Moderate; weekly rates include lodging, meals, daily maid service, horse, ranch activities, guided fishing trips, and daycare for older children. Discount given during off season. Special rates for children between 2 and 12; children under 2, free. Extra charges: afterhours babysitting, van rides to Cody, overnight pack trips, extended horse pack trips, airport shuttle to Cody or Billings. Cash or check only.

How to Get There: Located 1½-hour drive from Cody and 3 hours from Billings, MT. Follow Route 20 north to Route 296; 296 is a dirt and gravel road that can be treacherous in rain; follow signs to Sunlight Basin Ranger Station; sign for ranch is ½ mile past ranger station. From Billings, MT, follow Route 212 south over Beartooth Pass into Wyoming; turn south on Route 296 through Sunlight Basin until you see ranch sign. Regional airlines service airport in Cody; ranch pick-up from airports in Billings and Cody. Rental car recommended for local travel.

Northwest of historical Cody, the 7 D Ranch is tucked up into a remote canyon of the dazzling Sunlight Basin of northern Wyoming's Absaroka Range. Owned and operated by the Dominick family since 1958, the renowned ranch has been featured in *National Geographic*, *Vacationland USA*, and Mary Emmerling's *American Country West*. The 7 D is ideal for families who want reasonable access to the attractions of Cody as well as the recreational opportunities only a dude ranch can offer.

Comfortable log cabins have pot-bellied stoves, country curtains and bedspreads, and woven Indian rugs that cover hardwood floors. Everything blends together to create a rustic, mountain cabin feeling. Front porches and open stone fireplaces are additional features in a few of the cabins—all scattered throughout groves of aspen that impart a sense of privacy and serenity.

The 7 D's main lodge is a beautifully maintained example of a classic western ranch house. Polished log walls, exposed-beam ceilings, hurricane lamps, and displays of Indian artifacts and hunting trophies exude a mood of casual elegance. An extensive book collection fills shelves that line the walls, inviting guests to spend time lounging in the large, comfortable chairs throughout the rambling rooms. The main dining room and common living room share the same roof. A separate rec hall/game room, located across the meadow, has a spacious interior with polished wood floor and ceiling and a lovely stone fireplace.

Things to Do

The 7 D takes pride in scheduling weekly activities according to the particular wishes of guests. Daytime babysitting and supervised children's activities free parents to go their own ways. A herd of sixty horses guarantees that experienced and novice riders alike will be suitably matched. Surrounded by thousands of acres of the Shoshone National Forest and the North Absaroka Wilderness, the ranch can also provide access to a variety of riding and hiking trails. Morning, afternoon, and all-day rides allow guests to get as much time in the saddle as their hearts desire. Gymkhanas are planned for confident riders who want to compete in games on horseback. Artifact hunting, trap shooting, softball, and capture-the-flag are also popular pastimes. A recreation hall is equipped with billiard and Ping-Pong tables and a piano. Square dancing and slide shows on Rocky Mountain wildlife and local geology make for engaging entertainment during the evenings.

Guests can also explore the spectacular geography of Yellowstone Park and historic exhibits in Cody, home of that legendary figure, Buffalo Bill. Main attractions in Cody include Old Trail Town—a collection of pioneer buildings and relics of the Bighorn Basin area—and the Buffalo Bill Historical Center, which houses probably the largest collection of western artifacts and memorabilia found anywhere in the world. So extensive are its displays that more than a day is necessary to view all the exhibits. A great way to break up the day is to have lunch at La Comida, serving some of the finest Mexican food in Wyoming. Guests who want to spend the day rafting on the Shoshone River are assisted in making arrangements with local outfitters.

Fishing

The sparkling, boulder-strewn Sunlight River flows by only a few hundred feet from cabin doors. Its cold waters support healthy populations of brook and cutthroat trout averaging eight to twelve inches. Although the fish tend to run a bit small in the Sunlight River, which averages only twenty feet in width, angling success is virtually guaranteed. Over one mile of the river runs through ranch property and is closed to the public. Hip boots are sufficient to wade the Sunlight's gin-clear, shallow riffle waters that flow by at a leisurely pace.

Ranch guides will arrange daily fishing trips to many nearby lakes and streams within the Shoshone National Forest, the Beartooth Mountains, or Yellowstone National Park. The Clark's Fork, Soda Butte Creek, Lamar River, and Slough Creek, and Copper, Beartooth, and Gardiner lakes are a few of the better-known fisheries easily reached from the ranch. Guided day trips, complete with canoes or rubber boats (for lake fishing) are available to guests at no extra charge. The 7 D also provides guides, cooks, horses, and camping equipment for longer pack trips into remote wilderness regions of the national forests and the park.

It's important to have an assortment of flies in various sizes to cover all the angling possibilities within proximity of the 7 D. A good selection of patterns (#10–16) includes adams, irresistibles, royal coachmans, grasshoppers, and humpies. Muddler minnows and woolly worms along with common nymph patterns are also productive.

The Fly Shoppe in Cody has the best selection of patterns tied to match local hatches as well as a knowledgeable local fly fisher on staff. One-, five-, and ten-day, and all-season licenses can be purchased at the ranch.

SHERIDAN

Sheridan Area Fisheries

Bighorn country is the historic heartland of the rough and lawless West. Pioneers arrived via the Bozeman Trail, and the Johnson County wars brought an end to the open range of the American Indians. This is also the area where dude ranching had its earliest beginnings as an offshoot of the cattle industry.

This region of the Bighorn National Forest encompasses the Bighorn Mountains in north central Wyoming, a fairly isolated part of the state. Its commercial hub is comprised of the towns of Sheridan and Buffalo and it is often overlooked by tourists drawn to the natural spectacle of the Teton Range.

Fisheries are primarily small, brushy streams and mountain lakes reached on horseback or by foot. Rainbows and browns found in lower elevations average ten inches with an occasional fish up to fifteen and eighteen inches. Native cutthroats and cutthroat-rainbow hybrids predominate in the higher elevations, with golden trout appearing in lakes above ten thousand feet.

Tongue and Powder River Drainages

The Tongue River and tributaries of the Powder River such as the North and Middle forks of Crazy Woman Creek and Wolf, Piney, and Clear creeks are also popular with anglers visiting the Bighorn region. The Tongue, along with its north and south forks, drains the northern end of the Bighorns. Public fishing west of Dayton is easily reached since U.S. Highway 14 parallels the river most of the way through the Bighorn National Forest. The main branches offer fair to good fishing for six- to twelve-inch rainbows and a few browns, while smaller feeder streams carry good numbers of small rainbows and brooks. The Powder River watershed offers good fishing for rainbows up to twelve inches, smaller brooks, and a few large browns depending on the drainage. A section of the river's middle fork, Outlaw Canyon near the town of Kaycee, is a designated blue-ribbon trout fishery. Anglers should inquire with locals before approaching any of the Powder River fisheries as most of them are on private land and access can be tricky.

Favorite dry flies (#14–18) include renegades, mosquitos, royal wulffs, and adams. Licenses and a full line of gear and tackle can be purchased either at Ritz's, in Sheridan, or at the Sports Lure, in Buffalo.

Sheridan Area Attractions

Some local sites worth a visit are the Jim Gatchell Museum in Buffalo, which houses western artifacts, and the Old Kendrick Mansion in Sheridan, a classic period piece of architecture. Outside Bighorn, the Bradford Britton Monument is an old ranch house mansion with one of the finest private collections of western art open to the public.

Rodeos, horses shows, and 4-H and county fairs are traditional summertime events in Buffalo and Sheridan. Sunday polo games played near the town of Bighorn have been carried on continuously for over seventy-five years as an offshoot of the horsebreeding English nobility who settled the area. The Piney Creek Triathalon in July and the Renaissance Fair held in Sheridan in September are two big annual events that provide the impetus for a family outing and a break from a busy dude schedule.

HF BAR RANCH

Saddlestring, WY 82840. Phone: (307) 684-2487. Contact: Hank Horton and Margi Schroth Bliss. Total capacity: 70–100. Open June 15–September 15. Peak season: July 15–August 15. Reserve 9 months in advance. No pets.

Accommodations: Twenty-six cottages with private bath and wood-burning stove or electric heat; most have porches.

Meals: Three family-style meals daily on Americn Plan; a la carte breakfast menu, breakfast cookout and picnic ride, cold and hot lunch, dinner. Chef will prepare fresh-caught fish to order. All alcohol is BYOB.

Rates: Moderate; daily rates include lodging, meals, horse, and ranch facilities. Discount for children under 12. Extra charges: mountain camp pack trip, round-trip transportation to Sheridan and Buffalo airports, babysitters. Cash, check, or travelers checks.

How to Get There: Reached by taking the Shell Creek exit off I-90 north of Buffalo; follow signs over 8 miles of gravel road to ranch. Commercial airlines service airports in Denver, CO, and Billings, MT; regional airlines service Sheridan airport. Ranch pick-up can be arranged. Rental car recommended for local travel.

Incorporated in 1902, the HF Bar is the second oldest dude ranch in Wyoming. Still run by descendants of the original owner, Frank "Skipper" Horton, the HF Bar offers one of the most authentic dude ranch vacation experiences found anywhere in the West. Its specially designed program for children attracts big families that return annually. Anglers have plenty of time to wade through fifteen miles of well-stocked streams on the ranch or to venture out on an overnight pack trip to a tent camp near the Cloud Peak Wilderness Area for spectacular high-country trout fishing.

Situated along the brushy banks of the North Fork of Rock Creek, each of the ranch's cabins was built by different family friends who prompted "Skipper" to take up dude ranching to accommodate their frequent visits. Additions to many of the original cabins give them the appearance of hobbit homes: nooks, crannies, and turrets are connected in eccentric ways. Wood, log, and stucco exteriors enclose cozy abodes furnished in a rustic western motif embellished with American antiques. Porches overhanging Rock Creek have been added to most.

A main ranch house is located downstream from the cabins. It houses dining facilities, a library, and a parlor. Spacious, glass-enclosed rooms overlook manicured lawns rimmed with gardens of wildflowers. Across the yard, a dirt lane leads down to the log dance hall, a coin laundry, post office and general store, barns and corrals, and a swimming pool.

Things to Do

Horseback riding, hiking, and fishing in streams meandering through sagebrush meadows are the main activities at the HF Bar. Guests are assigned a horse upon arrival and from that moment on they are free to ride (or hike) as they wish on miles of scenic trails through the heavily timbered slopes of the Bighorns. Weekly rodeos are an event looked forward to by novice and advanced riders alike. Treasure hunts, hayrides, hikes to find Indian artifacts, aerobic classes, and swimming in a heated outdoor pool are other favorite pastimes guests enjoy on the ranch. At night the dance hall becomes a backdrop for festive evening entertainment including square

dancing, movies, amateur theaters, and costume parties.

Fishing

Approximately fifteen miles of the North and South forks of Rock Creek run through the HF Bar. Native rainbows, cutthroats, and browns average eight to ten inches, although unusually large fish—twenty inches and better—have been caught. The fishing is challenging as most banks are lined with overhanging willows and heavy underbrush. However, even the most inexperienced anglers are sure to see some action if they keep at it.

The trip to HF Bar's mountain camp located at ten thousand feet on Piney Creek requires a packer, guide, and four to five hours in the saddle. The creek connects two high mountain lakes—Frying Pan Lake and Willow Lake—that occasionally yield large mackinaw up to twenty-five pounds. These big lake fish work their way into Piney Creek to compete with its predominate

population of eight- to thirteen-inch cutthroats and rainbows for western coachmen and mcgintys (#12–14) fished dry or wet. It's not unusual for anglers to hook more than a dozen plump, vigorous trout within an hour where Piney Creek empties into Willow Creek. Several other lakes and streams reached by an easy day's ride from the camp produce large numbers of rainbows and cutthroats in the nine- to eleven-inch class.

HF Bar's guests also have easy access to Clear and Crazy Woman creeks, tributaries of the Powder River, from the ranch. It takes a little longer to reach productive spots on the Tongue River, which drains the northern end of the Bighorns.

Brown and yellow elk hair caddis (#12–14), all colors of mayflies (#16–20), and dark-colored stoneflies (#8–10), are all-around favorite patterns to use. Hoppers, ants, beetles, and royal and gray wulffs are also productive, depending on the month and weather conditions. Wet fly choices include woolly buggers, muddlers, and rubberleg patterns such as yuk bugs and girdle bugs. The montana and gold-ribbed hare's ear are the preferred nymph patterns. A noted Rocky Mountain fly fisherman visits the ranch frequently to conduct informal clinics, streamside demonstrations, and fly-tying workshops. Impromptu casting lessons and flies tied to match the hatch are usually provided by several ranch staff who are avid anglers in their spare time. The HF Bar fishing policy restricts tackle to the use of flies only; all fish over ten inches must be released. The daily bag limit is one fish under ten inches per person.

HF Bar's General Store sells Wyoming licenses and a limited selection of leaders and flies. A large selection of tackle and equipment is available at Ritz's Sporting Goods in Sheridan or the Sports Lure in Buffalo.

SPEAR-O-WIGWAM RANCH

Box 1081, Sheridan, WY 82801. Phone: (307) 674-4496. Contact: Jim and Barbara Niner, managers. Total capacity: 30–35. Open June 15–September 15. Peak season: July and August. Reserve 6 months–1 year in advance. No pets.

Accommodations: Seven rustic log cabins with hot water and gas heat sleep 2–8. Daily maid service; laundry facility.

Meals: Three family-style meals daily on American Plan; breakfast cooked to order; hot lunch or trail lunch, full dinner, western-style cookouts and picnic rides once a week. Wine and beer available; all other alcohol is BYOB.

Rates: Moderate; weekly rates include lodging, meals, horse, and ranch facilities; daily rates also available. Special rates for children 2–11. Extra charges: pack trips, pick-up from Billings, MT, airport. Cash, check, or travelers checks.

How to Get There: Located 30 miles southwest of Sheridan, WY. From west, take U.S. Forest Service Road 631 off Highway 14, 5 miles south of Burgess Junction; take gravel road 28 miles to ranch. From east or north on I-90, take State Road 335 (Red Grade Road) through town of Bighorn; ranch is 15 miles from end of paved road. Though short, this road is steep, rough, and suited to 4-wheel drive vehicles. Regional airlines service airport in Sheridan; free pick-up from Sheridan.

The great American writer Ernest Hemingway claimed to have loved only two places on earth, Africa and Wyoming; it was to the Spear-O-Wigwam that he retreated to put the finishing touches on his epic tale, *A Farewell to Arms*. Spear-O-Wigwam, surrounded by the Bighorn National Forest near the boundary of the Cloud Peak Primitive Area, has a high rate of repeat clientele who will attest to how well the ranch blends warm, western hospitality with quality resort comfort.

The rustic log cabins' western motif features classic oak furnishings, log-hewn bedsteads, and a variety of color schemes that lend a unique personality to individual cabins. The main lodge, built circa 1934, is a one-of-a-kind log-and-mortar structure. Built in the shape of a "spear-O," the lodge has a massive stone fireplace that dominates the head of the spear. This is the large social area of the lodge, decorated with historic photographs, topo maps, and Indian artifacts and rugs. Located here also are a library, piano, and a small bar where guests are invited to gather each evening before dinner. The shaft of the spear contains the dining room, and the O is a circular log wigwam that houses the large, modern kitchen, cook's quarters, and crew dining room. A rec hall where guests play pool and Ping-Pong near a warming fire is located across the road from the main lodge.

Things to Do

Riding and fishing are the primary activities at Spear-O-Wigwam. Guests are assigned a horse and saddle for the duration of their stay and are free to come and go as they please. Photography is enjoyed on horseback rides and hikes on miles of trails within the Bighorn National Forest. A summer tent camp maintained sixteen miles from the ranch near the Cloud Peak Primitive Area requires at least three days minimum on the trail. Relaxing moments on the ranch are spent playing Ping-Pong or pool, taking a refreshing dip in the fish pond, or settling back with a good book.

Fishing

Spear-O-Wigwam provides easy access to numerous alpine lakes and small, brushy steams at elevations between eight thousand five hundred feet and ten thousand feet. Native browns, brooks, and rainbows rarely exceed twelve inches with the average being between eight and ten inches. Serious fishermen usually opt for a pack trip into the ranch's tent camp, centrally located near remote lakes that hardly ever receive any angling pressure. The ranch also keeps canoes and rowboats for guests to use on several lakes at lower elevations, including man-made Park Reservoir.

The East and West forks of Big Goose Creek and Little Goose Creek, which produce nine- to ten-inch rainbows and brooks, are the major stream fisheries within an easy horseback ride from the ranch. The Tongue River and its major tributaries are accessible by longer drives from the ranch.

Anglers can pack along a good supply of (#14–18) renegades, adams, mosquitos, and royal wulffs from home or take advantage of flies tied to match local hatches available at the lodge. Licenses and equipment can be purchased in Sheridan at Ritz's Sporting Goods. Licenses are available on the ranch.

DUBOIS

Dubois Area Fisheries

East of the popular Jackson Hole area on the opposite side of the Continental Divide lies the Upper Wind River Valley. The broad grassland and sage-covered valley is defined by the southern Absaroka mountain range to the north and the Wind River Range to the west and south. Both ranges are included the Shoshone National Forest—the largest of the sixteen national forests in the Central Rocky Mountains—which encompasses nearly two and a half million acres and three major wilderness areas. The Washakie Wilderness in the Absaroka range is typified by deep, narrow canyons and broad flat-topped mountains and plateaus created by ancient volcanoes. The Fitzpatrick Wilderness and the Popo Agie Primitive Area along the backbone of the Divide on the eastern slopes of the Wind River range are two spectacular, rugged areas carved by glaciers—even today. Great granite cirques jut up above seven of the largest glaciers in the lower forty-eight states. Gannet Peak, Wyoming's highest peak, is also located here.

Upper Wind River Drainage

The Wind River, along with its tributaries, is the primary watershed in the Upper Wind River Valley. The broad-chested Wind River begins its journey near Togwotee Pass on the east side of the Continental Divide and travels southeasterly along U.S. 287 towards Dubois and the Wind River Indian Reservation. The Little Wind River, which flows in from the west, and the three forks of the Popo Agie River, which join from the southwest, are the major tributaries of the Wind River. Rainbow, brown, and cutthroats averaging twelve inches with larger ones not uncommon inhabit the long riffles and deep pools of the Wind River near Dubois. The river averages seventy-five feet wide in this section, broadening out considerably as it winds through the Wind River Indian Reservation before eventually being dammed to form the Boysen Reservoir.

Some of Wyoming's best and most easily accessed fishing is found in native American Indian

territory. Fall spawning browns in the lower Wind River are reputed to range between two and four pounds. Expensive permits required of nontribal angers—which tends to reduce the number of fishermen—and the closure of tribal regulated waters to the public during the seventies have created an immensely rewarding fishing situation. Alpine lakes and tributary streams of the Wind River and its East Fork, which have an abundance of plump goldens and rainbows, are reached only by foot or on horseback. The numbers of rainbows, cutthroats, and browns inhabiting the lower elevation fisheries of Ocean Lake and Boysen Reservoir diminish in comparison with warm-water species that predominate, such as perch, bass, walleye, and crappie.

West of Dubois, the Wind River is drained by innumerable small lakes and streams flowing out of the southern end of the Absaroka Range to the north and the Wind River Range to the west. The rugged high country of the Washakie and Fitzpatrick wilderness areas in the Shoshone National Forest offer spectacular fishing. Glacier-fed lakes yield hard-to-get goldens and rainbows averaging twelve to sixteen inches. A few select lakes producing golden trout up to two pounds and cutthroats over eighteen inches are the well-guarded secrets of anglers who trek here annually. Mid- to high-elevation fisheries also have plenty of smaller eight- to fourteen-inch cutthroats, cutthroat hybrids, rainbows, brooks, grayling, mackinaw, and some browns. The Dinwoody Glacier Wilderness Area, Whiskey Basin, and Ring and Trail lakes all offer a variety of rich angling opportunities in the Dubois vicinity.

Productive dry fly patterns (#14–18) include adams, irresistibles, royal coachmans, and royal wulffs. Effective patterns that work well below the surface are freshwater shrimp (#16), matukas (#8), muddler minnows (#10), and woolly worms (#10). Light rods and long leaders are recommended for delicate fly presentation required on alpine lakes. Boats and motors are permitted on a few of the mid- to lower-elevation lakes that can be reached via roads. Heavier gear and chest waders are recommended on the larger river fisheries.

Fishing licenses and supplies can be purchased at a number of locations in Dubois. The Whiskey Mountain Tackle Shop is probably the best source, along with the Dubois Mercantile and the Coast to Coast Hardware store.

Dubois Area Attractions

Dubois is the commercial and social center for livestock and guest ranches in the Upper Wind River Valley. Downtown hosts a variety of western shops, casual restaurants, and motels. Museum fare includes a rare collection of North American wildlife on display at the Wildlife Exhibit and the Dubois Museum. Exhibits in the museum depict the early history of western life in this small timbering and ranching community. Golfers will enjoy the nine-hole golf course at Antelope Hills and tennis buffs have access to several municipally maintained courts. Bring along a pair of binoculars to observe the largest herd of Rocky Mountain bighorn sheep in the continental United States, which is frequently spotted grazing on the outskirts of town.

Dubois' summer calendar is highlighted by events re-enacting its heritage as a western timber community; men's packhorse races in May and Museum Day demonstrations of pioneer crafts and labor in July. In August, the Wind River Rendezvous features rifle and black powder shoots and tomahawk–knife throwing contests. Rodeos, art exhibits, and community barbecues are scheduled throughout the summer.

West of Dubois, spectacular beauty awaits travelers along the Union Pass drive and Togwotee Pass area. Togwotee is the gateway through the Rockies connecting Dubois to Grand Teton and Yellowstone parks and all the attractions of the Jackson Valley. Historic sites in the vicinity include the Tie Hack Memorial and Union Pass Historical sites on U.S. 26/287. The area has abundant fossil finds and specimens of petrified wood, agates, and various gems and minerals. Indian petroglyphs and arrowheads, old logging campsites, and tie flumes stand as mute reminders of days gone by.

East of Dubois lies the vast Wind River Indian Reservation. Encompassing over 2.25 million acres, the reservation is home of the Eastern Shoshone and Northern Arapahoe tribes. The towns of Fort Washakie, Crowheart, Ethete, and Arapahoe located within reservation boundaries draw large crowds to the annual powwow celebrations each August. Tribes from all over the West convene to take part in parades and pageantry and to compete in dancing contests.

A day on the reservation should include a visit to Ocean Lake. This twelve-thousand-acre wildlife refuge maintained for public use by state and federal agencies is a haven for waterfowl hunting. Fishing for crappie, bass and winter ling is tremendous. Castle Gardens, located in the reservation's southeastern quadrant, is an area where spire-and-pinnacle sandstone formations rise abruptly ten to one hundred feet above the sagebrush. Petroglyphs imprinted on these eerie outcroppings depict scenes of animals, weapons, and Indian life. Just over the reservation's southern boundary in Sinks Canyon State Park, the startlingly beautiful Popo Agie (Po-Pó-sha) River disappears into a canyon wall cave only to violently reemerge one-half mile downstream in a crystal-clear trout-filled pool.

Historic sites found on the reservation include the graves of legendary Indian girl guide, Sacagawea, and one-time leader of the Shoshone Indian nation, Chief Washakie. A valuable and fascinating collection of Arapahoe artifacts is on display in St. Michael's Mission.

ABSAROKA RANCH AND WILDERNESS OUTFITTERS

Star Route, Dubois, Wy 82513. Phone: (307) 455-2275. Contact: Budd or Emily Betts, owners. Total capacity: 15–20. Open June 10–September 15. Peak season: July and August. Reserve 6 months in advance. No pets.

Accommodations: Four rustic cabins with electric heat and private bath sleep 2–4. Daily maid service; laundry facility.

Meals: Three family-style meals daily on American Plan; breakfast, a la carte lunch or sack lunch, full dinner, weekly cookout rides and picnics. All alcohol is BYOB.

Rates: Moderate; weekly rates include lodging, meals, horseback riding, and ranch activities; daily rates also available. Special rates for children under 12; children under 2, free. Extra charges: overnight camping trip, airport pick-up in Jackson Hole or Riverton, Yellowstone and Grand Teton parks tour, pack trips. Cash or check only.

How to Get There: Located 16 miles northwest of Dubois. Follow U.S. Highway 26/287 east 45 miles; turn north up Dunoir Valley Road to ranch. Commerical airlines service Jackson Hole airport; airstrip for small planes 3 miles outside of Dubois.

Surrounded by the Shoshone National Forest, the Absaroka Ranch is situated on the slopes of the Absaroka Mountains overlooking the immense Dunoir Valley. Over the last fifteen years, Budd Betts, owner and head guide of the ranch, has guided for some of the most reputable outfitters in northwestern Wyoming, followed the rodeo trail, and worked the range as a cowboy. Owning the Absaroka is his way of ensuring a continuance of the life-style he and his family love so well.

Rustic, sap-stained log cabins have cozy furnishings that rate a cut above rustic. In the quaint log cottage serving as a main lodge, which perches up on a knoll above the meadow rimmed by the widely spaced cabins, a large fireplace and bouquets of freshly cut wildflowers add a touch of elegance to simple furnishings accented by C. M. Russell prints. A separate rec room has bumper pool, darts, and a jukebox. Across the yard, a spacious redwood sauna is perched above rippling Five-Mile Creek which runs through the ranch.

Things to Do

Horseback riding is the mainstay of a vacation at the Absaroka Ranch. Guests have virtually unlimited territory to explore throughout the Shoshone National Forest surrounding the ranch. Hikers and photo-enthusiasts can wander the same trails at a more leisurely pace. Guided excursions to nearby lakes and trout streams are set up each morning, when everyone gathers with the crew to decide the day's agenda.

Guided pack trips into the Teton, Wind River, and Absaroka ranges lead through verdant river valleys and lush alpine forests tucked between snow-capped mountains. An abundance of wildlife, wildflowers, and high Continental Divide vistas make these rides unforgettable. Absaroka Outfitters provides clean, spacious tents, warm sleeping bags, and hearty meals on extended back-country trips. The ranch also provides a vehicle and guide for guests interested in day-long sightseeing trips into Jackson Hole and Yellowstone and Grand Teton national parks.

Fishing

Guided day trips on the Wind and Dunoir rivers are the main angling attraction for fishermen

who choose not to pack into the wilderness. Ranch guides have access to river sections running through privately owned land that receive very little fishing pressure. Lively fighters found in these stretches include ten- to fourteen-inch native and stocked rainbows, cutthroats, and a few larger browns.

Absaroka Outfitters also specializes in fishing the headwaters of the Shoshone River. The Teton and Washakie wildernesses form part of the Yellowstone ecosystem and, combined, include over 1.5 million acres of wilderness territory. The Shoshone headwaters drain the backside of the Absarokas at the top of the Wind River Valley, then flow down towards the town of Cody. Budd is partial to these uplands because they have some

of the best brook trout fishing in Wyoming with fish averaging ten to twelve inches. "The biggest challenge is finding something they won't bite," he claims. Anglers who prefer lake fishing have a chance to catch large mackinaw (recorded up to forty pounds) in June when Brooks Lake is still partially covered with ice.

The ranch supplies spinning gear for novices; most experienced anglers prefer to bring their own equipment. Ranch guides are well stocked with a variety of fly patterns to cover daily conditions and local hatch activity. Fishing licenses and a complete line of angling merchandise are available at the Whiskey Mountain Tackle Shop in Dubois.

CM RANCH

Dubois, WY 82513. Phone: (307) 455-2331. Contact: Leslie Shoemaker, owner; Erroll Peterson, manager. Total capacity: 50. Open June 15–Labor Day. Peak season: August. Reserve 6 months in advance. No pets.

Accommodations: Twelve cabins with private bath, wood-burning stove, and front porch sleep up to 6; 3 rustic cabins with no electricity or plumbing reached only by mountain trail located 13 miles from ranch. Daily maid service; laundry done for nominal fee.

Meals: Three ranch-style meals daily on American Plan; breakfast cooked to order, buffet lunch or trail lunch, full dinners, weekly cookout. All alcohol is BYOB.

Rates: Moderate; weekly rates include lodging, meals, horse, and ranch activities. Children under 5, free. Extra charges: pack trips to cabins at Simpson Lake, airport pick-up in Jackson Hole or Riverton. Cash, check, or travelers checks.

How to Get There: Located 6 miles east of Dubois off U.S. Highway 26/287; a 2-hour drive from airports in Riverton and Jackson Hole. Turn south on Fish Hatchery Road onto a graveled road leading to ranch. Regional airlines service airports in Riverton and Jackson Hole; airstrip for small planes 3 miles outside Dubois. Rental car recommended for local travel.

Situated on the eastern slope of the Wind River Range, the CM Ranch lies in a broad valley that funnels into Jakey's Fork Canyon. Ranch lands are contiguous to the Fitzpatrick Wilderness Area of the Shoshone National Forest on the south. To the west, the nearest neighbors are over forty miles away across the Continental Divide.

In operation as a stock ranch the greater part of the year, the CM was established by Charles C. Moore in 1917. The Shoemakers purchased the ranch from the Moores in 1952 and have been very active in its management ever since. Their love of the outdoors is something they enjoy sharing with their guests. As the Shoemakers have grown older, the management of the CM has fallen to Errol M. Petersen and his wife, Lisa, who carry on the operation with skill and enthusiasm.

Cabins are widely spaced along Jakey's Fork and throughout the grassland meadows that make up the ranch. Some of the original log-and-mortar cabins date back to the 1920s and their basic character remains unchanged. Rustic but well-maintained rooms are large and light with simple furnishings. Bouquets of fresh flowers, country-spun curtains, and braided throw rugs covering wood floors combine to create a cheerful tone. Heat is provided by old-fashioned wood-burning stoves.

The CM also maintains three very rustic log cabins located thirteen miles from the ranch within the Fitzpatrick Wilderness Area and reachable only by mountain trail. Everything had to be hauled in on horses to build these cabins. There is no electricity or plumbing to be had here—only the bare necessities are provided.

Log ranch house buildings containing common guest facilities surround a central meadow bordered by Jakey's Fork. A small office/post office lies off to the side of the main dining hall. The dining hall is an attractive log structure with exposed-beam ceilings surrounded on three sides by a large open air porch. A large recreation hall warmed by crackling fires is located across the creek via a bridge. Young and old alike are fascinated by an old player piano, while others play the regular piano, Ping-Pong, and darts. The decor blends western artifacts, antiques, and dated wicker furniture. For those who'd rather be soaking up the sun during the horse's midday siesta, a large heated swimming pool perches atop a knoll with expansive vistas of the valley below.

Things to Do

Ranch life at the CM is very informal and geared toward engaging guests in wholesome outdoor recreation. Horseback riding on trails throughout the surrounding Shoshone National Forest heads the list of daily activities. A rodeo arena provides a place for guests to compete in gymkhanas, horseback games, and contests. Geology trips, nature hikes, and wildflower walks are organized whenever enough guests want to take a saddle break. The rec hall, swimming pool, and impromptu lawn games also attract a fair share of guests between excursions. In the evenings, the rec hall becomes the social center where guests gather for square dancing, storytelling, and other entertainments.

Many CM guests also enjoy taking time off from the ranch to relax in the secluded environs of Simpson Lake. A wrangler/guide and cook can pack up to six people along with all their food

and gear to the lakeside cabins. This is not an adventure for those dependant on the undivided attention of the hosts. Once at the lake, guests are on their own to enjoy the peace and tranquility of the wilderness.

Fishing

Five miles of small, fast Jakey's Fork run through ranch property. Full of naturally reproducing brook, rainbow, and brown trout averaging ten to fourteen inches, this stretch of Jakey's Fork is reserved for the exclusive use of guests. It's a narrow, overgrown creek with a relatively steep and steady gradient that is rewarding to fishermen accustomed to fast water. The creek's brushy banks and swift current can be frustrating for beginning fly fishers; however, experienced anglers return year after year for the challenge. Standard caddis and mayfly patterns (#12–16) and popular attractor flies such as wulffs and humpies are favored on Jakey's Fork.

Dozens of high-country lakes and streams brimming with fat goldens up to two pounds, and rainbows, cutthroats, and brooks averaging ten to fourteen inches are within easy hiking distance from the Simpson Lake cabins. Angling pressure in these rugged areas is virtually non-existent. Unsuspecting trout are easily spooked by clumsy casts on the one hand yet eager to snap up delicately presented artificials on the other. Aquatic food is scarce in many of these glacier-fed lakes which often remain ice-bound until mid-July. Typical dry fly patterns (#14–18) that will attract hungry trout are adams, royal coachmans, gray wulffs, and irresistibles. Mickey finns (#8–12) cast out a ways and stripped back with small jerks are sure to entice brookies—fishing for which is reputed to be fabulous throughout the entire Wind River Range. Small freshwater shrimp (#14–18) also work well.

Many CM guests like to take a day or two to fish the Wind River on the Indian Reservation. Plenty of trout and relatively little angling pressure on the reservation create a very rewarding fishing experience. See Dubois Area Fisheries for further fishing information.

Fishing licenses, tackle, and equipment can be purchased at the Whiskey Mountain Tackle Shop in Dubois as the ranch does not stock any of these items.

SPORTING GOODS AND FLY-FISHING EQUIPMENT

California

California Department of Fish and Game, 1416 Ninth Street, Sacramento, CA 95814, (916) 445-3531

South Lake Tahoe: Carson River Area

Sporting Goods
Markleville
   Monty's Trading Post, (916) 694-2201
Reno, NV
   Reno Fly Shop, (702) 851-0151
South Lake Tahoe
   The Outdoorsman, (916) 541-1660

Northeastern California: Fall River Area

Rick's Lodge, (916) 336-6618

Northern Sierras: Feather River Area

Sporting Goods
Quincy
   Sportsman's Den, (916) 283-2733
   Quincy Sport Center, (916) 283-1445
   Kiene's Fly Shop, (916) 486-9958
   Bob's Bait 'n Bull, (916) 258-3775

Outfitters and Guides
   Mill Creek Pack Station and Mountain Base Camps, c/o Russell and Beth Reid, P.O. Box 487, Graeagle, CA (916) 836-2491

Northern California: Klamath River Area

Sporting Goods
Yreka
   Don's Sporting Goods, (916) 842-5152
   Ken's Sporting Goods, (916) 842-7664

Outfitters and Guides
   Klamath River Guide Association, Klamath River, CA 96050

Quartz Valley Pack Outfit, c/o J. Santone and Steve Moore, 12712 Quartz Valley Road, Fort Jones, CA 96032
Wilderness Adventures, P.O. Box 938, Redding, CA 96099

Northern California: Trinity River Area

Fly Shop
Redding
   The Fly Shop, (916) 222-3555

Sporting Goods
Trinity Center
   Wyntoon Resort and Store, (916) 266-3337
Weaverville
   Brady's Sporting Good, (916) 623-3121

Mammoth Lakes: Owens River and Hot Creek

Sporting Goods
   Filson's Sporting Goods, (619) 934-2517
   Kittridge's Sporting Goods, (619) 934-7566
   Mammoth Lakes Sporting Goods, (619) 934-3229

Outfitters and Guides
   Agnew Meadows and Reds Meadow Pack Train, c/o Bob Tanner, Box 395, Mammoth Lakes, CA 93546
   Convict Lake Pack Train, c/o Lou and Mary Roesner, Box 61, Mammoth Lakes, CA 93546
   Frontier Pack Train, c/o Dink Getty, Box 18 Star Route 33, June Lake, CA 93529
   Mammoth Lakes Pack Outfit, c/o Lou and Mary Roesner, Box 61, Mammoth Lakes, CA 93546
   McGee Creek Pack Station: (summer)—Star Route 1, Box 162, Mammoth Lakes, CA 93546 / (winter)—Star Route 1, Box 100A, Independence, CA 93526
   Pine Creek Saddle and Pack Train, c/o Brian and Donica Berner, P.O. Box 968, Bishop, CA 93514
   Rock Creek Pack Station, c/o London and Dohnel, Box 248, Bishop, CA 93514

Central Sierra Nevadas: South Fork of the San Joaquin River

Sporting Goods

Fresno
  Herb Bauer Sporting Goods, (209) 435-8600
Shaver Lakes
  Shaver Lakes Store, (209) 841-3341

Colorado/New Mexico

Colorado Division of Wildlife, Department of
Natural Resources, 6060 Broadway, Denver, CO
80216, (303) 297-1192
New Mexico: Game and Fish Department,
Villagra Building, Santa Fe, NM 87503,
(505) 827-7899

Antonito, CO, and Chama, NM: Conejos
River Area

Sporting Goods
Antonito, CO
  Fox Creek Store, (303) 376-5881
  Jim Fulton, Superior Trout Flies,
  (303) 376-2203
La Jara, CO
  Bob's Sinclair, (303) 274-5964

Outfitters and Guides
  Lobo Lodge/Outfitters, Box 565, Chama, NM
  87520, (505) 756-2150

Steamboat Springs, CO: Elk River Area

Fly Shops
  Bob's Float Fishing, (303) 879-0650
  Buggywhips Fish and Float, (303) 879-8033
  Steamboat Springs Sporting Goods,
  (303) 879-1240
  Straightline Products, (303) 879-7568

Outfitters and Guides
  All Season's Ranch, (303) 879-2606
  Bob's Float Fishing, (303) 879-0650
  Carl Creel/Outdoor Adventures (fishing trips),
  (303) 879-0199
  Hassle Haven Ranch (pack trips),
  (303) 879-3850
  Ladies of the West, Guide Services,
  (303) 879-3906
  Andy Popejoy, (303) 276-3321
  Red Barn Ranch, (303) 879-4580/4545
  Straightline Products, (303) 879-7568

  Sunset Ranch, (303) 879-0954
  Vista Verde Guest Ranch, (303) 879-3858

Rafting
  Adventure Bound, (303) 879-1100
  Buggywhips Fish and Float Service,
  (303) 879-8033
  Colorado Adventures, (303) 879-2039
  Colorado Custom Canyon Raft Trips,
  (303) 879-3034
  Wild West River Riders, (303) 879-6215

Treks
  Llama Trekking, The Home Ranch,
  (303) 879-1780
  Ultimate Adventures in the Rockies,
  (303) 879-6318

Aspen, CO: Fryingpan River Area

Fly Shops
Aspen
  Fothergills, (303) 925-3288
  Taylor Creek Fly Shop, (303) 920-1128
Basalt
  Taylor Creek Fly Shop, (303) 927-4374

Climbing
  Colorado Mountain College, (303) 925-7740
  Rocky Mountain Climbing School,
  (303) 925-7625
  Smith Mountaineering, (303) 925-9476

Outfitters and Guides
  Aspen Trout, Box 8982, Aspen, CO 81612,
  (303) 920-1050
  Moon Run Outfitters, (303) 923-4945
  Red Mountain Horse Centre,
  (303) 925-9287/1659

Water Sports
  Aspen Kayak School, 611 E. Durant, Aspen,
  CO 81611, (303) 925-4433
  Aspen Water Sports Center (kayaking, sail-
  boarding, raft trips), (303) 925-5405
  Blazing Paddles River Rafting, Box 2127,
  Aspen, CO 81612, (303) 925-5652
  Colorado Riff Raft, Inc., Aspen,
  (303) 925-5405/Snowmass, (303) 923-4871
  River Rats, 318 S. Mill St., Aspen, CO,
  (303) 925-7648

Snowmass White Water, Inc., P.O. Box 5929, Snowmass Village, CO 81615, (303) 923-4544

Wildlife Expeditions
Aspen Center for Environmental Studies, (303) 925-5756

Fort Collins, CO, & Laramie, WY: Laramie River Area

Fly Shop
Laramie, WY
   West Laramie Fly Store, (307) 721-8175

Sporting Goods
Fort Collins, CO
   JAX Surplus, (303) 482-4177
   Montgomery Ward, (303) 482-1110

Rafting
   Colorado Whitewater Specialists, (303) 493-3369

Central New Mexico: Pecos River Area

Fly Shop
Terrero
   Terrero General Store, (505) 757-9590

Outfitters and Guides
   Huie Ley, P.O. Box H, Terrero, NM 87573, (505) 757-6193

Telluride, CO: San Miguel River Area

Sporting Goods
Telluride
   Olympic Sports, (303) 728-4477
   Telluride Sports, (303) 728-3501

Outfitters and Guides
   Far Flung Adventures, (303) 728-3895
   John Mansfield (guided fly-fishing trips), Box 95, Telluride, CO 81435, (303) 728-4661

Estes Park, CO: Upper Colorado River Area

Sporting Goods
Granby
   Fletcher's, (303) 887-3747

Tabernash
   Nelson Fly and Tackle Shop, (307) 726-8558

Rafting
   Estes Park Adventures, (303) 586-2303
   Rapid Transit Rafting, 1-800-367-8523

Creede, CO: Upper Rio Grande Area

Fly Shop
   Ramble House, (303) 658-2482

Outfitters and Guides
   Write c/o Upper Rio Grande Fish and Game Association, Hank Chafin, Star Route, Creede, CO 81130. Winter phone: (303) 852-2700

Rafting
   Spruce Ski Lodge, P.O. Box 181, South Fork, CO 81154, (303) 873-9980

Raton, NM: Vermejo River Area

Fly Shop
   Vermejo Park Ranch, (505) 445-3097

Meeker, CO: White River Area

Sporting Goods
Eagle
   Eagle Pharmacy, (303) 328-6875
Meeker
   Buford's Hunting and Fishing Lodge, (303) 878-4745
   Miller's Ace Hardware, (303) 878-4608
   Roaring Fork Angler, (303) 945-0180

Idaho

Department of Fish and Game, 600 S. Walnut Street, P.O. Box 25, Boise, ID 83707, (208) 334-5159

Ashton: Henry's Fork of the Snake River Area

Fly Shop
   Three Rivers Ranch, (208) 652-7819

Southern Idaho Panhandle: Lochsa River

Sporting Goods
Lochsa Lodge, (208) 942-3405

Montana

Fish, Wildlife and Parks Department, 1420 East Sixth Street, Helena, MT 59620, (406) 444-3186

Dillon and Twin Bridges: Beaverhead and Ruby Rivers Area

Sporting Goods/Fly Shop
Bozeman
    Bob Wards, (406) 586-4381
    High Country Angler, (406) 587-2331
    Rocky Mountain Angler, (406) 587-5121
Butte
    Bob Wards Sporting Goods, (406) 494-3445
    Fran Johnson's Sport Shops, (406) 494-5558/723-3802
    The Sportsman of Butte, (406) 723-7714
Dillon
    Hitchin' Post, (406) 683-4887
Twin Bridges
    Four Rivers Fishing Co., (406) 684-5651
Sheridan
    Hutchinson's Fly Shop, (406) 842-5868

Wisdom: Big Hole River

Sporting Goods
Wise River
    Frank Stanchfield's "Troutfitters," (406) 832-3212
    Complete Fly Fisherman, (406) 832-3175
    Also see Butte under **Dillon and Twin Bridges**

Fort Smith: Bighorn River

Fly Shop
Bighorn Angler, (406) 666-2223

Missoula: Bitterroot River Area

Sporting Goods
Hamilton
    Frustrated Fly-fisherman, (406) 961-3401

Angler's Roost, (406) 363-1268
Missoula
    Streamside Angler, (406) 728-1085
    Clark Fork Landing, (406) 728-3575
    The Montana Fisherman, (406) 721-6839

Livingston: Boulder River, West Fork

Sporting Goods
Bozeman
    The River's Edge, (406) 586-5373
    Powderhorn, (406) 587-7373
Livingston
    Dan Bailey's Fly Shop, (406) 222-1673
    George Anderson's Yellowstone Angler, (406) 222-7130

Bob Marshall Wilderness Area: Flathead and Sun Rivers

Sporting Goods
Great Falls
    Fly Fishers Retreat, (406) 453-9192
    Montana River Outfitters, (406) 761-1677
Kalispell
    Big Sky and Tackle, (406) 755-1911
    The Sportsman, (406) 755-6484
    Rainbow Sports, (406) 257-5454
    Snappy Sports Center, (406) 257-7525
    Rocky Mountain Outfitters, (406) 752-2446

Lewistown: Judith River Area

Sporting Goods
    See Great Falls under **Bob Marshall Wilderness Area**

Ennis: Madison River Area
    See Ennis under **Yellowstone Park Area**

Nye: Stillwater River Area
    See Livingston under **Yellowstone Park Area**

Yellowstone Park Area

Fly Shops
Ennis
    Bob's Tackle Box, (406) 682-7234

Madison River Fishing Co., (406) 682-4293
Headwaters Angling, (406) 682-7451
The Tackle Shop, (406) 682-4263
Gardiner
Parks Fly Shop, (406) 848-7314
Livingston
Dan Bailey's Fly Shop, (406) 222-1673
George Anderson's Yellowstone Angler, (406) 222-7130
Wilderness Outfitters, (406) 222-6933
West Yellowstone
Madison River Outfitters, (406) 646-9644
Bud Lilly's Trout Shop, (406) 646-7801
Bob Jacklin Fly Shop, (406) 646-7336

Oregon

Oregon Department of Fish and Wildlife, 506 Southwest Mill Street, Portland, OR 97201, (503) 229-5406

Eugene: McKenzie River Area

Fly Shop
The Caddis Fly, (503) 342-7005

Outfitters and Guides
McKenzie River Guides Association, Vida, OR
Cascade Adventures, 1-800-321-4395 (in Oregon), or call collect, (503) 549-1047

Rafting
Oregon Outdoor Experiences, Joe Estes, Jr., (503) 747-9231
River Expeditions, Inc., Neil Scott, (503) 822-3214, or Wayne Gardner, (503) 896-3215
Whitewater Fun For All, Ken Helfrich, (503) 741-1908

Sisters: Metolius River Area

Fly Shops
Bend
The Fly Box, (503) 388-3330
The Patient Angler, (503) 389-6208
Camp Sherman
The Camp Sherman Store and Fly Shop, (503) 595-6262

Stables/Packers
High Cascade Stables and Pack Station, (503) 549-4972/5802
Black Butte Stables (Memorial Day, September), (503) 595-6152
Lake Creek Stables, (503) 595-6158

Roseburg: North Umpqua River

Fly Shops
North Umpqua Feather Merchants, (503) 496-3512
Steamboat Inn, (503) 496-3495/498-2411

Outfitters and Guides
Dave Hall, (503) 496-0215
North River Guide Service (Bill Conner), (503) 496-3252
Steamboat Inn, Jim Van Loan, (503) 496-3495/498-2411
Umpqua Fisherman's Association, Box 2083, Roseburg, OR 97470

Rafting
Walk on Water, Ralph and Sandy, (503) 496-0245

Gold Beach: Rogue River

Sporting Goods
Gold Beach
Jot's, (503) 247-6676
Rogue Outdoor Store, (503) 247-7142
T & R Sporting Goods, (503) 247-7621
Illahe
Cougar Lane Store, (503) 247-7233

Outfitters and Guides
Oregon Guide and Packers Association, P.O. Box 3797, Portland, OR 97208

Raft and Jet Boat Trips
Court's Rogue River White Water Trips, Jot's Resort, P.O. Box "J," Gold Beach, OR 97444, (503) 247-6676
Jerry's Rogue Jets, P.O. Box 1011, Gold Beach, OR 97444, (503) 247-4571/7601
Rogue River Mail Boat Trips and Wild Water Trips, P.O. Box 1165, Gold Beach, OR 97444

Rogue Whitewater Excursions, Grants Pass, OR 97526, (503) 476-6401

Klamath Falls: Williamson River Area

Fly Shop
Take It Easy Resort, (503) 381-2328

Washington

Washington Department of Game, 600 North Capitol Way, Olympia, WA 98504. (206) 753-5710

Olympic Peninsula: Hoh River Area

Fly Shop
Forks
Tackle Box, P.O. Box 2061, Forks, WA 98331, (206) 374-9601

Outfitters and Guides
Olympic Peninsula Guides Association, c/o George Wing, P.O. Box 1432, Forks, WA 98331, (206) 374-9601

White Salmon: Klickitat River Area

Outfitters and Guides
Phil's Guide Service (float fishing trips), Route 1, Box 552, White Salmon, WA 98672, (509) 493-2641
Mount Adams Adventures, Dave Heitzmena and Don Warner (back country packers), (509) 395-2561/(503) 663-6599
Whitewater Adventure, c/o Tracey and Lori Zoller, 38 Northwestern Lake, White Salmon, WA 98672, (509) 493-3121

Chelan: Stehekin River and Lake Chelan

Sporting Goods
Chelan
Coast to Coast, (509) 682-4114
Kelly's Hardware, (509) 682-2815
Stehekin
McGregor Mountain Outdoor Supply, Stehekin, WA 98852

Outfitters and Guides
Cascade Corrals Packing Service, The Courtney Family, Stehekin, WA 98852

Wyoming

Wyoming Game and Fish Commission, 5400 Bishop Boulevard, Cheyenne, WY 82002, (307) 777-7631

Pinedale: Green, New Fork, and Upper Gros Ventre Rivers

Sporting Goods
Pinedale
Wind River Sporting Goods, (307) 367-2419

Outfitters and Guides
Green River Outfitters, Bill Webb, P.O. Box 727, Pinedale, WY 82941
Richard Miller, The Fishing Guide, Box 555, Pinedale, WY 82941
Skinner Brothers, Box B, Pinedale, WY 82941
Also see **Jackson**

Jackson: Snake River Area

Fly Shops
High Country Flies, (307) 733-4944
Jack Dennis Outdoor Shop, (307) 733-3270

Sporting Goods
Jack Dennis Outdoor Shop, (307) 733-3270
Jackson Hole Ski and Sports, (307) 733-3461
Spike Camp Sports, (307) 733-4406
Wilderness Sports, (307) 733-4297

Float Trips
Barker-Ewing Float Trips, (307) 733-3410
Charlie Sands Wild Water River Trips, (307) 733-4410
Dave Hansen, (307) 733-3273
Fort Jackson Float Trips, (307) 733-6340
Lewis & Clark Expeditions, (307) 733-6858/4022
Mad River Boat Trips, (307) 733-6203
Riverwind Float Trips, (307) 733-4821
Snake River Park Whitewater Trips, (307) 733-7078

Sunlight Basin: Sunlight River

Sporting Goods
Cody
   Jack's Sports, (307) 587-4531

Sheridan: Tongue and Middle Fork of the Powder Rivers Area

Sporting Goods
Buffalo
   Alabams, (307) 684-7452
   Just Gone Fishin', (307) 684-2755
   The Sports Lure, (307) 684-7682
Sheridan
   The Ritz Sporting Goods, (307) 674-4101
   The Sports Stop, (307) 672-5356

Dubois: Wind River Area and Upper Wind River Range

Sporting Goods
   Coast to Coast Hardware, (307) 455-2838
   Dubois Mercantile, (307) 455-2455
   Whiskey Mountain Tackle Shop,
   (307) 455-2162

Bureau of Indian Affairs, Programs Office, Fort Washakie, WY 82514, (307) 255-8324. For permits and specific information: Wind River Indian Reservation, Fort Washakie, WY 82514, (307) 255-8301.

INDEX

BIBLIOGRAPHY

Bell, Lloyd. *Fishing Stehekin Waters*. Seattle: Trade Printery, Inc., 1983.

Black, William C. *Flyfishing the Rockies*. Boulder, Co.: Pruett Publishing Company, 1976.

Brooks, Charles E. *Fishing Yellowstone Waters*. Piscataway, N.J.: Winchester Press, 1984.

Casali, Dan, and Diness, Madelynne. *The New Henning's Guide to Fishing in Oregon*. Portland, Or.: Flying Pencil Publications, 1984.

Charlton, Robert E. *Yellowstone Fishing Guide*. St. Anthony, Id.: Robert Charlton, 1980.

Dennis, Jack H., Jr. *Western Trout Fly Tying Manual*. 2 vols. Jackson Hole, Wy.: Snake River Books, 1974–80.

Graetz, Rick. *Montana's Bob Marshall Country*. Helena, Mt.: Rick Graetz, Publisher, Montana Magazine, Inc., 1985.

Kelley, Tim. *Tim Kelley's Fishing Guide: Official Colorado & Wyoming Guidebook*. Denver: Hart Publications, Inc., 1983.

Sample, Mike. *The Angler's Guide to Montana*. Billings, Mt.: Falcon Press Publishing Co., Inc., 1984.

Woolley, Jane. *Following the Adams and the Humpy*. Palm Desert, Cal.: JW Publishing, n.d.